Hsiao-Hung Pai is a Taiwanese-born w

Nick Broomfield's film Ghosts. Her undercover work for *Invisible*
also forms much of the basis for a documentary made by Broomfield
for Channel 4. She lives in London.

http://hsiaohung.squarespace.com

'This is investigative journalism at its best. Fearless, rigorous and
compassionate, *Invisible* is a shocking exposé of Britain's shadow world
of sex slaves that enthrals and shames by turn. A master storyteller,
Hsiao-Hung Pai opens a door onto one of the most secretive and least
understood communities in the UK. Essential reading for anyone
interested in the real price of sex.'
James Brabazon, author of *My Friend the Mercenary*

'Hsiao-Hung Pai has done it again; she went undercover, smelled the
sweat of violence, cried hidden in a brothel bathroom and videotaped
the underworld of pimps and madams who profit from the enslavement
of women in need. To navigate the sex trade of Chinese women in the
UK with *Invisible* is to feel the desperation of thousands of women
who enter sex work as the only option for survival ... *Invisible* seeks
deflate the myth of sex work as a free choice for migrant women.'
Lydia Cacho, author of *Slavery Inc.*

'A profound, disturbing and compassionate account of the tragic
lives of women migrant workers who live and suffer in our midst ...
Once read there is no place for denial or complacency – they can be
invisible no longer'
Helen Bamber OBE

INVISIBLE

Britain's Migrant Sex Workers

Hsiao-Hung Pai

The Westbourne Press

Published 2013 by The Westbourne Press

First published in Great Britain in 2013 by The Westbourne Press

The Westbourne Press
26 Westbourne Grove, London W2 5RH
www.westbournepress.co.uk

A full cip record for this book is available from the British Library.

ISBN 978-1-908906-06-9
eISBN 978-1-908906-07-6

Printed and bound by Bookwell, Finland

This book is dedicated
to all migrant women workers in their struggle

Contents

Author's Note

This book is a work of non-fiction. All names have been changed to protect individual identities.

Introduction

'Why are you so interested in sex and sex work?' 'Why do you want to write about it?' These are questions I've been asked many times while working on this book.

Actually, sex work was not one of the occupations I was looking at when I started researching my first book, *Chinese Whispers*, which explores the lives of undocumented Chinese migrants working in Britain. I talked to and visited migrants working on salad farms and construction sites and in food factories, restaurants and takeaways. At the time – this was around 2005 – there had always seemed more Chinese men than women in these workforces, but every now and then I heard stories, told mostly by men in private conversations, about Chinese women entering the sex trade.

As my workplace research progressed, I noticed a rise in the number of women I was seeing. I was told by migrants themselves that the proportion of female migrant workers is now around 20 per cent, compared with 10 per cent at the beginning of the twenty-first century. This is indicative of a well-recognised trend towards the feminisation of migration resulting from increasing poverty and structural inequality in the global economy. And it is a trend that's growing.

China's increased participation in the global market-place during the past three decades has changed the position of women beyond recognition: privatisation of public services has pushed them back into the carer role within the family, while at the same time the dismantling of state-owned enterprises and privatisation of national industries have made millions of working women jobless and marginalised in the job market, pushing them to find alternative means to feed their families.

As in the former Soviet-bloc countries, economic liberalisation has been accompanied by a boom in the sex industry in China. Sex tourism has flourished alongside a growing eroticisation of popular culture and commodification of sexuality, particularly over the past two decades. Women have once again become objectified and second-class – much more so than ever before. While economic reform has created new opportunities for some, working-class women and women from rural China particularly have seen their status degraded in the transformation.

During the last decade, as migration has continued to feminise globally, we have seen ever more migrant women filling the lowest-paid British jobs. In the course of my research, I began to hear more and more stories of what was happening to migrant women as the most vulnerable group of workers in a variety of workplaces. I heard of cases of sexual harassment of waitresses and kitchen workers. I became acquainted with a Chinese single mother who was raped while working as a nanny in Birmingham. She told me she wasn't the only one. I listened to the stories of Filipino and Indian domestic workers who suffered from abuse behind closed doors in the households of celebrities and wealthy businessmen. I also met new arrivals from Romania and Bulgaria and learned how these women struggled through low-paid work and gender discrimination in the hospitality industry. Some of them have discovered Britain's trade unions and become members, but the majority fight their battles in isolation.

Then, in 2006, while working undercover as a leek picker in Northamptonshire, I befriended a woman who told me she worked as a maid in a brothel when there was no farm work available. She had been robbed before during a raid by a local gang, but that experience didn't deter her from returning for more work in other brothels. She introduced me to a precarious world in which migrant women have found themselves trapped, one in which sex work stood out as the employment option with the highest potential rewards but also the highest risks to women's personal safety and well-being.

After completing *Chinese Whispers*, I decided to investigate further. *Invisible* is the result. I began my background research by contacting the London-based British organisations that promote health care and health awareness in the sex industry. These groups were finding it hard to reach migrant sex workers, there being no migrant community organisations working with them and also a great deal of prejudice towards them from their own communities.

Through my contacts in the migrant communities, I learned more about the industry and was introduced to a number of people working in it. I discovered that there are 80,000 sex workers in the UK, 20,000 of whom are migrants. In the EU, research into the sex industry conducted by the Amsterdam-based TAMPEP project, among others, has found that the number of nationalities has increased over the years, from at most thirteen during 1993–4 to sixty in 2008. This is a clear indication that the number of migrant sex workers has grown and that the industry has been highly 'ethnicised'.

I also learned that in 2000 there were already up to half a million migrant women working without documents as sex workers in EU countries. That number has undoubtedly grown since then as such underground work has attracted increasing numbers of migrant women, despite its risks and social stigma, largely due to their illegal immigration status.

The social stigma attached to sex work makes research difficult. In the British Chinese communities, for instance, sex workers are subject to a great deal of contempt and discrimination and prostitution is treated as a taboo subject, even though sex is sold in every town and city across the country. Understandably, few sex workers are willing to share their stories without trust and the guarantee of confidentiality. And trust takes time to build. This was why, initially, I relied on my existing contacts for introductions. This way, I got to know Ming, a courageous Chinese single mother who was reserved, dignified and kind. And through her, I became acquainted with others working in the trade.

Not wanting to rely entirely on my contacts, I began a more direct, 'door-to-door' search for women who might be willing to share their stories. I trawled Soho, and many times I had doors slammed in my face. Eventually, though, my strategy worked and I found Beata, a single mother from Poland, who was pleased to have someone to talk to. Since then, we have had numerous chats over coffee and cigarettes in the flat where she works, her local café and her bedsit in Finsbury Park. I also became acquainted with the maid, Pam, who looked after the place where Beata worked. Pam was very approachable and chatty. She, too, shared her story with me.

I visited other cities: Nottingham, Manchester, Portsmouth. I became convinced that I'd never understand what really goes on in the trade simply by conducting one-off interviews, so I began to get more 'personal'. In Manchester, I met with local pimps, letting some of them buy me dinner, visiting them in their local bars and, on one occasion, even meeting a brothel owner in his house. It took time to gain such access, but it gave me an invaluable insight into how the industry works and how those within it operate.

At this stage, though, I remained an observer. When I went to these meetings, I was seen as a reporter trying to do her job. I was someone with a particular agenda. An outsider. We would agree on a venue and always be in a controlled, well-managed situation. But although it is standard journalistic practice to adopt an objective stance as a neutral observer, doing so removes the possibility of ever obtaining an entirely unfiltered account of the issues you want to write about. As an outsider, all interaction is based on social presumptions about your role and your understanding. You are fed the standard line. You lose the opportunity to build the closeness and intimacy which precondition truthfulness.

The paradox is that sometimes we need to put on a different identity in order to understand how different social relations and identities really work. We need to deceive in order to expose deception. As journalist Günter Wallraff, who posed as a Turkish migrant to research the lives of West Germany's often badly exploited migrant workers, famously said, 'One must disguise oneself in order to unmask society; one must deceive and dissimulate in order to find out the truth.'

Through my research, I realised that an 'observer' approach wouldn't be enough to get to the bottom of the subject matter. How would I ever understand how Beata and Ming really felt if all I could do was to listen to them? How could I discover the extent to which their experience of exploitation is shared among migrant women in the sex trade? And how could I test the theory that the nature of sex work conducted by migrant workers is determined by inequalities of gender, ethnicity and class?

I had a framework in mind: not only did I want to examine the process by which migrant women left their homes to enter the sex trade and to detail their exploitative working conditions, I also wanted to understand their sense of economic powerlessness and their perception of the reality of entrapment – and in some cases, control – that I believed were characteristic of their lives as sex workers. I didn't want to portray the migrant women as merely victims of oppression (although they clearly are victimised, as they have no control over the material circumstances that determine the course of their lives and no control over their wage structure and work regime), but to document their reconciliation and their resistance against their circumstances.

I knew that the best and only way to do that would be to adopt a 'participant approach'. Inevitably, that would involve subterfuge, but I considered that a necessary means to an end – the exposure of exploitation and its mechanisms in order to uncover and question the lack of institutional protection for workers and to reveal the failure of government immigration policies as one of the causes of such workers' vulnerability. In my opinion, it would serve the public interest to achieve these aims. A little subterfuge was clearly justifiable, and I decided, as I had with the farm workers, to work undercover. I would live and work in the sex industry in order to witness its reality and experience at least some of it first-hand.

My first step was to get a job inside a brothel, as a housekeeper. Looking through the papers, I saw many ads repeating this identical message for punters:

'Oriental. Very young and busty. All services. Reasonable price.'

Amazingly similar in tone to the ads placed by migrant job-seekers found in many West German newspapers – 'Foreigner, strong, seeks work of any kind, including heavy and dirty jobs, even for little money' – when Wallraff started looking for a job for his undercover research in March 1983.

An old London contact told me he knew of someone who was looking for a housekeeper in Burnley. He had never met the man, but believed that it was a business recently set up in the depressed Lancashire town. I dialled the number he gave me, and was offered the job straight away. Finding work through word of mouth is very common among migrants, and the brothel owner suspected nothing unusual about my call.

Although this was not the first time I'd worked undercover, I was aware that this would be a much harder industry to work in, and a much more dangerous one. On the train north I rehearsed my cover story: my name is Li Yun. I'm thirty-eight, a single mother. Without papers. I remember my heart beating fast during that train trip. What I knew of the industry from the interviews I'd conducted didn't fill me with confidence. I could only speculate about the risks involved.

The brothel owner turned out to be a harmless-looking man, a former kitchen worker, quite smartly dressed, from the north-east of China. He met me at Blackburn, from where we took the train to Burnley. 'Call me Li,' he introduced, handing me a can of Coke. He told me that he had closed down his business in east London and relocated in the north 'because there were too many robberies in London'.

I was to be paid £180 for a seven-day week and was to have only one day off per month. I was also instructed not to leave the premises during working hours. These, I found out later, were all common conditions in the Chinese-run sex trade. Inside the brothel I was told by the madam not only to do all the household duties and keep accounts, but also keep an eye on the girls 'in case they cut short on working time'.

The madam ruled her charges harshly, forbidding unnecessary communication, despite the fact that the women were here for only a week at a time and there was little chance of rebellion against an employer who openly treated them as commodities to be distributed among the parlours. When I asked one what food she liked the madam intervened to tell me that the workers' needs were irrelevant to the business.

The girl in question was called Mei. Like all the others, she was there to be worked like an animal to the maximum – till around 2 a.m. each day. When she came to say good-night to me on the last evening of her stay, she'd removed her make-up and looked like herself. She's a single mother, too, just like my undercover identity Li Yun. Wearing an exhausted expression after working more than sixteen hours, she said the words that I was to hear from every single mum working in the trade: 'I'm doing this to support my child.'

She told me she was leaving for Blackburn the next morning to work in another brothel for a week. She worked a circuit of four different sex businesses in four Lancashire towns.

As it turned out, the Burnley experience confirmed my expectation and theory: migrant women are compelled to enter the sex industry by the low-wage economy in which they become trapped as soon as they arrive in Britain. Within the sex trade, they are trapped once again: their freedom of movement is restricted, most of the money they earn is extorted and both their health and safety are put at risk.

I wasn't a resounding success as a brothel maid. My first assignment lasted only three days, mainly because I couldn't stomach sharing a bed with the madam (the place wasn't large enough for me to have my own room). But it had given me a taste of what it was like to work in the trade, and prepared me for my next position – as a brothel housekeeper in dull, suburban Bedford. As you'll later learn, the set-up there was even worse than in Burnley, the employer ruling with a rod of iron. But it was all good experience, and the various interviews I conducted with brothel maids, sex workers and their employers enabled me to build up a clear picture of what life is really like for a migrant worker in the sex industry.

So when film-maker Nick Broomfield contacted me to discuss making an undercover Channel 4 documentary about the sex trade, I felt quite confident that I would be able to do the job. This time, I was not only going to record the daily happenings in my diary, but also film them using a camera concealed in a pair of glasses. The footage would be saved on memory cards which I was to exchange with the crew as often as possible.

Once I'd learned how to use the glasses, I scoured the Chinese newspapers to find a job. Predictably, there were more vacancies in London than anywhere else: a staggering 80 per cent of women sex workers in the capital are migrants.

This time my cover identity was Xiao Yun, a forty-two-year-old single mother from Zhejiang province in southern China. (I chose Zhejiang because the social networks of the Zhejiangnese migrants are not as established as those of the Fujianese or north-eastern migrants. Therefore it was less likely that my deception would be discovered.) I had come to the UK three years earlier on a business visitor visa that had since expired, so was now an 'illegal'.

My first job interview was in an upmarket brothel called the House of Leisure in affluent St John's Wood. From its decor, it might have been a four-star hotel. A woman named Ling Ling, who looked to be in her early forties, came up to the top of the road to meet me, looking around warily all the time, as if to check that no one was following us. I hoped she hadn't spotted Nick in his spy glasses down the road. As we walked on, she told me that her premises, close to the famous Abbey Road recording studios, was a 'high-class place for wealthy locals'.

Although Ling Ling and I had talked only about housekeeping on the phone, when we finally sat down inside her room – the only place in her otherwise pitch-dark flat that had any sunlight coming through – she asked me whether I would consider sex work. 'Haven't you thought about that before?' she said in a soft voice. I was surprised, as this was the first time a brothel madam had asked me this openly. I demurred, saying I was too old.

'No, no, many women of your age do this work, believe me,' she persisted. Then she looked at my spy glasses and added, 'If you do decide to do this job, though, you can't wear your glasses during work.'

Ling Ling was obviously uninterested in hiring a maid. Back in the office, I dialled the number given in another job ad and got through to a woman named Ah Qin, based in Stratford, east London, who was looking to exploit the business opportunity offered by the forthcoming Olympic Games. That was my first job for our documentary, though I was no more successful there than I'd been in Burnley. A week later, as it became clear that Ah Qin's new venture wasn't going to work out, I appeared to be the major dispensable item and was dismissed after being paid half of what was promised. Fortunately, one of my co-workers at Stratford, a girl from Taiwan, tipped me off about a new housekeeping job in Finchley, where I was subsequently employed for six weeks.

This turned out to be toughest assignment I have ever undertaken. Partly, it was because both my task and my agenda were different from previous undercover jobs. Filming without permission was difficult enough, but I also had to make sure that the battery in my glasses stayed charged as well as recording the footage onto memory cards, changing the cards when they were full and smuggling them out. And all without letting anyone suspect what I was up to. (There was a full day when I simply couldn't find a place to recharge the battery and therefore couldn't film.) Apart from these technical difficulties, I had to develop my relationship with the women around me and deal with Grace, my harridan of an employer, who began to pressure me to 'help out with sex work' almost as soon as I arrived.

As someone experienced in undercover work, I'd never imagined that I wouldn't be able to cope with life inside a brothel. I had thought that the only challenge for me would be to produce visually satisfactory material for a documentary. To my surprise, within two weeks I began to feel so emotionally and physically exhausted that I felt a desperate need to leave the place. It affected my performance inside the brothel and I was losing concentration even in the everyday tasks my job as a housekeeper obliged me to do: cleaning, cooking, opening the door to customers and keeping track of each girl's daily earnings.

I tried to control my own feelings and not allow despair to creep in. I constantly reminded myself that I was doing an undercover job and that I mustn't become emotionally involved. But things continued to deteriorate. My stubborn refusal to take up part-time sex work in addition to maiding had infuriated Grace, resulting in constant verbal abuse on a daily basis. It was becoming unbearable and I was ready to give up.

At the time, my reaction puzzled me, but I later realised the reason for it. I had focused on filming and writing about the women I had met and talked to and their relationship with their employer. I had observed the daily life of the women without trying to reflect on what was happening to me and my own feelings. By ignoring my own emotions, I wasn't understanding them. I had participated emotionally in all that was happening around me. I had internalised the pain and hardship these women were suffering and the inhumane relations I had witnessed. Simply put, I had let it get to me. When Grace gave me her harsh moralistic lectures on how to earn money for my family, I tried to hold back my tears and smile it away. But soon enough, I found myself crying uncontrollably behind the closed bathroom door. By my fourth week into the job, after each session of bullying and verbal abuse I was locking myself in the toilet in order to find some individual space where I could try to put myself together again.

I had become Xiao Yun. How could I not? I had adopted the identity of a single mother working without papers and willing to do anything in order to support her family back home. Desperation motivated Xiao Yun, and everyone around her could see that. Grace saw that very well. She wanted to make sure Xiao Yun would yield to her pressure to take up sex work, for then she would become even more desperate, even more malleable. I experienced what was inflicted upon Xiao Yun, as I was meant to. The problem was that Xiao Yun and I were now one. I took personally everything that was happening to her. I felt everything that she would possibly feel.

I survived only because I knew there would come a moment when I could leave Xiao Yun behind. At the end of the assignment I could walk away and shed her like a too-tight skin. I would be able to leave this underground world, never to return. But Xiao Yun and her kind would not be so fortunate.

Günter Wallraff's undercover persona, Ali, suffered similarly. Through Ali, Wallraff saw the racism of German society, the hypocrisy and brutality of the ruling ideologies; in his words, he saw an apartheid within a 'democracy'. Through Xiao Yun, I saw the sacrifice of all those migrant mothers who are like her. I experienced what they have to endure in a society that has consigned so many migrant women to a subhuman existence.

London Calling

I met Ming for the first time five summers ago, when a friend of a London kitchen fryer known as Brother Li introduced us. But it took more than one phone call to convince her she could trust me. At the time, Ming was a thirty-two-year-old single mother from the outskirts of Shenyang in the north-east of China. For most of her adult life she had worked her heart out in a state-run brewery, until 2003, when the company laid her off, along with fifty others. Ming told me she'd been the victim of so-called 'reform' that had swept across the industrial north-east of the country resulting in mass job losses. The minimal compensation she had received on her dismissal had lasted barely two years, and she had found it increasingly difficult to support her seven-year-old daughter and elderly parents. Decent jobs in her city were few and Ming eventually felt she had no option but to go abroad. She borrowed what was, for her, a large sum of money and left the country to seek a livelihood.

I was anxious to hear Ming's story, but when I finally sat her down to talk about her life in Britain, she had other things in mind. She wanted to tell me about Xiao Mei, a murdered fellow migrant whom she'd never met, but whose own tale Ming had somehow internalised. Ming seemed haunted by Xiao Mei's misfortune. 'It is so sad,' Ming said frowning solemnly, stirring the hot chocolate in front of her in a café in Chinatown, the only place she would meet me. She raised her thick eyebrows as she spoke, her dark brown eyes shining movingly with melancholic compassion. Her straight dyed brown hair, long to the top of her jeans, looked reddish against the sunlight through the window.

It all started on a sunny day at the open market on Whitechapel Road, Ming told me breathlessly. The midday hustling and bustling had only just begun, right below the first-floor room where Lenin had stayed during his years in exile. Here, British Asian street sellers of cheap garments and handbags busied themselves with more customers than usual – when the sun was out, business prospered. Meanwhile, young South African nurses and Lithuanian builders and labourers strolled along during their lunch break from the Royal London Hospital across the road.

A few steps away, old men clutched half empty bottles of drink outside the Blind Beggar, waiting for it to open. (Back in 1966, the much-feared East End gangster Ronnie Kray shot his rival George Cornell in this pub when he was enjoying a gin and tonic, because Cornell had publicly called him a 'big fat poof'.) That morning, Ming related, a group of young Chinese men and women arrived outside the pub – all with bags and rucksacks of DVDs on their shoulders. They made a space of a few yards between each other, and formed a line of street sellers in front of the underground station. Each of them watched the movement of the pedestrians warily, alert for plain-clothes police officers – men who often confiscated counterfeit DVDs but kept them for their own consumption.

Like all the others, Xiao Mei carried hundreds of DVDs in her bag, ready for a long working day. To protect her eyes from the strong sunshine, she pulled down a white straw hat she had brought from home, a tiny village in Jiangjing, central Fujian. Xiao Mei had left Fujian with her husband a year before, but had already outgrown her nostalgia for home. Eking out a meagre living on a tiny plot of land was not something either of them wanted to return to. For the same reason, tens of thousands had left villages around Jiangjing to come to Britain to work in the past fifteen years.

At the time, Xiao Mei and her husband's primary aim was to pay off their suffocatingly heavy debts to the moneylenders from whom they had borrowed to pay the smuggler's fees. Their need to earn fast had taught them to be accepting of all the available work choices and conditions in Britain, no matter how difficult. But it had become increasingly hard to get any sort of employment in the Chinese catering trade, so the couple had decided to go into DVD selling on the street, exactly as many of their relatives and neighbours from their village had.

They had moved into a crowded first-floor flat on Cannon Street Road, just off the busy Commercial Road, with their cousins and villagers who'd come to Britain earlier. The group kept to themselves, constantly aware of the risks of exposing their place of residence to the authorities. Luckily, everyone else in the building seemed to like minding their own business, too. Their next-door neighbours were a group of young Ukrainian men and women who never tried to strike up a conversation with anyone outside their flat. The only thing the Chinese knew about the Ukrainians was that they seemed always to return home late in the evening – perhaps they worked shifts as cleaners or bartenders?

Despite its modest surroundings in the more run-down part of the area, Cannon Street Road was a perfect place for the

Chinese migrants – it was relatively secluded and only a few blocks from the main street where they did their DVD selling. But one unlucky workday, Xiao Mei's husband hadn't run fast enough when the police officers showed up on Whitechapel Road. He had been arrested and jailed, a devastating development. Xiao Mei hadn't blamed him for being careless, nor the police officers for catching him. She was modest and accepting, quite like Ming, as I found out later. Xiao Mei blamed her own fate instead. After all, it was fate that had condemned her to a life of poverty as a *nongmin* (peasant) in Fujian; she had only the heavens to cry to.

Xiao Mei had no idea if her husband would be deported at the end of his prison sentence. Thus the burden of debt she carried on her shoulders had become even heavier. She had to make more money, even faster, to be able to pay off their debts. Only then could her two sons back home finally benefit from any improvement in their lives. Xiao Mei was aware of the many risks around her: not only of police raids, but robberies by local youths who targeted Chinese street sellers. She knew also that for many local men she was viewed as an exotic sex object on display. Xiao Mei and every other female DVD seller knew that many of the men who walked past were not interested in buying DVDs; many seemed to have a fetish for East Asian females.

Ming sneered and shrugged her shoulders at this point. It was as if she herself had had similar experiences. On Whitechapel Road, most of the Chinese women selling DVDs didn't mind the local men's over-friendly approaches, patting them on the shoulders or touching their arms, so long as they took a few pounds out of their pockets and bought a couple of DVDs. As one told me later, 'There's always the risks of being troubled and harassed; there's no way around it. But the main thing is to sell the goods. We'll tolerate most things in order to achieve that, and local men know it – they know we'll put up with their rude manners and talk.'

Often, local men would approach the most attractive of the Chinese women asking them whether they 'liked to fuck'. Initially, the women didn't know how to respond. They would giggle and wave the men away. But some men took it a step further, asking the women to return home with them 'to try out the DVDs first' before buying them. It couldn't have been easy to refuse such requests, Ming said, shaking her head, sighing. After all, these men were their local buyers, and losing only one of them meant losing potential income on this street.

Under such pressure, some felt compelled to agree, in spite of the dangers. For these women, the risks did not seem as frightening as being arrested and deported back to China. And once again, they trusted to fate. 'It all depends on luck, whether you stay safe or not,' one of Xiao Mei's fellow villagers later told me.

Knowing the migrants were without papers and all on their own, certain local men felt free to do anything they wanted. Some women had been sexually assaulted or even raped in customers' homes. Others felt they had no alternative but to accept money for sex.

The day Xiao Mei was murdered had been a slow one, Ming said. After several hours Xiao Mei had sold only five DVDs, earning a mere £10. She had begun to feel restless. But the sellers couldn't be too aggressive with their sales pitches. Police raids had increased in the area and everyone had to be vigilant. For fear of attracting the authorities' attention, sellers had to wait for buyers to approach them.

'Miss,' a voice said from behind her.

Xiao Mei looked back and saw one of her regulars – an overweight forty-something white man. She remembered him well because of the paleness of his face. He was wearing a rucksack on his shoulders. He smiled at her uneasily.

'You want DVDs, Mr Brown?' she asked automatically. These were among the few words of English that she knew.

The man stared at her, not uttering a word. What was he thinking? Xiao Mei dared not look into his eyes.

'DVDs? I have many,' she pressed on nevertheless, taking a handful of samples out of her bag. All the latest blockbusters.

The man took the discs in his hands and flipped through them quickly, clearly not really interested.

'Which one you want?' Xiao Mei asked, hoping for a sale.

He rubbed his dark brown hair and shook his head, saying, 'I've no idea if these are of good quality. They aren't always good.'

'Good quality! Very good quality!' Xiao Mei responded enthusiastically, with her thumb up, eager to persuade him.

'Well,' said the man, shaking his head again as if to make sure that Xiao Mei understood. 'As I said, I've bought these DVDs before and they were all crap. I'll have to try them at home before I can pay you for any of them.'

As Xiao Mei anxiously looked for words to respond, he stared at her again and asked, 'I can try these at home now if you like. If they are all right, I'll buy them.'

Xiao Mei nodded gratefully. She had been to his place a few times before. As she had described it to her co-workers, it was in a strange part of London called Rotherhithe, just one stop away on the underground. Feeling desperate to sell at least a few copies today, she saw no alternative but to go with him.

Xiao Mei's co-workers watched her leave with the middle-aged white man, disappearing inside Whitechapel tube station. They saw nothing odd about it. No one knew where he lived, because sellers kept their regular customers' contact details a secret from each other, to avoid competition for sales.

Xiao Mei's co-workers and relatives recalled that she had always blamed herself for not understanding customers properly. She blamed herself for not speaking much English. Without the language, this regular customer's long, vacant gaze, his expressionless face and his tendency to repeat questions would not mean very much. This language barrier served to benefit Brown – it protected him from becoming recognised for who or what he was.

But even if Xiao Mei had been able to understand English well, how could she ever have known that this man had been reading a copy of Nigel Cawthorne's *Killers: The Most Barbaric Murders of Our Time* that he'd borrowed from a local library? How could she have known that he was a convicted rapist? He was a fan and a determined follower of Jack the Ripper who murdered at least five women in the Whitechapel area in 1888. And how could she possibly have known that he'd also been studying the 'Yorkshire Ripper' Peter Sutcliffe, who murdered thirteen women between 1975 and 1980.

Xiao Mei certainly had no idea that this forty-eight-year-old man sitting right next to her had brutally murdered twenty-four-year-old Bonnie Barrett a few weeks previously, in the very flat to which he was now leading her. Bonnie had worked in the red-light district of Commercial Street just down the road and she had been paid for sex by Brown. She was a single mother of a seven-year-old boy.

For him, Xiao Mei was a particularly soft target: a Chinese migrant without papers, trying to make a living in a much criminalised community. On top of this, she was selling counterfeit DVDs. She knew few people in this country and spoke little English. As her killer, Derek Brown, later said in court, he thought that 'she would not be missed'.

That evening when Xiao Mei did not return to the Cannon Street Road flat to cook dinner with her relatives, they became alarmed. She knew no one outside their circle of new Chinese migrants; she would have nowhere to go after work but home. In the days that followed, Xiao Mei's cousins scoured east London in a vain effort to find her, calling all their contacts and village friends. They couldn't believe that she had just vanished. Weeks went past, and there was no trace of her. Eventually, they gave up hope. But no one reported her disappearance to the police, for fear of deportation.

Ming became more saddened as she carried on. She said she was very frightened on hearing from her flatmate about Xiao Mei's death. Her body was never recovered, but the details of her brutal death eventually emerged during the trial of her murderer many months later, just after Ming arrived in England.

The murder had rocked the small community, and the tragedy quickly became ingrained in Ming's mind. As a migrant working mother, Ming told me, Xiao Mei had been a victim of choiceless choices. Ming, too, felt that she was such a victim. Ultimately, she said, without capital there was no such thing as free will.

Ming was not alone in such sentiments. Over the past decade, an increasing number of Chinese women had been compelled to become the sole breadwinners of their families and had 'chosen' to migrate abroad in search of a livelihood to sustain their families. In China, economic reforms and the opening-up (*gaige kaifang*) to the world market had dramatically changed – and lowered – the social position of women. The institutional framework that used to offer certain basic levels of security in women's livelihood before the late 1970s has been taken away. Women have also become increasingly marginalised in the job market. Not only were women disproportionately affected by the mass redundancies from state-owned enterprises, they also received less state support than their male counterparts after being laid off, and they had less chance of re-employment.

As Ming said, women in China today no longer 'hold up half the sky'. Gender equality has been much eroded under *gaige kaifang*. 'We women have to fight for our own survival,' she said.

Thus, today, women comprise a large proportion of Chinese migrant workers, and many have become the main earners of the family. But they still tend to migrate into female-dominated, female-specific occupations bound up with traditional gender roles. In Britain, more and more migrant women have been compelled to take up temporary work as carers, cleaners, domestic workers, masseuses and sex workers. In this context, Chinese women in Britain have found themselves at the bottom of the lowest-paid casual employment. The threat of exposure of their illegal status, job insecurity and the need to seek better options to improve income mean that these women are highly mobile, ready to change from one type of casual job to the next, seeking to maximise opportunity.

When Ming first arrived in Britain, she went searching for work in London's Chinatown. There she met a woman of her age from Shenyang, who had been working in the catering trade for a long while and knew someone working in a Chinese restaurant in Elephant & Castle. She said they were looking for a kitchen worker, *da-za* (sorting bits: a kitchen porter). Ming immediately asked for her introduction to the restaurant manager and got the job.

To be near work, she moved to Elephant & Castle, an area which she found unpleasant and 'stinky'. There was litter everywhere, she said, and the second-floor flat was terribly crowded, with ten of them sharing three rooms. But her flatmates all reassured her that it was the best place they'd found in London.

So Ming arrived at the Phoenix Tower restaurant – a name typical of a thousand others scattered across Britain – for her first job in England. It was a few bus stops away from her flat, and a few blocks away from a well known Chinese restaurant owned by a Mr Big in London's Chinese communities. Mr Big, from Fujian, had set off his career by working as a people smuggler. During the peak of his business, he was moving 20,000 people per year. He accumulated his wealth and became head of a well known Chinese community organisation. Mr Big is obviously a popular man. Or at least this was what everyone told her on her first day in the kitchen. They said Phoenix Tower, with only twelve tables, is tiny in comparison with their rival restaurant. And their boss, a fifty-two-year-old originally from Hong Kong, is a nobody. 'But big or small, the food these restaurants offer is more or less the same,' Brother Li whispered to Ming. 'This is called the *guilao* [ghost: a Westerner] food, unauthentic Chinese food made to fool the Westerners.'

Ming listened, amazed. 'No wonder there was a smell of stale sweet and sour fish the moment I entered the restaurant. Guess it's very popular around here.'

'Definitely,' Brother Li giggled. 'For the locals, it is our national dish.'

Ming couldn't help laughing at the idea, but quickly restrained herself when 'Fat' Fai, the chef, turned his head. She then murmured to Brother Li, 'I haven't the slightest clue about this food, though. We north-easterners don't eat much that's sweet.'

'No worries,' Brother Li smiled, pushing up his glasses. 'Your job doesn't involve much cooking. All you have to do is chopping and cleaning up after the others.'

So Ming started working, ten hours per day, six days a week, under Fai's nose. Fai was known for always trying to exchange his 'protection' for sexual favours from female workers. A chef has a lot of power in a kitchen, deciding who stays and who goes. If you get on the wrong side of the chef, you're on your way out, Ming explained. Fai constantly harassed her, both verbally and physically, but she had little means of avoiding him. If she moved away, it caused great offence. So she stopped saying no.

Ming felt as if she was prostituting herself – swallowing her pride when it was being trodden upon. Besides cringing inside at his crude groping and gestures, she also had to put up with a constant stream of invective from the Cantonese-speaking manager, for whom it had become a habit to abuse all the kitchen staff.

'Bosses and workers can never sit on the same bench,' Ming told me, quoting a Chinese saying. She knew that the two could never be equals. She'd had to lower her head while being exploited and abused. Sometimes she felt they were trying to push her to the limit, just to see how much she could take.

Brother Li told her that Phoenix Tower was a small, family run business, like many Chinese restaurants, that profited by squeezing sweat and blood out of its workers. These catering businesses had increasingly relied on asylum seekers and migrants without papers from China for their staff over the past decades. Wages were kept impossibly low and work conditions were punishing. Ming herself was earning £200 for a sixty-hour week. 'Wages stagnate in this trade,' Brother Li told her. 'Take London Chinatown, for example: twenty-five years ago, the average wage there was just over £3 per hour for the waiters. Today it is barely £5, well below the national minimum wage – and the kitchen workers without papers always get less. Things seem able to remain the same for eternity.' Brother Li shook his head.

And the workload increased for Ming. Soon she was asked to arrive an hour early to start her food preparation. Often, she was made to work an hour late, with no extra pay. Brother Li's statement that 'all Chinese restaurants are the same' was no consolation. Every day she dreamt of giving up her job and walking out the door. She fantasised about spitting in their greasy faces and tearing off all the tablecloths during the restaurant's rush hour. But instead she bit her tongue and kept her head down, busying herself with her duties and restraining her contempt.

One late night after a very long day, Ming caught the bus back to her flat, as usual. When she arrived home at 1 a.m., the streets had quietened down, and even the Chinese superstore next door had closed for the night. In their tiny room lit by a dim light, her room-mate Ying was still awake, sitting on her mattress and talking to a friend on her mobile phone. 'Want some snacks?' she offered, pushing a plate of duck towards Ming's mattress. It was the leftovers from the kitchen where Ying worked. She was now an experienced fryer and was able to bring food home sometimes.

Ming nibbled the bits of duck on her plate. 'What a hell of a day,' she sighed, as soon as Ying finished her phone conversation. 'I really can't stand that place. The work is killing me. Just over three pounds an hour for all that bossing around! And I'm supposed to appreciate the favour and shut up.'

'Join the club! Everyone's doing tough work for shit money,' Ying said, with an angry edge to her voice. 'You just have to clench your teeth and get on with it, like everyone else. We're all *laobaixing* [common folk] back home. If you never suffered a day in your working life in China, you wouldn't need to come here, either. Am I right?'

A few minutes later, Ying's impatience mellowed. She picked a duck bone out of her mouth. 'You know, better-paid work comes with its own price,' she remarked. 'You want to know how to get the best-paid work in this country?'

Ming looked up at her and nodded.

'Open your legs! A friend of mine has got herself a job in a massage parlour. She's making a minimum of £150 a day! She moans about having a bad day when she earns even that. If there are less than six customers in a day, she gets insecure and calls me to ask if I think there's a problem with her Chinese nose! Given all her "bad days", she's nearly paid off her debt, while I'm still struggling to keep this stupid job! Pity that I don't have pretty legs to open!'

Ming lay on her bed, without saying a word. She didn't want to reveal to Ying that she had actually thought about this option. The idea came to her on each of her bad days in the kitchen. Who wouldn't want to pay off debts of 100,000 yuan (around £10,000) within a few months? She was desperate to send money home to her parents and to her seven-year-old daughter, Ting Ting.

'I've seen the ads in the newspaper,' Ming said.

'Lots of Chinese girls sell sex,' said Ying. 'There's a big market for foreigners in the sex trade here. Chinese massage parlours are nothing but *ji-dian* [chicken shops: brothels]. You'll be hard-pressed to find a real Chinese massage parlour that only does massage. When you see the ads of massage parlours in the papers, they're all brothels, without exception. You can tell by the language.'

Ying took out a Chinese newspaper and showed the ad pages to Ming, pointing out a relatively famous brothel: *Red Tower. Seven Sisters (light blue line) underground station exit 1. Three minutes by foot. Newly arrived beautiful ladies from Asia. Elegant environment. Thorough service. Plus professional massage and foot massage. Open 3 p.m.–3 a.m. Young and beautiful ladies are very welcome to join us. Kind boss. Safe place. Weekly income can reach £2,500. For Chinese customers.*

'Two and a half thousand a week! How could that be possible?' Ming could scarcely conceive of such earnings.

'Another popular one here,' Ying said, ignoring Ming's reaction and pointing to the next ad down: *Palace. Situated in zone one of London. Close to Marylebone and Baker Street underground stations. One minute by foot. High-class residential area. Reasonable price. Newly arriving Chinese, Japanese, Korean and Malaysian girls every day. Providing you with warm and complete service. Opening hours: 2 p.m.–4 a.m. Also recruiting young and beautiful Chinese, Japanese and Korean ladies. The highest share of wages in the UK. Including base salary. £3,000 weekly income.*

'Three thousand pounds per week! Is that really true?' Ming asked with astonishment.

'If you work really hard. It's flexible and depends on you. You'd be like a self-employed person – the only difference is that you don't pay tax. You decide how much you want to earn. Hard work is rewarded with good income. My friend in the parlour told me so,' Ying replied. They carried on looking through the pages and spotted an ad for a massage parlour nearby in their area: *Situated in Elephant & Castle. Two minutes from underground station. Our motto is: Dare to visit? We will make you come hard! Urgently recruiting young and beautiful massage ladies. Excellent rewards. £2,500 per week. No experience required.*

'There's such a big market that many Chinese medicine clinics now include sex along with massage therapy. They're practically brothels with Chinese medicine as the front of the shop!' Ying said. 'You're pretty enough, Ming, I'm sure any of these parlours and clinics would take you on immediately.'

Ming hesitated, puzzled as to why Ying was so eager to encourage her to *xia hai* (go into the sea: enter the sex trade). 'I'm not really pretty,' she said. 'And look at me, I'm not exactly thin.' Ming showed Ying her thighs. 'Flabby. I wouldn't pass the test.'

'Don't be silly. Do you think all *xiaojies* [female sex workers] look like Zhang Ziyi [a Chinese actress]?' Ying challenged her. 'Your age is perfect for this. Thirty-two. Not too young to be scarred by the experience. Not too old to collapse during your first session! Besides, those simple-minded Westerners don't know the bloody difference. Tell them that you're in your twenties and they'll treat you like a goddess. We Chinese look younger than our real age anyway. The only places that you might not be able to pass the test are those for Chinese customers – Chinese men are more fussy about age.'

Ming frowned. The idea of sex with strangers disturbed her; more so the idea of doing it for money. And the ten-hour work day she'd just finished had left her exhausted. She switched herself off to Ying's words and fell asleep. That night she dreamt she was dressed in a red silk dress she'd seen many times in a shop window in a bustling street of central Shenyang. The dress was her favourite, even though she'd not been able to afford it. Now in her dream she was wearing it and the silk hugged her frame closely.

Ming realised she was late for Ting Ting, who was waiting to be picked up after school. She looked across the street and saw her daughter standing there. The little girl waved and flashed a broad smile. Her ponytail made her look much younger, as she had when her father was still around, a much happier time in their life. 'Ting Ting! Wait for me there!' Ming shouted.

Ting Ting didn't hear. Eager to reach her mother, she stepped into the street. A bus turned the corner and couldn't stop. Ting Ting was still looking at Ming and running towards her when the bus hit her. Ming screamed, but for some reason her voice didn't make a sound. It was as if it wouldn't be allowed out. Time had stopped, and Ting Ting had stopped. Only her blood flowed: she was covered in red, and so was the zebra crossing.

Ming opened her eyes in desperate shock, finally able to scream out loud. Then she saw her room-mate Ying lying next to her on the mattress, breathing heavily as she always did in sleep. Their white walls still gleamed in the dark. No blood stain. This was Ming's first nightmare in England. But she had never felt more relieved in her whole life, because Ting Ting was all right.

In spite of this knowledge, the image of Ting Ting in front of a bus haunted her. Was it a bad sign? Ming was not a superstitious person when she first came to Britain, but since arriving in the UK her thoughts had become more inclined towards the mystical. Perhaps it was the unpredictable nature of her working life here that had changed her. She would hate to think that a nightmare could be a premonition. When she woke the next morning, she decided to call her parents before she went to work. They reassured her that everything was fine. Ting Ting chatted to her on the phone about her school lessons and the latest exams. 'Ma, I got the highest in Maths in my class!' she reported happily. Ming reminded her not to forget to study English in the after-school lessons that she was paying for.

'If you don't want to work so hard like Mama now, then you must study English,' she warned her.

Another month went by and Ming was still working in the kitchen. The long hours of chopping, washing and cleaning in the dim light and the lack of ventilation were beginning to make her ill. She often felt dizzy at work, as if she was about to faint. She sometimes had to ask Fai's permission to have a sit down. Fai was playing hot and cold with her every day. Sometimes he would try to flatter her. 'You are too good to be *da-za* in England!' he said. At other times, though, he would fly into a rage, shouting at her for not responding to him quickly enough. 'Listen to me, you old rag! I've been pitying you or you'd have been kicked out of here long ago!' Day after day, Fai and the manager's voices became like a swarm of buzzing flies around her.

Each day Ming could hear the clock ticking above her on the wall. She felt every minute of her remaining youth draining away in this terrible place. And the worst thing was that no one knew and no one cared. She felt as if she was living in silent torture. One day, as Fai piled yet another huge amount of work on her, she bit her tongue and turned away. 'Stop sulking,' he said, trying provoke her. But neither of them expected what happened next.

They heard people screaming from the front of the restaurant. Heavy boots. Men walking about, talking loudly on mobile phones. Metal sounds. And the English words 'Don't move!'

One of the waiters ran into the kitchen to inform them that five or six officers – immigration officers and police – had stormed into the restaurant. As their raised voices came closer, Brother Li was urgently leading the staff out through the back door.

'Run!' he shouted. 'We must run, now!'

Ming's instinct told her that Brother Li was right. She ran as fast as she could behind him, too frightened to look back. She didn't know if anyone was chasing them. She was too scared to think. Ming and Brother Li didn't stop running for forty minutes, and when they finally stopped, exhausted and out of breath, they realised they'd run all the way from Elephant & Castle to Brixton.

Go West

Not ten minutes' walk from Whitechapel tube station, just past Commercial Road, will bring you to the red-light district bordering the City of London. It is a far cry from the street where the weary-looking Chinese DVD sellers work. Here you will reach a cluster of 'gentlemen's entertainment' venues, the most popular of which are Club Oops on Alie Street and Whites Gentlemen's Club on Leman Street. Unlike the socially inadequate single men who harass the Chinese women DVD sellers for sex, the clientele around Aldgate East are bankers and brokers looking for a lavish way of spending their evenings after work.

At 4 p.m. the ground-floor bar at Club Oops has just opened. The lap dancers are downstairs in the basement getting dressed and made-up, chatting about who's looking her best this evening. Soon they will climb the narrow stairs to start their evening's shift, clad in scanty silk dresses. They will flock to the shiny marble bar, seeking out lone punters and asking what type of service they require. Most men start out with a few drinks at a table accompanied by a smiling escort; later they will graduate to other services offered elsewhere in the club. Club Oops is no different from a dozen other strip venues scattered across

London: about half of its girls are migrants from eastern and south-eastern Europe. Many of these women never imagined they would wind up working in the British sex trade.

Beata is one such woman. When she left Poland five years ago, she thought she would find herself an 'ordinary job' that required little English and would remain in it until she returned home. She had no idea that the precarious employment environment in which she found herself trapped soon after she arrived in the UK would lead her into selling her body for money.

Beata was from Katowice, a tired-looking southern Polish industrial city which used to be known as Stalinogród up until Stalin's death in 1953. Its exhausted concrete landscape recalls a bygone nineteenth-century industrial boom and says something about the reasons for the departure of many of its youth in the past decade. There, Beata struggled through every day contemplating a change, an escape from her despair.

Some might think that Beata was fortunate enough. She worked as a quality controller in a busy electronics firm in central Katowice. It wasn't exactly a management position, but many of her peers envied her promotion prospects. She was good at her job and was well respected by those around her. The problem was her monthly wage, which was the equivalent of £200. Although it was a regular income, it hardly covered the day-to-day living costs of the entire family whose livelihood she bore on her shoulders.

Beata's father was a carpenter and her mother worked in a food-processing factory. They were, she told me, a 'typical, working-class household in Katowice'. The family shared a four-room flat, and the monthly rent of £200 was partly paid out of her mother's meagre monthly wages of £150. Life became even tougher when Beata's parents reached retirement. They could barely afford a basic standard of living on their monthly pension.

When Poland joined the EU, which by then had twenty-five member states, on 1 May 2004, Polish working-class people felt optimistic about the forthcoming changes and the potential for increased prosperity. However, while the country quickly attracted investment from abroad as a result of its low labour costs, many Polish workers became unwilling to put up with an average hourly wage approximately six times lower than that in Germany, just next door. They made their plans to migrate to take advantage of the higher-paid work and better career prospects in western Europe.

For Beata, the turning point came when she felt she could no longer meet the needs of her six-year-old son Tomasz. It was very painful for her to admit that in Poland she could not afford to care for him as she wished. It hadn't helped that her husband Mariusz had been an absentee father.

'Where's Mariusz?' Beata asked her mother when she walked into the flat after each long working day.

'Where do you think?' her mother replied, shrugging her shoulders. 'He's out drinking again.'

Mariusz had taken to drink and that seemed to be all he ever did after work.

'He's in trouble, isn't he?' her mother asked. 'He's drinking more than ever.'

Beata knew that Mariusz was no longer the man she had married six years previously. It wasn't that he'd ever betrayed or mistreated her – in fact, he had never raised his voice to her, even when she lost her temper and yelled at him – but something had certainly changed.

She tried to rationalize the situation. Mariusz was a plumber, a good one. Perhaps he'd been overworking, or was finding their cramped living conditions too claustrophobic. Perhaps he just needed more space, away from the family environment. Mariusz was a simple man and the only way he was able to relieve his stress was to drink. Things would get better; that was what she hoped.

But things got worse. Mariusz became an alcoholic. He rarely saw his son. And as his addiction took hold, he became unfit for work. Before long he had lost the job he was so good at, and Beata had become the sole breadwinner for three generations.

The strain began to wear down the love she had for Mariusz. She didn't want their relationship to end, but despite trying so hard, she just couldn't feel the same about him any more. Instead, she began to feel hopelessly trapped, bitter at all that life had thrown at her. She needed a way out of the marriage that had failed her – and escape from the desperately lonely and unhappy place in which she found herself.

After listening to all Beata's troubles, her best friend Anna presented her with a solution: 'Why don't you leave Poland and go to the West?'

The idea of seeking employment in western Europe was not totally unfamiliar. After all, Poles had been venturing into western European countries for work well before the EU enlargement in 2004, many without papers. In Britain they had helped fill the labour shortfalls in food-processing, agriculture and construction. They had gained a reputation abroad as both hard-working and willing to endure harsh working conditions.

Like most Poles, Beata and Anna already knew quite a lot about western Europe. In the years following the collapse of the Eastern bloc in 1989, western Europeans had exported their culture to central and eastern Europe. Of course, there was the highly visible consumer culture that was clearly incompatible with the local living standards and completely at odds with the lifestyle of the majority of the population, but there was also a distinctively new and developing urban environment shaped by the growing numbers of visiting tourists from western Europe.

Following the EU enlargement in 2004, travel to central and eastern Europe became much easier and cheaper, and sex tourism prospered in the new accession countries, particularly Poland, the Czech Republic, Latvia, Lithuania, Estonia, Hungary and Slovakia. Despite the fact that prostitution remains officially illegal in most of these countries, cities like Krakow, Warsaw, Prague, Riga, Tallinn, Budapest and Bratislava soon became popular with sex tourists. A culture of eroticisation and commodification of women's bodies soon developed. 'Eastern European' femininity became an idealised product, sought after by wealthy Westerners. This growing demand also led to a boom in women from the Eastern-bloc countries working in western Europe's sex industries.

TAMPEP, an Amsterdam-based international health-care foundation for migrant sex workers, recently produced a research report that shows this east–west divide by highlighting the striking differences in the EU sex industry. In most western European countries the vast majority of sex workers are migrants, for example Denmark has 65 per cent, Finland 69 per cent, Germany 65 per cent, Greece 73 per cent, Italy 90 per cent, Spain 90 per cent, Austria 78 per cent, Belgium 60 per cent, France 61 per cent and the Netherlands 60 per cent. But in the former Eastern-bloc countries, the reverse is true. For example, 98 per cent of sex workers in Slovakia, Romania and Bulgaria, 90 per cent in Lithuania and 66 per cent in Poland are of national origin.

In Katowice, the type of western European that Beata and Anna, both in their late twenties, would most often have encountered was a tourist. The perception among young Poles is that many of these visitors are sex tourists. In the alleyways of central Katowice, you will find many sex tourists from Germany and Britain, lured to Poland by the cheap strip clubs scattered across the city.

Further south in Krakow, one of the most popular Polish destinations for Westerners, the increase in the number of British visitors has created a culture of sex tourism which has boomed since Poland joined the EU. Although sex work per se isn't illegal in Poland, profiting from it or running a brothel is. Sex workers' income is not taxed, and sex work is perceived as, if not illegal, then certainly immoral by most of the population in this largely Catholic country. The growing number of sex businesses, therefore, are scattered and hidden, sex work often being covertly provided by escort agencies officially registered as other organisations. Brothels are found all over town, some near the train station, others dotted around the city centre, rather than concentrated in a designated red-light district. In the 'tourist-infested' Old Town are bars where young women offer visitors both company and sex, but English-language signs for strip clubs can be seen even in the middle of the countryside.

A hostel worker who has met many western European sex tourists told me, 'Sex tourism is relatively new, and it caters particularly for the British.' They have made Krakow one of the major markets for stag-night events and activities. One stag-night tour operator, Maximise, advertises that 'Krakow is now one of the hottest tickets in stag weekend locations. With Krakow having a higher than average female population, you can't help but have a great time!'

Here in Krakow, Polish femininity is on sale. Another popular stag operator, The Krakow Pissup, advertises 'Beers, Babes and Bullets'. Its activities include the six-hour, Krakow Tottie Tour, a pub crawl followed by visits to three lap-dancing clubs in town, one of which will offer a free table dance. 'The tour specialises in strip bars that are packed with beautiful Polish women,' the ad says. For all that, the excursion boasts a price of only £26. There's also the best-selling, two-hour-long Krakow 'Babes in Oil', which takes place in a bar in the city centre. The operator describes the 'exotic Pole' as 'weighing a hundred pounds, tall, blonde, long-legged, a big-busted twenty-four-year-old'.

'You'll get three rounds of wrestling, with two slippery bikini-clad Polish beauties fighting in oil just for your pleasure.' For that, the stag crowd of nine will each pay £35. All these services can be found with the same operator in Bratislava, Budapest, Prague, Riga, Tallinn and Warsaw, where sex tourism for western Europeans is also booming.

At the same time, the aforementioned cities are the major exporters of economic migrants from central and eastern Europe. For many women like Beata, their home cities no longer offer the opportunities they need to improve their lives.

Months passed after Anna raised the idea of going to work abroad, and Beata's situation got no better. Beata began to talk to Anna more seriously about leaving Poland, and England in particular seemed to be the most favourable among the few EU countries that did not impose too many restrictions on the movement of workers from the new accession countries. Apart from the fact that the pound was strong, they'd also heard that it was relatively easy to find employment in Britain, where there were already several well-established Polish communities.

'I have heard that we Poles are the largest migrant group in Britain,' Anna told Beata. 'There are more than a million, if you include the first-generation Poles and the second generation who went there before 2004 and those who went afterwards.'

'That is a lot of us!' Beata said, feeling greatly encouraged. 'There must be a lot of work around.'

'Sure there is. The Poles are all working hard and making a life for themselves there,' Anna carried on. 'I heard that many are working in flower and salad factories, others on large sweetcorn farms, supplying Britain's top supermarkets. I have a friend who was sent to work at World Flowers.'

'Really? What did she tell you about the work there?'

'She said it's not bad. It is tough work, but it pays the bills for her entire family.'

'That's what I'd like to do, too,' Beata said. After a pause, she asked Anna, 'Do jobs last in Britain?'

'I think so. I think we'll be all right over there. The Poles look after each other,' Anna encouraged Beata again. 'And no matter what happens, we'll have each other.'

Beata's spirits were lifted by the imagined prospect of working in Britain. For the first time in a long while she saw hope. Yes, she thought, there was nothing more important than improving her income and making life better for her son and her parents. Leaving home might also be the easiest way to end her dying marriage.

Beata approached a local agency and was told she would be given work as soon as she arrived in London. Anna promised to join her shortly afterwards.

However, the departure turned out to be much, much harder than Beata had ever imagined. On the eve of her journey, she put Tomasz to bed and told him her plans.

'I'll be away only for a little while, to earn some money for us,' she said.

'How long? When will you come back?' he asked anxiously.

Beata hesitated, not knowing how to tell him that she was planning to be away for six months.

'Two weeks? Will you be back in two weeks?' He'd never been parted from his mother for more than a day.

'I don't know yet, Tomasz,' she said, trying not to cry.

But Tomasz burst into tears. 'Please, Mama, tell me the truth.'

She just couldn't answer him, but held him tightly in her arms and they cried together. She tried to calm him down so that he would sleep. But he couldn't. He kept his eyes open all night.

Thankfully, by the early morning he had finally fallen asleep and Beata could leave without seeing the hurt in his eyes. She kissed him, said goodbye to her parents and left home for the airport.

She spent the entire flight crying and thinking of Tomasz. All the way from Katowice to London she could only ask herself whether she had made the right decision. Should she have stayed in Poland? How would Tomasz feel when he woke up?

Beata arrived in London with a pair of red, swollen eyes. Someone from the agency met her at Heathrow. He took her from the far west of London all the way to the far east, to a place called Ilford, where the agency head office was based.

'I've never seen anywhere quite so lifeless,' Beata described the Essex town to Anna on the phone. 'It's very frightening to be here. They led me into this cold little room that looked nothing like a head office. Who are they exactly? I haven't a clue.'

Before Beata had time to consider her options, she was taken to an overcrowded flat with other migrants from Poland, the Czech Republic and Slovakia and told to get ready for work the next day. All she was told was that she would be sent to work in a 'salad place'.

It was a salad-processing factory two hours away from Ilford by minibus, which meant that four hours were spent travelling to and from work each day. Beata had no idea where the factory

was, other than that it was in 'a village'. She barely survived
the first day of her new job because the temperature was so
low inside the factory and she had not been warned beforehand
to dress warmly. From then on, she always wore three pairs of
jeans and thick boots to work.

Every week, the agency sent her and the other migrants to
a different factory to process salad or pack fruit. She found the
constant change of workplace to be quite unsettling. However, as
other workers seemed to be able to keep their heads down and
cope with the ever-changing conditions, she did the same. She
worked tirelessly for twelve hours every day – harder than she had
ever had to work back home – and all for around £180 a week.

Even so, she was making nearly four times what she had
earned back home, and Beata would have been content to
carry on if the job had. 'It was tough then, but I was actually
quite happy in those days. I had more respect for myself,'
she recalled. However, the workers were getting fewer and
fewer hours. No one was given an explanation. Eventually,
the factory work was reduced to only one shift a week. When
Beata finally called the agency to inquire about the lack of
work, the staff mimicked her broken English and replied, 'We
have problem, problem with contract. So we get small hours.
Small hours, understand? Only one to two hours a week. No
more, understand?'

'It's not possible to live with so little work,' she said.

'Take it or leave it,' the woman said in her normal accent.

Beata spent the following days wandering around Ilford. If
she'd known about the job advertisements in *Loot*, she'd have
picked up a copy and started to apply. But she really had no
idea. Not a clue about how to start looking for work. So she
carried on exploring blindly, by foot. She wandered into places
along the high street and the byways of Ilford. She peeked in

through the window of a bakery, a café and many newsagents. She walked into two or three employment agencies and asked about any work. They took her name, registered her onto their system and told her she would be contacted when a vacancy arose.

One day, after she had walked for miles, searching aimlessly for jobs in shop windows, she stumbled across a place called Stratford. It stunned her. It looked like a bustling, 'happening' place where there might be more promising job prospects. She walked all round the indoor markets and through the arcades, looking for job ads in every possible window. For once, she felt hopeful about finding another job.

To Beata's delight, there were ads written in Polish in one of the shop windows along the arcade. She stopped to read them carefully. She looked at each one thoroughly, and couldn't help but feel inspired every time she read the words 'full-time job'.

'*Dobry rano*,' a gentle voice emerged from the bustle behind her. 'Looking for work, are you?'

Beata looked back. It was a young Polish man, his light brown hair shining in the sunlight that shone through the exit of the arcade.

'Yeah, I'm looking for work. You too?' she asked.

'Oh, no, I already have work. It's my day off today,' the man answered. 'Are you new here?'

'Yes …' Beata turned back to the ads in the window. 'I really must find some work soon.'

'Well, I know of a vacancy in a café, right here in Stratford. It's just outside the shopping centre.'

'You do?' Beata turned back to face him properly. She couldn't contain her excitement at this surprise. 'Where is the café? Could you take me there, please?'

'Sure! It's this way. Come with me. The café just put out the advert yesterday. So you're still early, I think. My friend works there and he told me about the job.'

Beata followed the man, speeding up her step, through the shopping mall and turned right onto the street.

'What kind of job is it?' Beata asked, her heart beating faster.

'You'll make sandwiches. I don't know anything else. You'll have to talk to the boss there.'

Eventually, they reached a busy café with metal chairs outside. Beata thanked the man gratefully and walked inside.

The employer, a local Englishman, seemed a bit too pleased at Beata's inquiry about the vacancy. In fact, his eyes lit up at the sight of her. Young, attractive – he probably thought she would be good for business. 'You're from Poland?' he asked.

'Yes. But I speak a little English,' Beata said.

'Good. Very good,' the boss looked her up and down, as if her looks were the primary requirement for the job. He nodded repeatedly. Then he got to the point: 'It's a very busy place. You'll work twelve hours a day, six days a week, all right? Your salary will be £200 a week.'

This is perfect, Beata thought. A lot better than the salad-processing and fruit-packing work. 'Please give me this opportunity,' she pleaded. His eyes kept switching between her lips and her bust.

'I've always liked your people,' he said patronisingly. 'We have a Polish boy here working in our kitchen. Good worker, he is. Never moans about doing a bit of overtime. You'll be making sandwiches and serving customers. You'll be our front-of-house face.'

It seemed obvious to Beata that she got the job because the English boss had a liking for 'foreign' women. She wasn't the type to use her looks to get ahead, but here in England, she felt like she was a guest. She felt she had to behave in a different way from how she would back home. She wanted to live up to the boss's expectations, to keep him happy and to keep the job. She found herself looking for tight tops with low-cut necklines to wear for work. He called her 'Polish babe' all the time and she accepted it. She secretly enjoyed his constant attention because it indicated job security for her. But at the same time she was aware that he wasn't really treating her as 'their kind'. She knew she was the 'exotic' selling point for this trendy sandwich bar and she was being used to help the business grow.

But over time the workload seemed to decrease and the pressure grew more intense. 'We're not doing that well here – not as well as we should, given the location,' the boss told her. Apart from the two hours between 11 a.m. and 1 p.m., there weren't that many people coming in. Beata felt the pressure to turn things round for the sandwich bar. She always put on her friendliest smile and greeted every customer sweetly and politely. 'How are you today?' 'Come back soon.'

However, nothing seemed to improve business. She wondered whether perhaps the sandwiches were a little over-priced. As the business continued to decline, the boss murmured about the burden of having too many people doing too little work. Beata feared the worst.

A short while later the boss announced that everyone's working hours were to be cut from twelve to eight a day. And their wages were to be reduced even more dramatically, down from £200 to £100 a week.

The cost of housing in London was high – the rent for her tiny room in a dingy flat in Stratford was £50 a week, a quarter of what she had been earning. Even so, Beata had been managing to send home about £100 a month to help feed her family. Now it would be difficult even to feed herself.

'I can't live on this money,' complained Beata. Her employer ignored her. No more 'Polish babe'. She was now struggling, sending home just £60 per month.

The worst was yet to come. Two months later, the boss gave them the news they were all fearing: the Stratford venture had failed. He would sell the business and relocate.

The workers were, naturally, upset. The Polish kitchen hand burst into tears. He had a family to feed back home.

'All finished! All finished!' he picked up his bag and walked out of the kitchen.

The boss tried to stop him, saying there was still work to be done.

The man turned to him and said, 'You say we all finish, we go now, not later!' The boss had given them no notice of dismissal, so the kitchen hand was simply doing the same.

Beata held her tears back. She wanted to maintain her dignity, too, like her Polish co-worker. She walked out of the sandwich shop without completing the day's work or looking back.

Jobless again, Beata began to search desperately for any opportunities in Stratford. Her friend Anna, having heard about her experiences, had decided against coming to England after all. Beata felt abandoned – and so helpless! She thought about her time here. Her months in England had taught her that someone in her situation had little chance of getting any remotely decent employment. 'Normal jobs aren't for us,' she said to Anna on the phone.

She would walk past employment agencies on Stratford High Road with their ads for clerical jobs. Without a good command of English, she knew she would only humiliate herself if she applied for office work. She knew she would only be able to get manual jobs, and despite the long hours and low pay, that sort of job wasn't easy to keep.

Beata found herself once again in front of the shop windows in Stratford shopping centre, jotting down phone numbers and the jobs they might lead to: 'Bakery assistant', 'Kitchen assistant', 'Cleaner'.

She couldn't help smiling as she looked at the words she'd written down. She had, after all, learned some English during her tragicomic job hunt. Perhaps she could eventually compile a dictionary of 'industrial English' for the Poles? She laughed at the thought.

'Hello,' a gentle male voice emerged from the bustle behind her once again.

She turned round, expecting to see the same Polish man who had told her about the sandwich-bar job. But instead it was a handsome dark-haired young man with a small beard. He looked southern European. He was wearing a high-collared black suit. 'Are you looking for work?'

'Yes ...' she replied, looking curiously at him.

'Where you from?' His eyes shone when he spoke.

'Poland.'

'Ah! Good, good!'

'And you?' she asked him.

'I'm from Albania.'

Beata knew nothing about his country of origin, apart from that severe poverty had driven many young men, followed by a growing number of young women, to Greece, Italy and Britain. Albanian authorities estimate their migrant population to have reached 50,000 in the UK, although little is known about this largely undocumented community.

'What do you do?' Beata wondered if he had an office job. Or he could perhaps be a salesman, with that suit.

'I work in a factory,' he said, looking kindly at her. 'Full-time work. My day off today.'

'You dress like this on your day off?' she said, smiling.

He shrugged his shoulders.

'You know about jobs in Stratford?' she asked. 'I'm looking for something like restaurant or bar work. A waitressing job.'

'I ask around for you,' he winked, smiling. 'You want cup of coffee?'

Why not? He might well get her a job somewhere. He was, after all, well dressed and seemed to be a cultivated man.

In a café nearby, Beata sipped the cappuccino he had bought her.

'Would you like a cake with the coffee?' he asked. She shook her head, watching him move his lips and his shining dark brown eyes.

'Don't look at me like that ... I'm shy!' he put his hand gently over her eyes.

That warm, solid feeling of his hand ... Beata secretly enjoyed that short moment of physical contact. She could sense that he didn't only want to help her find a job. As they sat facing each other, with cups of cappuccino in their hands, he introduced himself as 'Robert'. He said that he had been in England for a few years but had never been able to find anything much better than a factory job in Walthamstow. But fortunately, he said, he was single and didn't have a family to feed back home.

'You free tomorrow to see me? I take you to my friends. You like?' he invited.

Beata was delighted. She was hoping to get to know him better. They met in front of Stratford underground station the following day. Robert took her on the Central Line to a pub in Holborn. He said that he and his friends often met there for a drink.

Once inside the pub, Beata and Robert were greeted warmly by a group of young Albanian men, all drinking and talking in

Albanian. They had all brought their girlfriends with them: the women, all identically blonde, looked younger than Beata.

'This is my girl,' Robert introduced Beata. His girl? She was taken aback. They had only met yesterday. Robert's mates stared at her as if she were some kind of trophy that he'd just won and was displaying for their approval. She didn't mind the attention. In fact, she quite enjoyed it, as she was already becoming attached to him. There was something about him that drew her towards him. She didn't mind that none of his friends actually struck up a conversation with her.

Robert sat her down among the group of women while he carried on talking to his friends. Beata looked at the women, wondering where these men had found such girlfriends. They all looked like models! Meanwhile, the women were looking Beata up and down, scrutinising her with competitive blue eyes. None of the women showed the slightest interest in any of the others. They just sat there, looking uptight and drinking what was given to them by their boyfriends. To say the least, it was a very different social gathering from what Beata was used to back in Poland.

'Who are those women? Where are they from?' Beata asked Robert after they had left the crowd two hours later.

'Everywhere. Two Lithuanians. One Latvian. The others are Russian.'

'They didn't want to speak to me,' she said.

'Shy. They are shy. They don't speak English,' he said.

'Why did you take me there if I can't talk to them?'

'Oh, sweetie, I wanted to show you off, to my friends!' he said, taking her in his arms.

Beata remained confused about the gathering with Robert's friends. But she didn't want to carry on questioning him. He seemed genuinely to care about her and that was all that mattered.

At this time, she desperately needed to feel someone cared about her – and there was no doubt in her mind that he did. Deep down, she began secretly to envisage a future with him.

I was standing at the bar in Club Oops in Aldgate East, having brought a male friend with me to justify my presence among the almost exclusively male clientele. Within seconds of me leaving him alone at a table, a dancer had gone up to him and offered him her services. A fully nude private dance would cost £20. She had pointed to a large room at the end of the bar where punters, sitting next to each other, watched their chosen women dance for them on their laps. The dancer had then whispered to my friend, 'After that, you can have a session with me for half an hour or an hour upstairs.' By this she meant sexual services, which is against club rules. She was obviously moonlighting to boost her income.

After 6 p.m., dancers from eastern and south-eastern Europe come into the club and start working through the night. On the evening of our visit, a number of them were sitting in the sun outside, chatting cheerfully with their City regulars, some of whom appeared to be three times their age. We sat down at a table next to them. One of the youngest, whom I'll call Anca, was outspoken and open and she told me that she came from Constanta, on the Black Sea coast of Romania. She is one of four Romanian workers in this particular club.

The fair-haired Anca seemed to be very popular here, being only twenty-one years old. She was introduced to the job, her first in Britain, by a Romanian friend who also worked at Club Oops (and was now sitting across the table and half-listening to us). It is common knowledge among Romanians that work is hard to find in Britain, given the harsh employment restrictions on Bulgarian and Romanian nationals since the two countries joined the EU in 2007. Migrants from those countries can work only in the low-paid food-processing industry under the Sector Based Scheme (SBS), or in agriculture under the Seasonal Agricultural Workers Scheme (SAWS), which currently have small quotas of 3,500 (divided between meat, fish and mushroom processing) and 21,250, respectively. Alternatively, she might have found work, with prior authorisation, in the cleaning and service industries in London as so many Romanian and Bulgarian women have had to do. Such restrictions are one reason so many Romanian and Bulgarian women decide to enter the sex trade, working as lap dancers, escorts or in brothels. The marginalisation and pauperisation resulted from these restrictions is the main reason why Romania is the origin of the largest number among the total of sixty nationalities of migrant sex workers in the EU. (The top three providers of migrant sex workers in the UK are Romania, Russia and Bulgaria.) Although these restrictions will be lifted in January 2014, Romanian and Bulgarian migrants continue to be targets of discrimination in British media and society as the government carries on talking about limiting migrants' access to health services.

Anca had left Romania because she was unable to earn enough as a waitress to live on following the disintegration of her family life. After her mother died, her father married a twenty-four-year-old and told both Anca and her brother to move out, even though she was still at school. She found work as a waitress, using her small income to support herself and her brother.

Then she heard from a friend who was earning good money lap dancing in Norway, and decided to join her. She had been worried about working in a strip club, but circumstances had left her little say about the type of work she could choose. With her friend's reassurance, Anca began her life as a lap dancer.

Anca's story is not unusual. Most Romanian lap dancers are led into the trade either by acquaintances from their home towns or through one of the private agencies that have mushroomed in Romania over the past decade. A typical agency ad might read:

'We are an international agency that recruits and books showgirls, exotic dancers, entertainers and hostesses for employment in Europe at well known strip clubs and lap-dancing bars … Do you enjoy travelling and working at the same time? We can help you achieve your dreams!'

Since joining the EU, the sex entertainment industries in both Romania and Bulgaria have made huge profits, but the reality of these young women's working lives in western Europe's sex trade could hardly be described as 'living the dream'.

Like many new migrants, Anca didn't find life easy in Norway. She said that the men there like to have company when they drink. Her own isolation made it easy for her to fall into the habit of anaesthetising her feelings with alcohol. Soon enough, like her punters, she had become a heavy drinker. She was feeling uncontrollably depressed and feared becoming an alcoholic. 'I wanted to get out of the job and the lifestyle,' she told me. Eventually, she plucked up enough courage to leave and returned to Romania.

However, Anca had no desire to return to poverty, and soon learned about another lap-dancing job from a friend who was working in a London strip club and earning relatively good money. Although anxious about starting a new life in England, Anca felt that she had to give herself a chance.

She had been working at Club Oops for ten months and was content to continue working there. At the same time, Anca was well aware of the opprobrium heaped upon her by other women from her home city. 'Few of the women here in London from

Constanta work in the sex trade. They're more snooty and they think any sex work is beneath them,' she said. Partly for this reason, she has few Romanian friends in London apart from those she works with.

She paused, sipping her drink and said, 'But I'm no different from the other Constanta girls. I don't like being told that I have a nice body by these customers. I feel cheap. I'd like to be treated as a human being by a man. But making a living isn't easy for a Romanian woman in London, and I don't want to earn £180 a week as a cleaner.'

Here at the club, she could earn £800 on a busy evening, although the earnings fluctuated a lot and she only made around £50 on a quiet night. A quarter of the dancers' earnings went to the club. Anca said this wasn't such a bad deal because Club Oops didn't charge a base fee to work in its premises like some other clubs.

Here, the 'VIP dance' upstairs was a good source of income for the women workers as men would pay up to £380 for an intimate dance. Anca never offered sex to the punters because that's where she drew the line.

Despite the relatively good income, she felt insecure about the work – how long would it last? As a migrant, she knew that jobs could be hard to keep. And once a job was gone, there would be no income until she found another. She had felt insecure from the first day that she had worked in the club. This is why Anca worked every single day of the week, so she could earn as much as possible. She knew that anything could happen to her at any time. She sighed and said, 'My father and stepmother have been demanding large sums of money from me. They think money is easy to earn here. They have asked me to pay for my father's medical costs of up to £25,000.' Despite all that had happened, Anca still felt it was her duty to do so.

At Club Oops, as in many men's clubs in London, there is a growing demand among local punters for the 'exotic', particularly for 'eastern European' women, by which is meant Polish, Lithuanian, Latvian, Romanian and Bulgarian. Some punters would even call a Russian woman 'eastern European'. The term itself has acquired new meanings as the EU has expanded. It is the otherness of such women that inflames male desire. Their foreignness becomes a commodity to be circulated and marketed – lap dancers and strippers with an 'eastern European' accent are the most sought after.

This reflects a British sex trade whose landscape has changed beyond recognition in recent years. From the end of the 1970s, migration into Britain's (as well as Europe's) sex industry came mainly from outside Europe: South Asia, South America and Africa. This migration continued into the 1990s, when Europe's sex industry began to see increasing numbers of migrants from central and eastern Europe following the collapse of the Soviet Union and the Eastern bloc, a process intensified by the 2004 and 2007 expansions of the EU.

According to the TAMPEP report referred to earlier in the chapter, in 2009 migrant sex workers comprised 64 per cent of the entire workforce of the sex trade in the EU-15 countries, Switzerland and Norway. Of those migrants, 11 per cent were from Latin America and the Caribbean and 12 per cent from Africa, but by far the largest group was that from central, eastern and south-eastern European countries (including the Baltic and the Balkans), who accounted for around 70 per cent of the total.

Bedding in in Beds

It had been several weeks since Ming and Brother Li had fled through the back door of the Phoenix Tower, and Ming was still without a job. Brother Li had gone to his only 'local friend' in England, Sister Yan, who was generally known among the local Chinese community as the best source of help around.

Brother Li asked Sister Yan if she could put him up for a while until he found a new job. He was hoping that her English husband, William, would play the role of the 'kind German who hides a Jew in his loft'. But William said no. He had far too much to lose. With a good job in the City, a four-wheel drive and a house in the country, William wouldn't entertain the idea of 'harbouring illegal immigrants'.

Since then, Brother Li had managed to get himself a job in a Bournemouth takeaway. Ming heard later that 'Fat' Fai was OK, because he had been able to produce the proper papers. However, the second fryer had been arrested and detained at Tinsley House removal centre near Gatwick, and would probably be deported.

Ming was at a loss. Anyone in London without papers was finding it almost impossible to obtain anything other than casual kitchen work. The immigration authorities were stamping down particularly hard on the Chinese catering trade, depressing wages at the bottom layer of the workforce still further, employers citing the risk of a raid as justification for paying peanuts. Those workers who failed to keep their jobs had to resort to selling DVDs on the street.

The 'old-timers' in Ming's flat were discussing whether it was now time to return home. That wasn't an option for Ming: she'd only arrived three months ago and there was still a long way to go before she would be able to pay off all the money she'd borrowed.

One day, Ming was wandering round Chinatown searching for work opportunities again, just like when she first arrived. As she passed a Chinese medicine clinic in Lisle Street her attention was drawn to the two heavily made-up women standing right outside the shop. Like Ming, they were in their thirties, but both were wearing low tops and short skirts, looking provocatively at passers-by. What were these women doing? By the way they were dressed, Ming thought they probably came from a rural part of China.

Her flatmate Ying's words seemed to echo in the air. 'You have to pay a price to make good money.' 'No loss, no gains.' Ming shrugged her shoulders and turned right into Gerrard Street.

She'd never really liked Chinatown, despite the fact that it was the only place for newcomers to gather. The fact that all things 'Chinese' were here – the bright gold and red colours, the dragon and phoenix motifs that covered the arches, restaurants and shops – served only to make her feel alienated and alone. They brought no sense of 'home' to her. For her, it was just somewhere to seek work – a place containing only prospects of hardship and struggle. While the tourists and local passers-by were salivating over glistening greasy roast ducks in shop windows, she was watching the men in overalls pushing trolleys laden with heavy boxes of food down the road. She was surprised to see that quite a few trolley pushers had Western features, for such work used to be done only by her countrymen, who provided the cheapest labour in Chinatown. Who were they, these men who parked the trolleys outside a Chinese supermarket and carried the heavy boxes on their backs, starting to load them into the shop?

Ming reached the stalls outside the casino where people collect Chinese newspapers and magazines – the popular *Chinese Business Gazette*, the lifestyle-orientated *Chinese Weekly*, the anti-government *Epoch Times* that every Chinese has come to associate with Falongong (a spiritual practice, banned in China, combining Buddhist and Taoist elements), the *Euro-Chinese Journal* run by a controversial community leader, and a dozen others. She picked up a copy from each stall, and started reading them while walking along. At this moment, she was only able to think of those massage parlour job ads that Ying had 'enlightened' her with. It was now urgent that she found work, she said to herself. One ad grabbed her attention:

'Located in outer London. Catering only for Westerners. Busy. Comfortable living environment. Safety guaranteed. Now recruiting Misses from all over the world. *Housekeeper urgently required*. Female only.'

Ming had never heard of such a job: massage parlour housekeeper. However dubious it might sound, she understood that the work did not involve providing sexual services. This didn't sound too bad to Ming: it would bring a regular income, although small. It would give her the security that restaurants and takeaways wouldn't be able to these days. This couldn't be a bad idea.

What Ming never told anyone, though, and perhaps found it difficult to admit to herself, was that she was curious to find out about what went on in a massage parlour. It would be her way to finding out about the sex industry – to see for herself whether it could ever be a real option to make money. Working as housekeeper in the sex trade would be her way of putting off making the final decision about whether to take up sex work.

Ming dialled the number. A woman with a southern Chinese accent answered the phone, identifying herself only as 'Sarah'. Ming said that she was interested in the vacancy for a housekeeper.

'How old are you?' Sarah asked so coldly that Ming could picture the icy expression on her face.

'Thirty-two,' Ming answered.

'A little too young for a housekeeper,' Sarah replied. 'But do you have any experience of this type of work?'

'No … But I have worked in a kitchen. I did cleaning, chopping, things like that.'

'Fine,' this seemed to satisfy Sarah. 'Are you bringing all your luggage with you? Because I'd prefer that you do, so that you won't need to make any other trip to collect it. The work here is busy and we can't afford you to have to be going off all the time.'

'Sure … I understand,' Ming answered like a good school student.

'Fine. Let's see how it goes. Come and see me tomorrow. I'll wait for you at the train station.'

Since Ming didn't understand very much English, Sarah texted the name of the station to her: Milton Keynes.

That evening, Ying returned home with another plate of roast duck leftovers from her work. She was pleased to hear about Ming's job search in the sex trade. Almost too pleased. Ming looked at her exhausted face and the folded-up duvet on her mattress. Well, at least Ying would be able to enjoy occupying a two-mattress space for a few days from tomorrow, until the next tenant moved in.

When the light was out and everyone else was fast asleep, Ming lay awake thinking about Ting Ting and their life ahead. And she felt anxious about the new job in Milton Keynes. What if it didn't work out? What would she do then? Who could she turn to? The uncertainty with which she'd been living day after day in recent months had made her ill – there was a pain in her stomach that worsened whenever she tried to go to sleep; it wouldn't let her rest. Meanwhile, despite her outward confidence, she had developed a habit of self-blame over the years, just like Xiao Mei before her. This time, she was blaming herself for her inability to support her family without having to resort to an occupation viewed as 'bottom of the heap', at least in the eyes of her family and friends back home. She blamed herself for allowing her aging parents to bring up her child. She blamed herself for Ting Ting's tears when she left home on that fateful day. And, finally, for the countless, soulless days behind her and now stretching out in front of her.

Early the next morning Ming went to Euston station, bought a ticket and boarded the train to Milton Keynes.

It was around this time that I decided to find myself the same type of work, answering an ad in the same Chinese newspaper. The job turned out to be in the middle of affluent Bedford – no real surprise there, as many such massage parlours seem to be based in the suburbs. I wanted to compare notes with Ming.

A woman called 'Linda', with standard Mandarin, answered the phone. She said that she ran the place.

'Listen very carefully. I'll say the ugly words first. You will get the job if you accept the rules: first, you must keep the place completely and utterly clean and tidy. That's the first thing you need to do to keep the customers. Second, you will have one day off a week. The pay will be £200 per week. Third, you are not allowed to go out at any time during your working hours.'

As instructed, I arrived at Bedford train station at 10 a.m. A slim woman in her forties with long, straight black hair arrived a few minutes later, waving to me from the car park.

'Linda?' I greeted her, and I saw a frown on her face.

'I didn't even have a chance to wash my face – so busy!' she grumbled, now revealing more of a Beijing accent. Every time she turned to speak to me, I noticed her tar-stained, chain-smoker's teeth.

While driving me to my new workplace, Linda said openly, 'I'll make this clear – you will only get one day off every two weeks. OK?'

'Sorry? But you told me on the phone it would be one day off each week.' I was confused by this change in the arrangement.

'I never told you that! You must be joking! This is a very busy place!' she raised her voice and sneered at me.

Linda took a much longer route than was actually necessary, turning many corners, to get to the premises. I later realised that the place was in fact on the main road, a short walk from the train station. I believe that she did so to confuse my sense of direction, so that I wouldn't be able to escape easily.

Then she turned into a parking area situated behind a Victorian red-brick house. Before entering the flat, Linda remembered our conversation in the car and turned to me, warning me directly, 'You are not to bargain with me like that again!'

I nodded in acquiescence.

She continued, 'A previous housekeeper asked me for paid leave! Can you imagine that? Where are the rules in this world?'

Linda led me into a block of flats. The massage parlour was the first two-bedroom flat on the ground floor: a surprisingly open location. A first look at the sitting room reminded me of a well-lit doctor's waiting room, with a bunch of plastic roses in the middle of a table. A Chinese woman was brushing her long hair at the dining table, while a young Chinese man in his twenties was tirelessly mopping the floor.

Linda didn't introduce me to her existing staff. Something else caught her attention: 'Hurry up, you *niu-bi* [cow cunt]! You're taking your time!' she shouted at the man, whom I now realised was the housekeeper I was to replace.

Then Linda turned to me: 'You remember – clean properly or your money will be cut.'

I tried to digest this blatant aggression. I'd known Linda for no more than fifteen minutes, but she was clearly a deeply damaged individual. What had happened in her life to make her like this, I wondered.

She continued, 'This is also your job – keeping clear and good accounts. How many customers come in, when they come in, when they leave, how long did they stay, and how much you receive from them: £50 per half hour, £90 per hour, £40 per twenty minutes. You must write it down clearly here. And never sign the accounts on my behalf. When I get the cash from you when I come in, then I'll sign it. This *niu-bi* housekeeper signed it on my behalf, and that's why I'm kicking him out of my door! The mother-fucker should have minded his own business!'

The outgoing housekeeper kept his head down, apparently emotionless, and continued to mop the floor. Why didn't he answer her back? Surely he had nothing to lose, now that his job was gone. I looked at him and wondered about his lack of pride. What had this place done to him?

Apart from keeping accounts, my duties were cleaning the rooms and the toilet, and cooking two meals a day for the workers. My working hours were to be from 7 a.m. to 2 a.m. every day.

Suddenly, the phone rang. Linda looked at the number on her mobile phone. 'It's the Big Cunt calling!' (A regular customer, I later learned.) Immediately she put on her sweetest voice: 'We've got a Japanese girl, very sexy, very busty girl!'

The 'Japanese girl' she was talking about worked at her other massage parlour down the road and was actually Chinese. 'You got to go with what's in fashion. Always tell them we got Korean or Japanese girls. Do you understand?'

Like most Chinese madams, Linda placed a different woman in the flat every week, to ensure variety for the local customers. She restricted it to one to avoid accusations of running a brothel. In Britain, the sex industry is regulated primarily through criminal and public nuisance legislation. Selling sex and working alone as a prostitute are not prohibited, but associated activities (such as soliciting) are. Brothels – two or more women offering sex at the same premises – are prohibited under the Policing and Crime Act 2009. (The earnings of sex workers are in theory taxable, no part of the legislation refers specifically to the taxation of sex workers, and there is no special tax code for sex workers who register to pay income tax.)

This week's girl was Zhen Zhen, from Dalian in the northeast of China. She was coy about her real age, but I guessed that she was in her early forties. Like Ming, she was a single mother, with a daughter who had just turned eleven. Zhen Zhen had been in Britain a little longer than Ming. 'It wasn't easy at home,' she told me. 'After being made redundant at the factory, I began work as a restaurant waitress,' she said. 'The money was appalling – 800 yuan [£80] a month. But there were no other jobs around. I had to borrow £9,000 to come to England.'

Women of Zhen Zhen's background, aged between thirty-five and fifty and from north-east China, comprise around two-thirds of the workforce in the UK's Chinese-run sex industry. The majority are former workers in state-owned enterprises who have migrated in search of work after being laid off in the economic upheavals of the past three decades. With little English and little knowledge about the UK but an urgent need to earn money, they are one of the most vulnerable groups of migrants in the UK.

I called Ming to find out how she was getting on with her new job in Milton Keynes.

She sounded exhausted. 'I have been working without a break here,' she revealed. 'Sarah won't give me any time off yet. She says I have to wait another two weeks.'

I realised Linda wasn't unique.

Worse still, Ming was getting paid £180 a week, even less than I was.

'What is the actual work like? A little better than in the restaurant? A lighter workload?' I asked.

'Not really. On the physical side, it's not quite as demanding as in the kitchen. The pace of work isn't as fast. But the mental pressure is huge – as a housekeeper, you're always on the alert. This is a new type of work for me and, as you know, I only speak a few words of English. Now I have to memorise the trade vocabulary, to be able to tell the customers what kind of services are offered here.'

I recognised that level of pressure in my work in Bedford, too. As a housekeeper in the sex trade, you are the sentry, the security guard and the first line of defence in the unpleasant world of punters as well as the punch-bag for whoever runs the business. 'I know exactly what you mean,' I said with feeling, keeping one eye on the bedroom so I'd know when Zhen Zhen had finished her session.

Ming had just sent her girl a punter. She said she was picking up English words she'd never imagined learning before. 'When he came in, I thought he was going to ask for "oral without condom", which many punters request. But apparently he's a regular and has a special liking for "water sports", if you have any idea what that means. He wanted that for an hour.'

'I'm guessing he didn't mean windsurfing?' I said.

'Our *xiaojie* assumed he wanted to urinate on her,' said Ming. 'Or the other way round. Apparently that's what it usually means, according to Sarah.'

'And did he?'

'No! He wanted to have a bath with her,' said Ming. 'At least she's keeping clean. That's the second bath she's taken with a punter today.'

'Are you all right?' I could feel the weight of the tiredness in her voice. 'You sound like you've had a long day.'

'You bet. The work is non-stop.' She gave out a sigh. 'Just cooked lunch for *xiaojie* before the man rang. One task after another. And Sarah doesn't trust me – she keeps calling to check that I'm updating the accounts properly.'

Ming said that she could now hear *xiaojie* and her punter laughing in the bathroom. 'They're going to be in there for a while yet.' This punter was a regular, she said. A *guilao* banker who used to live in Hong Kong and had a Chinese wife. Since she died two years earlier, he had been visiting Chinese women for sex, as if they would bring back memories of her.

'He says he's always liked "things Oriental",' Ming said,

laughing. 'He says he appreciates our manners and our politeness. He loves it when I call him "sir". He thinks we all speak like that, all the time. Stupid.'

I could imagine the man's obsession with stereotypes leading him to a mail order Chinese bride at some point in the future.

A few days later I called Ming again.

'How was your day?'

'Different,' she said, sounding somewhat bewildered. 'A couple came in and asked for a session together with *xiaojie*. A man and a woman, can you believe it? As we say, one kind of rice breeds all kinds of people, doesn't it?'

I didn't think it was all that unusual, but let her continue.

'I told them talk to *xiaojie* directly because I just didn't have a clue what to say. The man told our *xiaojie* that the woman was his "ladyfriend". He was slurring his words – I think he was drunk. Anyway, our *xiaojie* didn't turn a hair. She said she'd done it before when working up north in another parlour. Afterwards, I asked *xiaojie* what they'd done. She said the couple wanted her to watch them have sex. The woman had breasts the size of watermelons, and *xiaojie* described her bouncing up and down on top of the man, making noises like the slaughtering of piglets.'

I had to laugh at Ming's lively depiction of the session. She continued, 'Then the man pulled *xiaojie* into the game while his girlfriend watched. But the blonde soon became aroused and asked to have a go with *xiaojie*, too. The couple giggled and laughed the whole time, though *xiaojie* said she couldn't understand much of what they were saying. They were getting so energetic that she was worried that one of them might be sick on the bed. They'd both had a lot to drink.'

One day I noticed Zhen Zhen taking some tablets with a glass of water. 'Aren't you well?' I asked.

'I'm all right. It's just that I caught something from a dirty old punter a couple of weeks ago. Since then I've been taking this medicine. Linda wouldn't let me rest for a few days. It's either work the whole week, or not at all.'

'What have you caught?'

'Syphilis? I don't know,' Zhen Zhen said, frowning, trying not to look embarrassed.

'And Linda won't let you off for a few days?'

'No, because I'm booked for the whole of this week, you see, and that's it, no argument. She won't even let me go to a chemist until my shift here is finished. In fact, she went and got this medicine for me from the pharmacy herself. But I really do need to see a doctor. She just won't let me out of this flat.'

Virtual imprisonment during work hours is very common among Chinese sex workers. This results from the 'double illegality' of their work: not only are the businesses trying their best to avoid attention from the authorities, but also the workers have no formal immigration status. Most employers, therefore, prefer to keep their workers out of public view. This can clearly pose health risks.

'What if your problem gets worse? You've got to see a doctor,' I said to Zhen Zhen.

'I will try to do that when I finish this week here before I start work at the next place.' Having said that, Zhen Zhen admitted that she didn't know where to get help and had to rely on a friend's advice. She had twice been refused registration with a GP – first, because she couldn't provide a passport with a valid visa (although the registration criteria at GP clinics do not include checking patients' immigration status) and second, because she didn't have a fixed address (although she should have been able to register with any GP as someone in need of 'immediate necessary treatment'). She certainly had no idea about the medical services available to sex workers. The only place she knew outside the four walls she worked in was London's Chinatown, where no such information was available. Apparently, mainstream health organisations such as Project: London have attempted to reach the Chinese communities and help new migrants access medical care, but many Chinese clinics are reluctant to publicise mainstream health services, for fear of losing out to the competition. Chinese migrants, particularly sex workers, have therefore found it difficult to access either information or help.

'And can you still work while you're ill?' I asked Zhen Zhen.

'Everything is possible when the boss wants to make money. But I'm in agony when I go to the toilet. And it's very painful during sex.'

'You have to be careful and look after yourself,' I said. 'Didn't the man wear a condom? Was that how you caught this?'

'Of course I always get the punters to wear condoms! But don't think it's always safe!' Zhen Zhen sounded anxious.

'You're right – it's not always safe. But it's the best protection you've got.'

'I think I caught it when I was working in London,' she carried on, frowning and shaking her head. 'The men there are crazy! Heaven alone knows how many places they've been! I was seeing up to fourteen men a day. I could have died on the job!'

I listened quietly, suddenly remembering the sunny optimistic evaluation of sex work by Ming's flatmate Ying in London.

Zhen Zhen continued, the anxiety in her voice turning into anger. 'I'm telling you – some men are just evil. They don't even care if you are going to be alive after the session. They might as well fuck a dead body! Some of the punters play tricks with you and try to take off their condom. You always have to watch out for that. And these days, more and more punters are demanding unprotected sex.'

I shook my head in disbelief.

'There was this man in London … He pressed me so hard on my back that I felt he was breaking me in half!' Zhen Zhen looked as if she was about to burst into tears. 'He treated me like a cushion, not human! One time, he pressed down so hard that I had to stop him and tell him to leave. There are some men I just can't work for, even if they paid me £500 per session.'

I listened and felt like telling her that there might be other work options out there. But she believed she was better off than many. 'Some of the Fujianese women work so hard. We north-easterners can't compete with them. They are younger than us and they can work up to fourteen hours a day, every day of the week, serving Chinese customers. Many are working around the Seven Sisters and Finsbury Park areas, the busiest places in London.'

The bell rang to signal the arrival of Zhen Zhen's next customer. He wanted to have her for an hour. As soon as the session ended and I'd seen the man out, Zhen Zhen rushed into the toilet, turning back and saying over her shoulder to me, 'It really bloody hurts!'

Zhen Zhen's health did not concern her madam in the slightest. At 5 p.m. Linda arrived. 'Get ready quickly!' she commanded Zhen Zhen. 'You have a half hour with a new customer. Be nice to him.'

A large white man in his forties entered the room. He looked like it was his first time in such a place. Luckily for Zhen Zhen, he finished his business in under a minute, pulled up his trousers quickly and left without a word. That was the easiest punter she had ever had.

I called Ming again that evening. Her *xiaojie* was also ill, though not with an STD.

'She's really poorly tonight,' Ming said sympathetically. 'She's burning up. It looks as though her cold has developed into a chest infection. What with moving from place to place non-stop, she hasn't had a chance to see a doctor. But Sarah wouldn't let her take a break or have a few hours off. She said there's no one to cover her. Instead of offering sympathy, Sarah has been moaning about how unlucky she is that so many of her girls get sick on the job. She said it openly to her cronies on the phone, right in front of *xiaojie*.'

'That's terrible. Perhaps you can get some medicine for her from the chemist?' I suggested.

'I'm not allowed to leave the premises at all,' Ming said. 'To be honest, I think unless there's a police raid or a fire, I'm chained to this place.'

'Surely these rules aren't even good for business,' I said. 'Punters don't want sex with girls who are sick.'

'I don't think they give a damn,' Ming sneered, and I could hear her bitterness. 'Neither the bosses nor the men.'

Both Ming's *xiaojie* and Zhen Zhen worked through the week despite their illnesses. On the day Zhen Zhen was in the most agony, she did two one-hour sessions and three half hours. Despite Zhen Zhen's discomfort, Linda moaned about business being slow. According to Zhen Zhen, though, Linda isn't doing too badly at all. 'Her minimum weekly profits are £1,700 here,' Zhen Zhen revealed. 'Apparently her other brothel in town is even more profitable because of its good location.'

Women like Ming's *xiaojie* and Zhen Zhen face serious difficulties in accessing mainstream health services and, typically, they are unaware of the range of alternatives available. I believed that both sex-business owners and prejudice from the wider Chinese community in Britain are to blame, but I needed to find out for myself.

First, I tried to find out where migrant sex workers could turn when their health was at risk. I talked to Fizza Qureshi at Doctors of the World UK, which is a part of the Médecins du Monde network, an international aid organisation that provides medical care to vulnerable people in sixty-four countries. Their health care project in Britain is known as Project: London. Formed in 2006, it operates as a free clinic for those who cannot access mainstream health care.

Dr Qureshi said that the project mainly targets vulnerable migrants, homeless people and female sex workers. At the beginning, the service users were mainly street girls based in Tower Hamlets, particularly from the Brick Lane area. Since 2008, the project has begun to work with migrant sex workers – from Romania (the largest group), Brazil, China, Bulgaria and Russia. It is estimated that around 17,000 of the 30,000 women working as off-street sex workers in England and Wales are migrants. Approximately half – around 9,000 in total – come from eastern Europe and a third, that is, around 6,000 women, are from Asia, according to ACPO (Association of Chief Police Officers) estimates.

Fizza Qureshi said, 'They need to be able to access mainstream health care. We publicise how we can help them in the various migrant communities via immigration solicitors and community organisations, GP's and A&E's. But the most common way for people to find out about our service is through word of mouth. With the Chinese migrants, we tend to advertise through the churches, like King's Cross Chinese Church. We emphasise that immigration status does not matter and that everyone's equal.'

She went on, 'We've seen cases where Chinese migrants have resorted to traditional medicine that has made their health problems worse. Some of them have found mainstream health care much too late ... We also know of cases of Chinese sex workers who became pregnant at work and had to resort to private abortions which damaged their health ... We need to get the information to them – and free contraception.'

But the resistance within the Chinese communities towards circulating sexual health information wasn't helping. Project: London's hard work initially bore fruit, not least following the appointment of a Mandarin-speaking support worker, but in recent years the number of Chinese users of the service has been static or falling.

As a result, Project: London sought partnerships with other organisations in order to reach migrant communities. They began to work with Open Doors, a female sex workers project, and more recently with CLASH (Central London Action on Street Health), an NHS project set up in 2010, referring women users to both organisations.

I visited Kim Leverett, an outreach nurse for Open Doors. Their work covers street workers in Hackney, who are mainly British, and off-street work in City & Hackney, Tower Hamlets and Newham, of whom 83 per cent are migrants, the majority from Brazil, Romania, parts of eastern Europe and Thailand. When Open Doors visits, two outreach workers give advice on contraception and other health issues, and inform sex workers about local medical facilities. The project also provides free and confidential consultations every Friday morning at the Ambrose King Centre, Royal London Hospital, as well as sexual health screening, blood tests, hepatitis B tests and emergency contraception.

According to Kim, 'The Chinese sex trade is the most difficult to reach. It's like there's a wall there.' As the team has found out, the owners of the Chinese sex businesses are rarely cooperative. 'In our outreach work, we can only establish contact with Chinese sex workers through Chinese owners of massage parlours … We got our Chinese-speaking counsellor to tell them what we provide, but there was very little interest … It's become increasingly difficult to get into working flats. When we phone, more and more premises refuse to allow us to visit.'

This lack of interest and social prejudice have combined to create mistrust among Chinese sex workers, particularly those over thirty-five who speak little English: 'They wouldn't speak to our Chinese support worker because she was from the same community as most of them.'

As a result, fewer than one in ten of the Ambrose King clinic's patients are Chinese. Open Doors has yet to establish the sort of regular relationship with Chinese sex workers that it has with other ethnic groups.

Similar difficulties have plagued the Soho-based CLASH, a specialist initiative of the Camden Primary Care Trust set up in 1987. It provides HIV prevention and sexual health promotion services for both female and male sex workers in central London. As well as two staff members conducting outreach work once a week in saunas and working flats, CLASH also runs sexual health clinics for female sex workers every Monday and Friday. CLASH's manager Andrew LaBray said, 'The changes in the European political landscape brought about changes in the origins of migrants coming into the industry … At the beginning, CLASH's main service users were local and Thai sex workers. Then, in 1998, Albanian and eastern European women began to enter the sex trade.'

Chrissy Browne, CLASH's health promotion specialist, told me more. 'The Albanian women without papers all say they're Greek or Italian … The Polish women are mainly self-employed, working alone in flats, whereas the Lithuanian women tend to be much younger and more vulnerable. We provide them with a translation service, through which we have gradually been able to identify their origins ... We provide a free and confidential service, and over time, we have managed to build trust, particularly among Albanian, Russian and Romanian women.' Today, CLASH works with a conglomeration of women of different nationalities and backgrounds. Albanian and Romanian women form the majority of CLASH's outreach service users. The users of its clinics are mainly Romanian and eastern European, though there are also some Chinese.

Andrew LaBray said that there has been no response from the Chinese community organisations about the health care needs of Chinese sex workers. 'They seem to prefer to keep a distance,' he said.

Chrissy Browne told me that it's been very difficult to engage with Chinese sex workers. 'A Chinese woman came in with bruises after being robbed at work ... When I asked her where it had happened, she didn't seem to know the location of the place.' Apparently, that wasn't unusual among Chinese workers. 'She came back after a second robbery and her arm was in plaster.'

With a limited budget, CLASH has been able to employ a Chinese translator for only one day a week in its clinic. Lack of communication has prevented the staff from building up a profile of Chinese workplaces or identifying risks that might be encountered during outreach activities. As Chrissy Browne said candidly, 'There's been some concern among our staff about gangs running some of the Chinese working flats. As we don't know which ones might be gang controlled, the staff are worried about their own safety when they visit.'

Lotus Bus (also part of the Médecins du Monde network), which offers free health care and consultations to Chinese sex workers in Paris, is a good example of how health care can be successfully provided to vulnerable migrants. I asked Tim Leicester, the health promotion worker at the Médecins du Monde office in Paris, why the project particularly targets Chinese women. He said, 'Lotus Bus is open to all, of course, but the Chinese are the largest group of migrant sex workers in France – making up 80 per cent of the total – as well as the most hidden and vulnerable.'

It is estimated that there are up to 1,000 Chinese sex workers in Paris, 600 of whom regularly use the Lotus Bus service. Most entered France during the past decade. Most are aged between forty and fifty and from north-east China. Most have backgrounds similar to Ming and Zhen Zhen: having been made redundant from state-owned enterprises, they chose to come to Europe to support their families. On arrival in France, most of them applied for asylum and subsequently had their applications rejected. Speaking no French and unwelcomed by the existing Chinese communities in France, these women led lives of complete isolation. Many worked as cleaners or in clothing factories. Eventually, many of them took up sex work to improve their income. Some still have two or three 'normal' jobs. They see sex work as a temporary measure to increase their earnings. Some Chinese women who are awaiting asylum decisions also choose to do street work, while those without documents tend to work indoors, either in a massage parlour or as a one-woman escort service.

Like their British counterparts, Lotus Bus have met with a complete lack of interest from the Chinese community organisations in Paris. Without Lotus Bus, the Chinese women workers would have nowhere to turn for help.

The Lotus Bus workers have put a great deal of effort into reaching this highly vulnerable group of women. They have made sure to recruit Chinese-speakers among the team's thirty-five volunteers. The Lotus Bus is regularly found on two to three evenings a week near the Strasbourg St Denis Métro station, where many Chinese and West African street workers gather at night. When I visited, there were three Mandarin-speaking French volunteers and one doctor aboard, and many Chinese women who wanted to talk to them.

The women stood in a long queue, chatting among themselves while they waited their turn. It appeared that the most common risk to health came from punters who refuse to wear condoms. On the Lotus Bus they were warned always to use condoms, no matter how much a client cajoled them, and were told about HIV prevention and treatment. The project also provided screening six times a year. Violence is also an important issue in Paris. Street workers run a high risk of assault, robbery and rape. Volunteers would take victims to hospital or the police, and advise them how to avoid a recurrence.

Many migrants remain unaware of their legal rights. The Lotus Bus volunteers would, for example, ensure that the migrants knew about the state health care and benefits to which they were entitled. Médecins du Monde also organises four workshops each year on issues of violence at work, health care and migrant rights (such as what to do when arrested).

Women visiting the Lotus Bus were given free condoms, lubricants, and plenty of individual advice in their own language on how to prevent STDs. The attraction of such projects is that the team dispense their advice non-judgmentally, unlike many doctors. 'They really do look after us ... with their professionalism and knowledge,' said one Chinese woman. 'Not only do they solve our practical problems, but they also stop us from feeling alone and isolated. With their warm and kind help, I've learned how to protect myself.'

Linda's lack of concern for her workers' welfare was also reflected in her food budget. She did all the food shopping (not allowing me to go out to do shopping for her) and it was always up to her what her staff ate. The weekly food provisions were a chicken, two beef steaks, a Chinese cabbage, celery, some tomatoes and eggs – these had to provide two meals a day, for seven days, shared between two adults. 'Be frugal in how you prepare the food,' Linda repeated her instructions to me firmly. 'I have a limited budget and I can't provide more than what you have in the fridge now. So if you cook too much food at one time, you'll starve for the rest of the week.'

In a normal Chinese household of two, a minimum of two dishes for an evening meal is generally expected. On the first evening, I planned hard with the limited resources that I had and prepared a tomato and egg dish – typical Chinese home fare – and fried cabbage with some leftover chicken drumsticks. But when Linda came in, she went mad.

'Are you preparing for a Man-Han *quanxi*?' (a Man-Han feast: a large meal combining Manchurian and Han-Chinese cuisines).

I froze, shocked rigid at her fury.

'Look, one dish is sufficient for the two of you. Now you'd better start being more economical around here!'

Not only food, but also hot drinks were restricted. Tea bags and coffee were only for customers. We workers had to bring our own provisions.

The only time Linda wasn't totally tight-fisted was on the odd days she felt less stressed about her businesses' income. At such times, she might also talk to her employees as though they were human – such as the evening she sat down on the sofa and started to confide in me.

'I didn't start up my business from nothing, you know. I came a very long way to do what I'm doing now!' she said with her mouth wide open, revealing her tar-tainted teeth. 'My first job when I first arrived in England three years ago was waitressing in a restaurant. They treated me badly and always made me carry heavy things. As a result I damaged my shoulders permanently – since then I've been unable to do any sort of manual work.'

I listened quietly.

'A friend of mine introduced me to a job as a receptionist for a massage parlour in Ealing. It was good work – painless compared with waitressing. And so later I thought about setting up a massage parlour myself.'

Then she turned to Zhen Zhen, who was dozing on the couch between sessions. Linda began a long monologue, insensitively ignoring the fact that the exhausted Zhen Zhen was trying to have a break.

'You know how difficult it is to run a business like this?' Linda started a lecture on her history in the sex trade. She spoke with animated intonation as if to make the story sound more interesting. It was like listening to a radio drama.

'You know how I managed that fucking place in Ealing? Do you have any idea?'

'Mmm.' Zhen Zhen tried to open her eyes. 'I know …'

'You know how I kept the customers? You know all that, don't you? Without me, the mother-screwing place wouldn't have stood a day! I made all the money for that *niu-bi* Alan!'

'Yes … you did,' Zhen Zhen didn't dare to disagree.

'I said to the punters, we got these nice girls, and the mother-screwing men all came! Who can compare with me? All the girls had to listen to me. If I liked the girls, I'd say to the punter, look, she's nice and provides a good service. But if a girl got on my nerves, I would never recommend her to the men and she would earn shit.'

'Right …' Zhen Zhen responded, her eyelids opened, but then dropped again. 'That's right.'

'You think everyone can maintain such a business? No way.' Linda waved her hand around excitedly. She then turned to me.

I immediately nodded at her little speech.

'As soon as I left that parlour, Alan's mother-fucking business went downhill,' Linda carried on. 'His luck went downhill, without me.'

I nodded, to show that I was still listening with interest.

'And as you know, that bloody idiot Alan was arrested in a police raid! Should I feel sorry for that *niu-bi*? His mother went to visit him in the police station, just a few days after she had been badly beaten up by him on Chinese New Year's Eve. He had left his mother bruised and homeless and she had had to find shelter in a church. On seeing his mother, the only thing Alan said to her was, "Bail me out with £3,000." The man's real trash and everyone knows that he couldn't have made any money without me.'

Linda's prolonged diatribe finally woke Zhen Zhen completely. She'd clearly decided there was no point in trying to have a nap with all this drama going on. She sat up, crossed her arms and regarded Linda through swollen eyes.

At midnight, Linda went off to visit 'Little Dick', one of the massage parlour's most frequent visitors, keeping him sweet. Her regulars were the only people she was nice to.

Zhen Zhen carried on working until her last client left at 2.30 a.m.

I was up again at 7 o'clock, following the instructions Linda had given me to clean and mop the flat. I was actually terrified of Linda's temper, even though I knew I could walk out at any minute, unlike Zhen Zhen and the others. I tried my best to make sure that the place was absolutely spotless before Linda arrived at 9 a.m.

However, it's no easy task to placate an obsessive boss. Linda was, as usual, furious. This time, it was the table mats.

'Why didn't you cut out the old newspapers to make table mats as I had told you?' She raised her voice.

'Because—' I was going to say I couldn't see the point, but she didn't let me continue.

'I've no time for your explanations! Sit there and do it now!' Linda ordered, the volume of her voice raised to the maximum.

When I looked puzzled at her anger, she lifted her hand as if to strike me: 'Do you want a slap? You'll get one if you don't do it now!'

I looked down and started cutting out the newspapers as ordered.

'And hurry up! You are supposed to do the hoovering as well!'

'But the floors are still shiny and clean,' I argued. I had cleaned the floors thoroughly only the previous day.

'If I say it is a daily task, then it is a daily task! I am not paying you to argue with me!'

After that, I became the target of Linda's constant verbal abuse. I told myself to ignore it: my boss was clearly insane.

But she wouldn't stop. One morning she came up and, staring at me fiercely, said, 'Guess what? I checked this morning. We are conflicting with each other. You are a Monkey and I am a Tiger. We contradict and clash. You also clash with Zhen Zhen. You are bound to reduce our wealth luck here.'

As I continued mopping the floor, I saw that coins had been placed in every corner of the flat.

'Don't you dare touch those!' Linda shouted behind me. 'They are for wealth luck! Unfortunately, your sign clashes with everyone and everything here, the wealth coins haven't worked properly since you arrived.'

I stood there, speechless. Can you ever reason with an astrological bigot?

My presence, in the boss's eyes at least, was harmful to the business. Clearly, I would soon be surplus to requirements. I would either have to resign or be sacked.

But before either could happen, the door bell rang again.

You Pay, We Play

Beata continued anxiously with her job search. She spent week after week looking for work in Stratford shop windows and in the small-ads she'd recently discovered in the local press. She felt that to take a low-paid waitressing job would be a repetition of failure, but the 'higher-end' hosting and bartending jobs seemed to require substantial previous experience. Days passed; a week. The longer she searched, the more isolated and alone she felt – it was as if she were the only unemployed girl in the world. She feared what might happen next; the future hung over her like an oppressive dark cloud.

Her rent was due and she had only £60 to her name. No job, little cash and certainly no money to send home. Robert was all Beata had; he was the only person she could talk to. And then, when she was at her lowest, he threw her a lifeline.

'Why don't you come and stay at my place for a while? Then you won't have to worry about the rent and you can concentrate on looking for work.'

Beata's faith in human nature was restored. No one in England had ever cared about her like Robert did. She gratefully accepted his offer, not least because she was falling for him. God must be looking after her somehow, she thought, for her to have met someone like him at the very time when she was most in need.

To her delight, he lived alone in a nicely furnished studio flat not far from the centre of Stratford. How could he possibly afford such luxury on his factory wages? This must cost £1,200 or more per month, but he'd told her he earned only £250 a week processing cheese twists.

Despite her doubts about Robert's unusual social circle and his unexplained source of income, Beata couldn't help liking him. He seemed a genuinely caring person, kind and happy to welcome her into his home. He talked endlessly to her about her past and future plans, and there was no doubt in her mind that he had her best interests at heart. One day, after coming home from work at the factory, he put on an apron and cooked a delicious moussaka followed by a fruit-and-yogurt dessert. He chatted about her day, listening patiently to her mundane stories about her fruitless job search.

'Don't worry, Beata,' he reassured her gently. Then he cleared his throat and said, 'I asked my friends today if they knew of any work for you and maybe something will come up soon.'

'Really?' Beata instantly cheered up. 'What kind of work?'

'Well, basic work, you know, like cleaning, waitressing, etc. The idea is that you start with the basic jobs and then you find something better later.'

'Yes, I know! I'll do anything!' she said, looking at him gratefully. She then lowered her head, tasting the yogurt on her spoon, thinking how lucky she'd been to have met him.

After supper, Robert ran a hot bath for her. His bathroom was spotless, different from the one in the dingy flat where she had stayed when she was doing the sandwich bar job. She saw the clean white bath towels that he'd laid out for her. Robert was so unlike other men she'd known. And he knew how to live a reasonably comfortable life, even with a factory job. There was something special about him, she thought, dozing in the scented, steaming water.

She was soon roused by a raised voice outside. It was Robert. He was arguing in Albanian on the phone, sounding furious. She'd never heard him shout and it worried her.

She quickly dried and dressed and went into the hallway, where Robert was opening the front door to one of the men she'd seen in the Holborn pub he'd taken her to. The two men went into the sitting room, speaking rapidly. She couldn't understand a word they were saying, but she heard her name mentioned.

'Hello?' She followed them into the room. 'Is everything OK?'

'Oh, you're here, sweetie.' Robert looked as if he hadn't expected her to get out of the bath so soon. His friend nodded at her politely, spoke a few more words in Albanian to Robert and then left.

'You look beautiful, Beata,' said Robert.

'I feel better now. It's hard being out all day looking for work.'

He clearly had something other than job seeking in mind. He kissed her, pulling her into his arms. He led her into his bedroom and undressed her gently. She felt herself melting and her body starting to respond to his passionate intensity as they made love for the first time.

Beata was head over heels in love. She dreamt of Robert, the smell of him, the gentle touch of his hands all over her body. She wanted him every evening when he came home, and they made love for hours on end. The only aspect of their love-making she didn't enjoy was when he encouraged her to be 'a little more wild'. But if he was a little sadistic and domineering at times, well, that was just the heat of passion, wasn't it?

After a month, Robert proposed. Beata was stunned. She had always wanted to be loved, fully and completely loved, the object of a man's devotion. She did not hesitate to say yes, she would divorce Mariusz and marry him as soon as possible.

Robert began to make arrangements for their wedding. They spent the evenings discussing venues and guest lists. She was thrilled! Although she still didn't have a job, she was no longer anxious or sad. She was on the verge of a new, happy and fulfilled life in England – with her fiancé looking after her, she had nothing to fear.

Two weeks later, as they sat down to dinner, he surprised her again: 'Listen, sweetie, do you remember when I said there might be some work you can do? Well, nothing has come up yet, and time is moving on. I know you must be worried about not being able to send money home for such a long time.'

Beata looked up at him, nodding.

'But look, if you want to make money sooner, I can show you how,' he said, holding both her hands in his. 'You do want good future for Tomasz, don't you?'

'Yes.'

'I really care about you, you know that, my sweet Beata.'

'Yes, I know.' She gripped his hands tightly.

'If you want to earn some quick cash, I can take you to special places to work.'

'What you mean, "special places"?'

'You'll see tomorrow. It will make you good money and fast. It's my day off tomorrow, so I'll take you for a visit.'

Beata thought it all sounded very mysterious, but she convinced herself that he simply wanted to give her a nice surprise. Maybe he'd already secured the job for her. Maybe he had got it with the help of his friends. At midday on the following day, Robert put on his black suit and drove Beata into central London. 'It's in the middle of Soho, a good area, you'll like it,' he reassured her.

They arrived in Soho half an hour later. As he drove through a warren of streets he said, 'It doesn't take a map and a compass to find this place, but you could easily walk past it.'

'Exactly what sort of work is it?' she asked.

'It's really no big deal. It's just a job to make you good money quickly. You'll be like a glamour model. You are very beautiful, Beata, my love. This job will be easy for you!'

'Model? I'll be a glamour model?' Beata was surprised. 'It's a modelling job?'

'Yes, sweetie. You get to show off your beautiful body to men and then provide some services to them.' Robert broke the news in that gentle tone of voice that she loved so much.

'What services?' She was suddenly anxious and confused. 'Tell me! What sort of services?'

'Calm down, Beata,' he said sternly. He had never taken that tone with her before. 'Just calm down, will you. Stop behaving like a child. Thousands of girls do the same sort of work. You are not the first and you won't be the last! You need work, badly, and I'm only thinking about your needs here. Tomasz, remember? He needs you to send him money. I am only thinking of you, Beata. I would never do anything to harm you. Never.'

Beata didn't know what to think. She cried and screamed, with her hands on her face, suddenly realising what the man she has fallen in love with – the man who said he wanted to marry her – was asking.

'I love you so much, Beata. I've never loved anyone the same way. I truly love you, my darling. But we must be practical. Think of your family; think of Tomasz.' He clearly wasn't going to take no for an answer. She started to shake and then sobbed uncontrollably, wailing and trying to get out of the car.

'Now put on your make-up. Hurry up.' Again, he was a different person – fierce, controlling and frightening. Beata stared, no longer recognising him. She was suddenly paralysed by fear.

He pulled her from the car and led her into a narrow alleyway off Lisle Street, on the edge of the always busy Chinatown. Tucked away inside the alleyway was the entrance to an old staircase, hardly noticeable between the mobile phone shops and cheap souvenir stores. In the middle of such a bustling tourist zone, it was very easy to miss. The only clues to what lay beyond were an entryphone and several small, colourful invitations to visit the 'models' upstairs. Robert shoved her roughly from behind and she reluctantly climbed the staircase, terrified by this stranger who seemed to have taken possession of her fiancé's body.

On the door of the first-floor flat was a large sign saying 'YOU PAY, WE PLAY: Slim, young model'. Next to it was another saying 'Models wanted', with an arrow pointing upstairs.

Robert told Beata that two sisters ran this place. The older one, Trish, was on the second floor and she managed the business on behalf of their boss – though Robert had never met him. The 'young' sister, Pam, who was herself in her seventies, worked on the first floor as a maid. The pair were responsible for recruitment.

Robert rang the bell of the first-floor flat and a woman opened it.

'Hello, Pam,' said Robert.

'Rob! Come in!' she welcomed him in a husky voice. 'Well, who have you brought this time?'

The flat had a sitting area no more than two or three metres square, containing a pair of worn-out armchairs and a small table. A tiny cooking area was right next to the entrance. A torn net curtain covered the room's single grubby window. In one corner was a door, from behind which came groaning noises and the sound of a creaking bed. Beata looked around the shabby flat, scared witless.

Immediately the doorbell rang and Pam hurriedly opened it a crack. Beata glimpsed a young South-East Asian-looking woman with hair down to her hips.

'Looking for a job, are you, darlin'?' said Pam.

'Yes, I look for job!' she answered eagerly. 'You have?'

'Can you come back in an hour, sweet'eart? I'm really busy 'ere!' Pam waved her away.

She then turned to Robert and Beata apologetically, pointing to the bedroom. 'Don't mind the noise in there – our Thai girl's still working. Sit down, please.'

Robert took the seat facing the window.

'You sit down on my armchair, love,' said Pam, waving Beata towards the other seat.

But Beata would not sit down. She stood there, still paralysed by fear and shock. There was a CCTV monitor on the wall above her head showing a picture of the alley. She saw a man walk up to the door and push the entryphone buzzer.

'Busy 'ere!' Pam shouted out. The man buzzed again, the noise loud as a circular saw in the tiny room.

She looked annoyed and opened the window. 'Told ya! Busy! Come back in half an hour!'

After waving him away, Pam turned and gave Beata a friendly grin, shared understanding between two women, shrugging her shoulders. 'Men!'

'This is Beata!' Robert finally introduced her.

'Beata!' Pam responded warmly. 'What a beautiful girl, Beata! How old are you?'

'Twenty-eight,' Robert replied on her behalf. 'But she looks much younger, don't you think?'

Pam looked at her up and down and said, 'All you'll have to do is replace that top and jeans you're wearing with working clothes. You know what I mean? You've got to provide those yourself. Good working clothes will make you look glamorous. You look like a glamour model already, Beata.'

Robert looked pleased to hear this. He put a supportive arm round Beata's waist.

'Where you from, love?' Pam asked.

'Poland.'

'Do you speak much English, dear?'

'Not so much. I learn.' As Beata spoke, Robert held her hands tightly, staring at her intensely as if to give her some kind of support for what she was saying.

'My little Beata wants a job, she tells me,' Robert informed Pam. 'Poor kid, she has come a long way from Katowice. She has a six-year-old son! Can you believe that this little thing is a mum?'

'And this is all she can do?' asked Pam, pushing up her glasses and looking him directly in the eyes.

'You don't know how many places she's tried! But the money's no good!' he said with a fake grin. 'Tell Pam about your work, little one!' He pressed Beata's hand.

'Yes, money in the other jobs was no good,' Beata said hesitantly. 'When I arrived in England, the Ilford agency sent me to work to make salads and pack fruit. Every week it was a different place. Each day was a long day, all for only £180 a week.'

'Oh, that's bad,' Pam nodded sympathetically, but at the same time looking up at the monitor on the wall, checking to see if anyone was entering the building.

'Have you had better luck since, darlin'?' asked Pam.

'Yes, I found a job in a café in Stratford, but my boss opened up another business at an other place and closed down the café. I lost my job.'

'You poor thing!' said Pam. 'I know the feeling!'

'What could she do? She cried all day. But it's no use!' said Robert. 'Her son has asthma and needs good medical treatment. Prescriptions are not free in Poland. Her mother also needs support to take care of her son. She's a pensioner.'

Beata was stunned at this speech of Robert's – it sounded as if he had been taking notes on her life history ever since they met. It was as if he had been quietly observing her in the dark, when she opened herself up to him. Her eyes were moist again.

'I can imagine what you've been through, dear,' Pam said.

Then Robert softened his voice a little more. 'And then one day I met little Beata in Stratford shopping centre. I was so happy to have met her.'

Beata looked up at him, fearful, wondering what he was really thinking. It was only yesterday that she'd invested all of her emotion in him. It was only then that she had completely and utterly adored him, believing that he always had her interests at heart. How had she grown so dependent on this man? A man she knew hardly anything about.

Robert then took out a note with Beata's mobile phone number and passed it to Pam. 'She needs a job. Call me when you get her a job.' He looked so familiar with the procedure that it was obvious that he'd done this many times before.

'Sure. In fact …' Pam picked up her work diary and began to leaf through it. 'Ah, actually, she can start work tomorrow. Let's see how it goes tomorrow, shall we? And then we can fix some more days for her. If it all goes well, she'll do three days a week and she'll work with me. Trish is very tied up now. You'd like to work with me, wouldn't you, darlin'?'

Beata kept quiet. 'Yes, of course she would,' Robert answered on her behalf.

'You'll be making a lot more than you did before! You'll earn £120 per hour 'ere, and £65 per half hour, and if you're good you'll get a tip from the regulars. A lot of men just come up 'ere for a quickie: £20 just for ten minutes' work. That's a good few hundred quid a day. A bit more than at the sandwich bar, ain' it?'

Beata didn't understand every word because of Pam's strong Cockney accent, but she got the gist.

'That sounds super, no? My little Beata!' Robert urged a response from her. 'Starting tomorrow, sweetie!'

She looked at him fearfully and nodded without a word. Then she left with him.

Pam told me later that she had conducted hundreds of 'interviews' with girls like Beata. After she and Robert left, Pam put on the kettle and made herself a cup of tea. She then sat back down in her armchair, lighting a cigarette. She coughed each time she had a puff. This was her third cigarette since she'd arrived an hour earlier. The room was filled with smoke. She picked up her phone and called her sister upstairs to tell her about the new worker.

'Trish, there's a new Polish girl starting tomorrow.' For her, it was simply another woman coming in to work. It didn't make a great deal of difference whether she was being pimped or was asking for work off her own bat.

Outside, it was another sunny day. Dozens of tourists were busy doing their shopping along the stores in the alleyway.

Pam took another drag, looking out of the tiny window of

the room in which she spent most of her day. She could smell and hear the beat of all that was out there: the pubs and shops, Chinese, Korean and Italian restaurants, the noises of London traffic and American tourists. Of all the places she had worked, this was her favourite. She liked to be in the centre of things and had always fancied the idea of working in the West End. She used to dream about it during her first job as a receptionist back in Shoreditch.

Her thoughts wandered into the past. In the sunlight that fought its way through the window, Pam's shoulder-length hair looked particularly blonde and bright. She knew she looked at least ten years younger with her hair down. Her blue eyes burned bright behind her thick glasses. With her limpid seductive gaze, she looked every inch the ex-working girl.

But looks can deceive, for Pam was never a sex worker. She saw herself as 'just another East End girl' living an ordinary life, albeit an occasionally turbulent one. Her working-class childhood had long accustomed her to material scarcity, and she had never had any aspirations for her life beyond meeting the day-to-day needs.

The 'turbulence' began when Pam was only a toddler. This was during the Second World War and there was bombing all over the East End of London. All she could remember from the age of five was a series of big bangs that destroyed her neighbourhood and her mum and dad being very upset and wondering where they could go.

Many children were evacuated to towns outside London, though not Pam, who stayed in Shoreditch for the duration. At the age of sixteen she set out to look for a job, and have the freedom she'd longed for. She was soon successful, working as a switchboard operator in a bedroom furniture factory on Kingston Road, just a few streets from home.

Pam was excellent at the job and soon taught herself to type. Before long, she was given responsibility for keeping the firm's books, an extra duty she accepted with pride as one further step towards independence. Like many girls in the fifties, Pam couldn't wait to start her own new life away from her parents.

When she was eighteen, she met the man of her dreams, 'a real handsome boy'. She thought that getting married would be the route to freedom, away from her father's strict control, but she couldn't do so under the age of twenty-one without her parents' permission. As she said, 'It was absolutely predictable that he would say no to me becoming someone's wife at eighteen.'

Three years later the young couple finally married and moved to Walthamstow. There she had her first baby, David, whom she completely adored. There was nothing in this world that could compete with her love for her first son. Soon, they had two other children – Ron and Tracey. Pam had never been so happy. Her life seemed perfect – almost too perfect.

Beata began work the next morning at 11 a.m. She doesn't know why she didn't simply run away. She imagines most women probably would. She thinks that probably she was overcome by the shock of Robert's betrayal, and with it the loss of her entire emotional investment in loving him. She felt empty, broken, unable to resist. She felt as if she was leaving her destiny to destiny.

As Beata arrived at the flat, Pam greeted her casually, as if she was just another working girl. Which, of course, she was. Another working girl coming to earn a living. Pam showed her into her work room, its size doubled by a large wall mirror. It contained a tiny dressing table and a double bed. This was where she was to spend her time making the much-needed cash to send home to her family.

Pam made sure that Beata was dressed properly for work – a pink bra and thong that Robert had bought for her in a shop on Charing Cross Road the day before. There was little time for any briefing about the job and the first punter of the day rang the bell shortly afterwards. Beata's first customer was a middle-aged white man and the session took no more than a few minutes. The man skulked out of the flat without saying a word.

The door was slightly ajar and Pam could see Beata – and her reflection – curled up under the sheet. The wall mirror reflected her fragile shape. She was sobbing when Pam pushed the door open wide.

'You want a cup of tea, love?'

Beata slowly sat up and got off the bed.

'May I have coffee, instead?' she said to Pam, covering herself up with a short, pink dressing gown. 'But real coffee, not English coffee, please.'

'How're you feeling?' Pam asked, putting two spoonful of Nescafé into a mug. 'There you go, only English coffee 'ere, I'm afraid.'

'I feel like the bottom of earth,' she replied. There was dark shadow under her eyes. 'I didn't sleep well last night. I didn't know what to do. I should have run away into the streets this morning when he dropped me in front of this flat, but my feet went numb. I couldn't feel a thing and I knew I had to come in.'

She burst into tears again.

'Don't be too hard on yourself, love. No one really knows what to do the first time.' Pam repeated the line she always gave to the new girls. She was very experienced in what she called 'after-first-session-consolation', having worked with so many young women.

'I'm Catholic. I don't want to do this to live. When I was with that man, I could only think about my son,' Beata said. 'I don't know how to feel or what to say. I hate this sex! I hate it! I felt as if I am nothing. Worthless.'

'Many girls feel the same way on their first day,' said Pam. 'But they soon learn how fast the money comes in. Then they always start asking why there isn't more work!'

'I want you to know – I wouldn't be doing this work if it wasn't for my son and my family. Both of my parents are retired and they don't have a good pension, you know, only a tiny amount for each of them. How do they live? Who doesn't want their own independence and to have money to help their parents? Who doesn't want to buy their own flat for their family?'

'Of course, darlin'. No one would do this job if they weren't desperate! It's just bollocks when people say women do this because they want an extravagant lifestyle or they actually enjoy it! I've never met a girl who said she enjoys it,' Pam said.

She sipped her tea and sunk back into her armchair. With a newly lit cigarette in her mouth, she carried on: 'You remind me of Christina, the first foreign girl I'd ever worked with in these flats. We got on really well. I remember she came up here one afternoon, just walked in and asked me, "Madam, you have vacancy here? I have experience." I looked her up and down 'cos I wasn't convinced that she knew this was a brothel. I told her the demand is high around 'ere. I didn't want no one dying on the job, you know what I mean?'

Beata listened quietly.

'She told me she had experience in Italy – she left Russia because a "friend" told her there was a waitressing job waiting for her in Italy and he arranged everything for her. When she arrived there, not speaking a word of Italian, this friend tried to pimp her. She had to do it to make money because she had already spent a fortune getting to Italy from Russia. In the end she had to pay more money to get into England. She had no visa, you see. But she really didn't look the type. She didn't look like she'd done the work, you know what I mean? Young, blonde, eyes the colour of the deep blue sea. But not incredibly attractive, or sexy. Yeah, she wasn't sexy. So I asked her why she wanted to do the job. She said, "For a pram and a cot – that's the first thing I want." I was just stunned. A pram and a cot!'

'I really feel for her,' Beata said. 'I understand her.'

'And then she said to me, "I am a single mother, Madam. I am from Russia. I am thirty-two years old. I need this job and I work very hard." She really pushed for the job.'

Christina had a purpose, and for her, the job was merely a means to an end. She had a timeline for how long she was going to do the job for and she had it all planned out. Work for three years in England, earn enough to support her two-year-old baby daughter, then return to Russia. She knew exactly what she was doing.

'Christina used to say to me, "My English is no good, but my head is very clear." She worked in this flat for nearly three years. Then, because new and younger foreign girls kept coming in, she began to lose her regulars. She realised that she might be getting a bit too old for the work. Fortunately, a maiding job came up in Mayfair, which she got with the help of a friend, and she was pleased to end the sex work. But she's a real tough girl.'

'I don't want to be tough. I don't want to be here,' Beata said sorrowfully. 'I didn't come to England to do this work. I imagined a regular job and OK money in a factory or doing a cleaning job in England. I never thought I would do a sex job.'

'Not many people have choices in this world, you know,' Pam said. 'You think I like doing this job really? It's not bad money but you have to put on a smile to stinking drunks and psychopaths all the time. If my son hadn't died and my husband hadn't left me, my life wouldn't have fallen apart and I wouldn't have ended up 'ere.'

Beata slowly wiped away her tears and tried hard to concentrate on what Pam was saying.

'When I was your age, I was doing a decent office job, you know. I was ambitious and I was saving up to move out of my parents' place and be completely independent. When I got married and had the kids in Walthamstow, I was so happy. I loved everything about our life ...'

Pam paused, taking another puff of her cigarette, and said, 'Back then, on my way to work sometimes, I used to wonder if this beautiful life of ours would continue. Sometimes I wondered if I was really entitled to it, if I deserved it. Then one day, twenty-two years later, my question was answered: my good life came to an abrupt end. My eldest boy, David, died of an asthma attack.'

Beata struggled for an English word that could express her sympathy, but she was only able to say, 'I'm sorry, Pam, I'm so sorry.'

'You see, bad things come without any notice! I said to my husband, "Bad things happen without notice". I wept next to my son's body. How could a twenty-two-year-old young man pass away so suddenly? Everything fell to pieces around me. I said to my husband, "Maybe this happens to some people, I don't know." But he became wordless. The loss was too much to bear and he had chosen to switch off so's to cope with it. I said to him, "I know David was the world to us. I know how you're feeling now. I know you can't cope. Well, I can't neither." But he wouldn't open up to me. Our feelings were all messed up.

'I had to leave work. I just couldn't face anyone in the outside world. But at home, we were isolating ourselves from

one another and that just made things worse. We both felt so
much anger towards each other. Maybe we were both trying
to blame one another for what had happened, to relieve our
own terrible feelings of guilt. Six weeks later, we started to fight
over some stupid trivial things at home. One time I shouted at
him, "Go on, I dare you. You'll never leave this place, will you?
You can't leave me, I bet you can't." But he did, the bugger. He
walked out on me and our other two kids there and then, and
he's never come back.'

Beata listened, her tears dried, and for this moment she
forgot about her own misfortunes. She stared at Pam with only
compassion in her eyes. She tried to imagine the kind of pain
this old woman must have lived through all those years ... and
now she seemed so strong and shrewd. Life can do so many
things to people. She thought back to her time in Poland when
she'd struggled to persuade Mariusz to stop drinking.

Pam carried on: 'Every day during the following weeks, I
would wake up in the middle of night because I thought I had
heard the door key turning. But it was never him. It was our
cat Gonzalez coming through the cat flap after a night on the
tiles. The loss of two members of the household one after the
other didn't seem to bother our moggy at all. Gonzalez carried
on scoffing his normal amount of cat food and making a racket
when he came through the cat flap – he was so noisy that my
upstairs neighbour told me he was "anti-social" and complained
about us to the council.'

Pam gave a bitter smile. 'Two months, it was, before I
realised that he was never coming back. I felt wrecked. Suicidal.
My days became pointless ... No one to expect home. No one
to spend time with. I felt numb. I couldn't sleep at night and
during the day I was too knackered to stay awake. I'd just lie
down on my bed in the middle of the afternoon and sleep.'

Beata didn't know what to say. She didn't have the English to show her sorrow at Pam's pain. She simply put her hand on Pam's and listened.

'I always felt better after a good sleep, and so I began to have more and more naps during the day. I didn't even want to open the curtains in my bedroom. I didn't want to face the world. The good life that I'd built had been taken away from me just like that. So I thought, why should I carry on being such a good girl and try to absorb the pain so I could live a normal life? I lived in that state for six long months.'

'What happened to your two other children?'

'Ron and Tracey saw that I was suffering from depression and they made allowances. They were good to me. But one day my sister Trish called. She said, "Are you looking after the kids, Pam? I saw Tracey the other day and she didn't look that well." That little warning sign pulled me back to life. I suddenly felt so desperate to keep what was left of my family together. I told myself I mustn't dwell on my guilt. I had to make sure that I was a good mother to Ron and Tracey. So I really tried to pull myself round. First of all, I knew I had to find myself a new job somewhere, and the sooner the better.

'I took the first thing I was offered – dinner lady at a school in Hackney. The job was hectic and didn't usually allow much free time for me to think about the past. I tried my best to focus. I was going to be the hardest-working dinner lady the school ever had. From ten in the morning to three in the afternoon I kept myself busy washing tins, cooking cabbage, frying chips and serving the kids and teachers who turned up every lunchtime. On top of all this, I had to clean the whole cafeteria before I went home in the afternoon. During those five hours, I'd never take a single break. I was only getting paid thirty quid a week, but I was content then. If you was to ask me now, I'd say it was bad money – even in them days. That was in 1983, and I didn't have high expectations. All I wanted from the job was for it to pay my bills, and it did. I felt that I couldn't ask for anything better, never deserved anything better, certainly not in the state I was in at the time.'

'Did the work help?' Beata asked.

'A bit, I s'pose. Now and then I would still have a little cry, and it was something I had no control over. The feeling of desperate loneliness and sadness came over me at unexpected moments – sometimes it was when I was dishing out chips or letting the grease drain out from the fryer ... sometimes it was when I bent down to sweep the filthy corners of the room. When the feeling came, I had to rush to the toilets, let the tears out, blow my nose, catch my breath, and then get back to work. Sometimes the tears wouldn't stop and I had to wait there in the bogs for the moment to pass. The other dinner ladies – a nice bunch of women, about my age – all seemed to understand and gave me time to recover. Most of them were mothers, you see, and could sympathise. But I just knew at the time that the job wouldn't last. I confessed to Trish. Told her I just couldn't cope. I knew David was gone for good, but I just couldn't accept it. Trish thought I needed an easier job. "You've got more than enough on your mind," she said. I thought she was right. An easier job. But where was I gonna find one?

'Then Trish told me that she knew someone in Stoke Newington who wanted a woman to answer the phone for one day a week. "It really is just answering the phone. You'll have no stress at all. And one day a week is probably enough for you at the moment, isn't it?" I said, "That will be perfect."

'So she gave me the address and off I went. To my surprise, it was a basement flat, with a staircase that stunk like a men's toilet. A young woman opened the door – she was wearing next to nothing. That was when I realised I'd come to work in a brothel.'

I met Pam, like Beata, during my research for this book, and over the course of several months we had many conversations, both in the Soho flat and at her home in north London. Unlike Chinese housekeepers such as Ming, British maids sometimes act as managers of the business. Relationships such as the one between Pam and Beata can be complex, marked by the closeness of shared experience as well as the animosity inherent in employer–employee relations.

Although the way in which Beata entered the sex industry is not uncommon, it is only one pathway among many trod by migrants. Beata's experience of sex work, however – its working conditions and her relationship with Pam – is far from unusual among the estimated 6,500 migrant sex workers in London, as I have discovered for myself. Sex work in Soho is characterised by its low pay, as will be evidenced by Beata's case in the following chapters, and pay rates for sex work have remained at the same level for many years.

One of the people I talked to about this was Hazel, a maid working in Old Compton Street. She has been in the trade for two decades, starting as a sex worker at eighteen, then as a maid since the age of twenty-five, cleaning and cooking for women from Brazil, Jamaica, Spain and Italy. She reports that the pay level has remained relatively static.

A spokeswoman for the English Collective of Prostitutes confirmed the stagnation of wages: 'In our experience, money in all areas of the sex industry has remained the same for the last twenty years with few exceptions. This seems to be true in every area of work (not just the sex industry) as wages have stagnated or gone down.'

Many sex workers in Soho work very long hours and can serve up to forty men a day. In the Old Compton Street flat where Hazel works, some women have loans of up to £20,000 to pay back to moneylenders, often at an extortionate rate of interest, and so tolerate the risks and the excessive workload. Hazel works with a twenty-three-year-old Thai woman who's been at the flat for the past two or three years. 'She's on contract,' said Hazel. 'At times she struggles to pay off the debt. Once I even had to lend her money. We're very close and she calls me her "English mum".'

The charges levied by sex businesses are sometimes extortionate. In Soho, workers can pay rental charges of £300 to £400 a day in a business characterised by high risks and lack of protection. Such risks are heightened by the criminalisation (as brothel keepers) of sex workers who work collectively. Both health service providers in Soho and sex worker activists agree that criminalisation has made matters worse. Chrissy Browne of CLASH said, 'The police activity and their zero-tolerance stance in recent years have silenced many women sex workers who might be in a vulnerable position. The police crackdown in the name of anti-social behaviour has driven workers further underground – workers have become reluctant to come forward to use health services, let alone seek help about the possible control at work ... The existing law has led to a more unsafe working environment.'

Her colleague Andrew LaBray told me that some Chinese sex workers seemed 'controlled'. 'However, without any of the women workers coming forward [for fear of exposing their immigration status and attracting police attention], there is no way of knowing how controlled they are,' he said.

Police activity, particularly under the Policing and Crime Act 2009 and other provisions such as the 'brothel-keeping' law, has halted the reporting of abuse and violence at work almost entirely. (Take, for example, Hanna Morris, a maid who reported a violent attack on 16 September 2009 when two men threw petrol around her flat and threatened to light it. After helping the police with the investigation, she was prosecuted for brothel-keeping and money-laundering. No charges have been brought against the attackers.) According to the campaigner Xanthe Whittaker, it has also led to some maids quitting their jobs (for fear of being arrested for brothel-keeping), leaving women working alone and therefore even more vulnerable to assault.

Police action against women working in the sex trade can only undermine women's safety. The English Collective of Prostitutes said, 'Surely after the tragic deaths in Ipswich and Bradford, and considering the high level of violence against women sex workers, no one needs reminding how deadly serious the situation is … Evidence from around the country shows that in any six month period, at least a quarter of sex workers working inside, experience violence by clients. If women are forced to work alone without the protection of a maid, or pushed out of premises and onto the street where evidence shows that it is ten times more dangerous to work, will the police be sitting back in satisfaction at a job well done?'

In its report 'Human Rights, Sex Work and the Challenge of Trafficking: Human rights impact assessment of anti-trafficking policy in the UK', published in October 2010, X:talk, the sex workers' campaigning collective for which Xanthe Whittaker works, argues for the removal of Section 21 of the Policing and Crime Act 2009. The 2009 Act introduced new powers for the courts to close, on a temporary basis, premises associated with certain prostitution or pornography related offences. X:talk argues that these provisions have done more harm than good: 'The police raids have affected migrant sex workers the most, increasing the risks in their work. Some of the women have been forced outside to work in the street,' said Whittaker.

Under Pressure

Another week in Milton Keynes brought Ming another *xiaojie*, and she was delighted to find that her latest charge was from her home town of Shenyang. Unusually, she had been driven the ninety miles from Orpington in Kent by her boss, a forty-year-old man nicknamed 'Old Classy'.

Ming was puzzled that Old Classy should be so considerate, but as she listened from the kitchen as he and Sarah sat chatting in the lounge, she discovered that he was doing the favour not for *xiaojie*, but for her boss of the week.

'It's difficult to trust people in this line of work,' Old Classy complained. Massage parlour owners often swap their workers with other parlour owners they trust. He told Sarah how he was also careful not to reveal too much of his background, in case of repercussions back in China. He tells everyone he comes from Beijing, a city big enough that anyone questioning him about it can be fobbed off with an obvious answer. Only a handful of close friends know his true 'roots'.

Old Classy turned up fairly often, and each visit seemed to bring some life to this quiet, secluded corner of Milton

Keynes. His foghorn of a voice and his comic way of *shuo-shu* (a traditional performance art of solo story-telling that began during Song dynasty, AD 960–1279) and the tongue-twisters he enunciated in his heavy northern accent always made Sarah laugh out loud. She especially loved the tales he told about his old days serving in the People's Liberation Army. She didn't stop laughing from the moment Old Classy stepped into the flat. Ming had never seen this side of her boss before – she'd thought that Sarah was in a perpetual bad mood. When Old Classy was around, Sarah's workers seemed to get a better deal, too.

'Let's go for a ride and then go fishing,' he said to Sarah one day, staring at her as they sat drinking tea on the sofa. 'I do it all the time in Kent. You can't just sit here worrying about how much money you're making. Got to get some fresh air as well.'

'If only I could relax like you,' said Sarah, still smiling.

'I can see why you get miserable here – Milton Keynes is such a dump. Concrete, lifeless. The town centre looks just like a tiny corner of Shenzhen. It's depressing. You've got to come down to visit me in the Garden of England, as they call it.' Old Classy put on his reassuring voice. 'Explore the country a little while you're here.'

Ming was mystified by Old Classy's concern for Sarah's welfare. She was no great beauty and was devoid of personality: her only interest in life seemed to be counting cash obsessively, over and over again. Perhaps he had a less romantic motive: Sarah had recently been granted permanent residency in Britain, which would make her an attractive business partner in this clandestine trade. Formal immigration status brings an essential benefit for anyone operating in the sex business: documentation, which is the key to renting property and opening bank accounts.

No doubt Sarah considered Old Classy an asset, too. He'd been in England for nearly nine years, and was well connected not only in the underground world of the sans-papiers, but also among the well-to-do in the mainstream Chinese communities. Not only was he familiar with half the Chinese-run sex businesses in the country, he also knew his way round related organisations such as Chinese medicine companies in central London, as he was happy to tell anyone who would listen.

'My good friend from Shandong who runs the medicine business in town is going to meet me for dimsum in Chinatown this weekend,' he told Sarah. 'We hang out a lot.'

'How did you get to know such an important man?' Sarah teased, obviously hoping Old Classy's contacts would be the ticket to her own future success and fortunes.

'Oh, he's my *laoxiang* [home-town folk],' Old Classy shrugged.

So, he's from Shandong, thought Ming in the kitchen. There goes his Beijing cover story. Perhaps Old Classy wasn't so classy after all.

It was an unusually busy morning in Bedford. Two punters arrived within the space of five minutes. Linda was over the moon. Was her wealth luck back at last? She could hardly contain her joy. After the first man handed the cash to me, he was led into the room to spend an hour with Zhen Zhen – who had barely recovered from the previous day's work. When he arrived a short while later, the other man said he didn't mind waiting.

It's a rule of the trade that punters should never meet each other. Confidentiality is everything: they could be neighbours or even come from the same family, for all you know. If that were to happen, you'd lose both men as customers.

The waiting punter – a white man with ginger hair in his forties – was starting to look restless and uneasy. He'd been glancing in the direction of Zhen Zhen's room and checking his watch every thirty seconds. He kept nervously rubbing his right arm, which had a large tattoo of a rose on it. It looked as if waiting was getting too much for him. Or maybe he just didn't like the thought of seeing Zhen Zhen straight after another man had finished. When the doorbell rang for a third time, Linda didn't know what to do. Turning away customers was unthinkable, but so was allowing two punters to meet. Linda had a problem.

'You want massage first while you wait, sir?' Linda asked the new arrival, using the gentle voice heard only by punters.

'Oh! That will be nice,' he replied, touching his moustache.

'It is free, just for you, sir!' Linda flattered him nauseatingly. She patted his shoulders and showed him into my bedroom, without even asking me. With a shock, I realised that my bedroom had just become a work room.

'Please, this way, sir!' Linda eagerly led him onto the bed. She then laid him face down – with his head on the pillow that I slept on – and undressed him. She took some massage oil from the dresser and began to massage his back.

'Go and entertain the other man!' she instructed me in Chinese.

Awkwardly, I sat down on the couch, looking at the embarrassed punter sitting opposite me. I kept thinking about Linda's words: 'No customer likes to wait and anticipate sex service in our presence. They want to minimise that humiliating moment. If the time drags on, they are most likely to leave. Your ability to keep a customer in this situation will show whether you are suited to the job.' I must try to strike up a conversation with him.

'So ... You are local?' I asked.

'Yes.'

'Is this your first, er, first visit?'

'No. I come here twice a week,' he said. 'Your ladies are nice here.'

'You're married?' I tried, but immediately regretted asking.

The man nodded. He clearly wasn't in the mood for a chat.

'Er ... Would you like to have a look at these?' I handed him a pile of outdated fashion magazines.

Then I heard Linda suddenly calling me from the bedroom. She had had enough of playing masseuse.

'Now you have a go,' she told me. 'Kneel on the bed and rub his back!'

This was definitely not part of the job description.

'I ... I don't know how,' I panicked. 'I've never done this before.'

'For fuck's sake! You'll never know how to do anything if you don't get your hands dirty! Do as I say!'

I looked at the man's greasy back. I felt dizzy. 'Linda, spare me, I really don't know how! I just can't do it!'

'I can see you are just no different from all the *niu-bi* maids before! All the same! Just filling your stomachs without doing the work! My mother-fucking luck!' she screamed, shivering from anger. It didn't look like she was going to recover from this.

'These *niu-bi* maids ... One of them asked for paid leave. One of them used far too much food. Another one didn't sit in the waiting area during the sessions. And the last one thought she was the boss of this place. And now, you! God, where am I going to find a good maid? Go on – get out!'

Suitably chastened, I returned to the lounge, grateful to discover that the uncommunicative punter was now Zhen Zhen's problem.

Linda continued to stare daggers at me for the rest of the day, so it was a relief when she announced that she was driving Zhen Zhen to her next appointment – on escort service for an hour. Zhen Zhen appeared heavily made-up for her outcall, and she seemed cheerful, mainly because Linda was always pleased when a booking for escort service was made.

Escort service is always good news for the boss: £100 for one hour in the daytime, £300 for a midnight-to-4 a.m. overnight session in the massage parlour, and a higher fee for an overnight stay at the customer's home or hotel room. The escort, on the other hand, loses what little protection is offered by working with a maid.

'Two customers rang me a while ago. They might turn up while we are gone. If they come, you must keep them entertained here and wait for us to come back. Understand?' Linda instructed me. I nodded.

While Linda was away, I was finally able to sit down and take a precious break. I made myself a cup of tea, sat back on the sofa and simply took a deep breath. This was the first proper break I'd had since I started working there, and it was over all too soon.

'Any customer while we were away?' barked Linda on their return.

'No.'

'But I told you, two men called and asked for the address here. They said they were coming. Didn't you hear the bell?'

'Honestly, no one came,' I answered truthfully.

Linda turned to Zhen Zhen. 'Can you see now? Haven't you noticed? As soon as I walked out of this door and left her on her own, the number of customers decreased. When Tiger is out, the Monkey claims his reign, and that's really bad news for the business.'

I kept quiet. I could see she was just trying to intimidate me. She'd clearly done it to others many times before. She was the one with the power; I was just a housekeeper without papers. I knew if I answered her back, I'd blow my cover. Just like a real housekeeper, I had little choice but to tolerate the abuse.

'Go and fetch me a clean ashtray from the kitchen!' she demanded.

'Of course!' I rushed to the kitchen, returning with a newly washed ashtray so that Linda might continue to chain-smoke among her non-smoking employees.

'I asked for a clean ashtray! Not a wet ashtray! All the ashtrays must be completely dry! Do you remember what I told you on your first day?'

'Er … But—'

'If you give me one more excuse, I'll fucking hit you to death!' Linda shouted. 'Now, give me a light.'

One night I spent an hour preparing and cooking shredded beef with celery for Zhen Zhen. I carefully made sure it was a small portion of beef, so that there wouldn't be a scolding from Linda.

Over dinner, Zhen Zhen and I talked about her daughter, her family and how she entered England and the sex trade. 'I wasn't earning much in my first job, in a restaurant kitchen, receiving less than £200 a week. I was struggling to send money home to support my daughter. Then, I met a woman from my home village. She's in the sex trade and encouraged me to join it. I was hesitant at first, but she said to me, "If you really need to earn fast for your family, this job is the only way." A week later, I asked her to introduce me to her boss, a Hong Kong man called Alan – the man Linda was going on and on about before. It was at his brothel in Ealing where I met Linda for the first time. That was where I started.

'I've been trying my best ever since, pushing my limit, to earn as fast as I can. In the first week at Alan's place, I was just adjusting myself to the pace of the work, and I was taking only four men a day, earning no more than £120. Alan was quite mean … always trying to push me to work more. After a few days he made me work the maximum number of hours, even beyond closing time. I never had enough sleep while I was working for him. But Linda's no better. They'd make a perfect couple! Anyway, as far as I can see, there is no such a thing as a good boss in the sex trade. They can laugh with you at times, as if you are best friends. But you know that's just a front. What they really want to do is to squeeze the most out of you. They are always going to tell you that without them, we'd still be chopping vegetables in a takeaway. Without doing sex work, we'd never be able to improve our family's situation.'

Zhen Zhen continued, 'Later on, I got bookings in busier places. Then I started to earn around £180 a day, around £1,200 a week. I began to see the final good cause for which I've been paying such a high personal price. As my food and accommodation is always provided by the parlours, I've been able to save my earnings, and over the past two years I managed to pay off my £9,000 debt – the money I borrowed from friends and relatives in order to come to England. Now I have sent home 700,000 yuan (about £70,000) in total. That has meant so much to my family. My suffering has finally paid off.'

I wanted Zhen Zhen to talk more about the personal price she has had to pay. 'Is this a fairly safe job?' I asked her, wondering about the risks involved. 'The punters look horrible, but they don't seem especially dangerous.'

'Don't be naïve!' she exclaimed. 'Anyone working in this

trade will tell you that sex work has become more and more dangerous and damaging to us. The risks are outside the door as well as inside.'

'What do you mean?'

'You see, from outside the door, we have the permanent risk of robbery. You might have heard of such things in London? That is the biggest threat to our personal safety that we can do nothing about due to our immigration status. You can't be too careful. We always have some cash here, something like £30 or £40 at least, so when you get robbed, you'll have something to give to them and to avoid a punch in the nose or worse!'

'Have you ever … ? I mean, has anyone ever been robbed here, in this flat?'

'I wouldn't ask that question in front of Linda if I were you,' Zhen Zhen warned, frowning. 'If we get robbed, that's expected and I shouldn't be too surprised. If we don't, that is luck only. But if you open your mouth to ask that question, Linda would think that it's incredibly inauspicious and that you're bringing bad luck. She's terribly superstitious, as you've seen.'

'Are we supposed to keep our mouth shut despite the high risks?' I said.

'Yes. It is a trade taboo to talk about risks.'

Seeing that I was anxious, Zhen Zhen tried to reassure me. 'There are ways to lower the risks. Look out for unexpected customers. As you know, Linda always calls you when there is a punter coming to the flat, because only her mobile number is advertised in the papers. So if she's not here and you have someone ringing the bell without her calling, then you know it's not a real customer. In that case, just ignore the bell.'

I nodded.

'Ah, also, never let in more than one customer at a time. When you open the door, if there is more than one man, you must shut the door quickly. Because some men can pretend to be customers and call Linda to book a session. Men in pairs or groups are potential robbers.'

'What's the danger "inside the door"?' I asked.

'Well, there is no protection at all in our work. Not only are the men threats and can harm us, but bosses like Linda don't have our interests at heart, either. If it will increase her profits, she is always prepared to sacrifice my well-being. The obvious example is that she has asked me so many times if I'd offer anal sex. I've told her I don't ever want to do that. She just keeps on trying to persuade me, saying that if I did, I'd definitely get a lot more work.'

When I called Ming that evening, she told me her *xiaojie* was in the same situation. Like Linda, Ming's boss Sarah encourages her workers to offer anal sex at the parlour in Milton Keynes. Those who do are promised more work.

'*Xiaojie* said that more and more punters demand "extra services" such as anal sex these days,' Ming told me. 'It seems that it has become normal, whereas *xiaojie* said it was very rarely asked for ten years ago.' As in all businesses, sex-trade bosses are keen to satisfy demand.

The next day I saw for myself how Linda tried to get her workers on board. First, she created a relaxed atmosphere while Zhen Zhen was on a break, ordering me to make a pot of green tea for them. Then she sat lamenting the lack of business and raised the spectre of shutting down if things failed to improve. Obviously, Zhen Zhen didn't want to lose her income, did she?

'Everyone in this business knows what will keep these men coming back for more,' Linda said, blowing smoke in my direction. 'We all know the basics of how to make our service appealing.'

'You are already swapping workers every week and they see

different faces all the time,' Zhen Zhen said. 'We are all doing our best to keep them sweet.'

'Keep them sweet?' Linda raised her voice slightly, but maintained her calm. 'Men will never be satisfied. They will always want more than they are given. This is why we've got to follow their desire, however insatiable it is. To put it simply, you've got to scratch where the itch is!'

Zhen Zhen must have had a good idea by now where the conversation was heading.

'You see, many of our customers will become our regulars if we have something to hook them.'

Zhen Zhen sipped her green tea quietly.

'These men will always come back if you offer them more than the ordinary, if you offer them special service. And I am speaking from the experience of so many girls who've been working for me.'

Even I could feel the weight of Linda's long-prepared, pressurising words.

'Linda, I'm not prepared to do that, I told you.' Zhen Zhen frowned, putting down her tea cup on the table. This was obviously a conversation she'd had with Linda numerous times before. She seemed determined to resist.

'Darling Zhen Zhen, it's not as painful as you imagine!' Linda just wouldn't give up. 'If you know how to do it, there's no pain at all. Use baby oil first, and then KY jelly – you'll find it an easy job!'

'Sounds like you're speaking from experience,' Zhen Zhen said, looking at her provocatively.

'I am, though not for money!' Linda admitted. 'My boyfriend wanted me to do it. It wasn't so bad.'

'Your boyfriend?' Zhen Zhen sneered. 'You mean one of the punters?'

'Zhen Zhen darling, be careful. Mind how you speak to me,' Linda warned, giving her a false, bitter smile.

'Linda, I don't mean to be rude, but please don't think I'll do absolutely anything for money. I've done enough already.'

Linda stared at her, shocked at the response. It seemed that Zhen Zhen had never answered her back before.

'Don't try to persuade me again – I'm not a child,' Zhen Zhen carried on, her voice quavering with a mixture of rage and anxiety. 'I've put up with men of all sorts and I think I've given enough of myself. I have already sold many things to these men, and I don't mean only my body. I've paid a big price for making money faster – my health is beginning to suffer. I have made enough sacrifices; I refuse to make more!'

Linda was shaking her head even before Zhen Zhen completed her sentence, showing her disappointment with her refusal to cooperate. 'You silly girl! People always want to do better, and better. You'll earn a lot more if you allow yourself … Ay! You know that Japanese girl who works for me? She used to think like you. But since she tried it, she hasn't looked back. Now she's making double what she earned before.'

'No, I am just not going to sell any more of my body!' Zhen Zhen stood and retreated to her room, furious.

Linda spat curses at her back. 'Keep your asshole for yourself, then, *niu-bi*. But you'll regret it!' Then she laughed loud, from deep in her belly.

The lack of formal immigration status of women like Ming and Zhen Zhen is common among non-EU migrant sex workers. It means they have no protection at work against what are often severe risks. Linda's attempts to pressurise Zhen Zhen into offering anal sex is a manifestation of a system that doubly disadvantages non-EU working girls (by adding 'illegality' to their already dubious occupation) and greatly increases their vulnerability.

Non-EU migrant sex workers are treated as inferior even to those from within the EU. Their interests seem to be no one's concern. In the past decade, the increase in the number of EU sex workers in Britain has coincided with the intensification of an immigration crackdown on undocumented migrants. While EU sex workers became increasingly visible, their non-EU counterparts were driven further underground and tried to make themselves invisible to avoid immigration controls. Non-EU sex workers inhabit a precarious world, unseen and unmonitored.

Dr Bridget Anderson of COMPAS (Centre on Migration, Policy and Society), University of Oxford, has pointed out how the informal immigration status of migrant workers has been exploited by employers seeking cheap, flexible and compliant labour. In her research report on the market for migrant sex workers between 2002 and 2006 she found similar vulnerabilities in both the sex sector and private households:

> Those who organise and profit from migrant sex workers observed that the vulnerability their immigration status brings about, alongside the fact that they were more likely to need money, makes them more reliable and less likely to quit at short notice ... From the viewpoint of the unscrupulous employer, the question is not whether migrants have been 'trafficked' or 'smuggled' or are otherwise illegally present in the country, but rather whether their immigration status and their desperation for work makes them, in the words of one

employer we interviewed 'so frightened that they're not going to pull any stunts'.

... The state is not closely involved in regulating employment in the sex sector as employment [similarly, it does not regulate employment of domestic workers in private households] ... There is little to protect migrant workers from exploitation and poor working conditions ... It means that the (illicit) contracts forged with workers in these sectors are treated as a private matter, and the state thus creates what is effectively a radically free 'free market'. However, 'sellers' and 'buyers' of services are not equal, and certain immigration statuses create marginalised groups who are vastly unequal to buyers.

I saw with my own eyes that Zhen Zhen had made huge sacrifices working in the sex trade. She truly worked non-stop. She lacked both sleep and nutrition. The cut-off time for customers was 2 a.m., and she had to be up again at 7 o'clock in case there were any early punters, so she had only five hours' sleep. And she found it very hard to get to sleep after a full day. 'I close my eyes and I just see their faces,' she confided to me.

At rare moments of reflection, Zhen Zhen revealed that she was anxious to return home. 'It won't be long before I can go back, to my daughter and my parents.'

Meanwhile, Zhen Zhen was still eager to earn as much as she could. In the daytime when it was quiet, she would sit at the dining table making phone calls. She was booking work for herself. She called round all the massage parlours in her notebook, one by one, asking if they had any vacancies. 'I'm setting up work for after October,' she said.

'I'm completely booked from now till October. But I need to make bookings early, otherwise the vacancies get filled up quickly. There are so many women out there doing the same work these days. And good and busy parlours never have vacancies for the following week. If they tell you they need more girls for next week, then you know they aren't making money and so you aren't gonna make much money there.'

Zhen Zhen hadn't had a break for nine months. 'Simply can't afford it,' she said. 'The only way I could allow myself to have a break is to work in a less busy place for two weeks – there I can serve only five or six customers a day. That would be a break for me. And then the next two weeks I'll be back into a busy place.'

'That's really tough,' I responded. 'I couldn't imagine working that hard.'

'But you know,' Zhen Zhen squeezed out a smile, trying to sound hopeful. 'I'm going to have my first real break, for one week, from the last day in June – because I need to spend some time looking for medicine and health products for my parents. There's a good clinic in London where I can buy these. Much better than in Dalian. They want me to send them home to them.' That seemed the only reason Zhen Zhen could justify a proper break for herself.

But at least she had been rewarded for her sacrifice. She was certain that it had been worthwhile. And as she said, 'Only you yourself can know if it is all worth the effort. No one else can judge or evaluate it for you.'

As Linda's verbal abuse continued, I made a judgment of my own. I decided that I had had enough and left the next morning, before she arrived.

Ming's duties were largely the same as mine. That is, until one Friday, when a new demand was made on her that would change the course of her life. When the doorbell rang that morning and

Ming opened the door as usual, the man standing there took her for *xiaojie*.

Ming had to explain quickly: 'Let me take you to *xiaojie*'s room. She will serve you.'

But he seemed instantly attracted to Ming. 'Please – you look lovely,' he told her.

Ming ignored his attentions and led him to *xiaojie*'s room.

'Sir, I shut the door behind us,' she heard *xiaojie* say, trying to get him focused after Ming had taken the one-hour fee from him.

Ming learned later what happened next.

The session had hardly begun when the man got up from the bed and insisted that *xiaojie* go back outside.

'No offence, but I like a bit of variety. Do you think you could go and ask that girl, the receptionist, to come in here?'

'Ah, you want to do *shuang-fei* [double-fly: a sex session with two women]!' *xiaojie* said. 'But … the problem is that our maid doesn't do this, you see. She only opens the door and collects money.' It wasn't the first time she'd been asked for *shuang-fei*, and it certainly wasn't the first time that a punter had become interested in a housekeeper who didn't do sex work. *Xiaojie* shrugged her shoulders.

The man wouldn't take no for an answer. 'Look, just go and tell your maid to come in here. I'll ask her myself,' he repeated.

Reluctantly, *xiaojie* went out of the room and told Ming what the customer wanted.

'What do you mean?' Ming was confused. She'd never been asked to do anything like this before.

'Can you just come to my room to help me explain to him?' *xiaojie* pleaded. The last thing she wanted was to offend a punter.

Ming shuffled in and stood there awkwardly. 'How I can help you, sir?'

'Come in here,' he said, putting on a smile. 'Come and watch us, that's all.'

'What?'

'I said, watch us, you understand English?'

Ming looked at her colleague for help. 'What should I do? Is he really serious?' she asked in Chinese.

'Yes, he's serious,' *xiaojie* said, shrugging her shoulders again as if she didn't mind. 'It's not unusual. We do get a few punters like this. Last month I was asked for exactly the same in a parlour down south. He wants you but can't have you, so he'd like you to at least participate by watching him having sex with me. Just watch us. I am sure he will pay you.'

It seemed that *xiaojie* had done this many times before. She wasn't at all embarrassed. Then the man requested oral sex without a condom.

'Another fool; they just love this flute-playing without the plastic cover,' *xiaojie* said to Ming in Chinese, sneering, but quickly putting back on a flattering smile when she turned to the eager punter. 'Darling, I do everything for you! Just £20 extra, please,' *xiaojie* reached out her left palm while rubbing the man's penis with her right hand. The man looked a little frustrated, murmuring to himself, but reached into his pocket to find the cash.

'He probably thought this service was free! Idiot!' *xiaojie* said to Ming, again in Chinese.

In this 'free, free-market' of unregulated sex, employers can sell what they like to whomever they like in order to remain competitive, regardless of the risk to their employees' health. Zhen Zhen wouldn't agree to unprotected sex, but some women workers were told by their employers to do so. In many Chinese-run brothels today, women feel obliged to accept employers' demands owing to their increasingly limited work options, and offer extras such as unprotected oral sex in exchange for a higher fee.

When the punter had had enough oral sex, he pushed *xiaojie* over the edge of the bed and started to penetrate her.

'Look here, darling,' he turned and stared at Ming, making sure that she was watching.

'You like it, sweetie?' he asked.

Ming had never felt so embarrassed. She tried not to look at her colleague's face.

'Look at me,' the man insisted.

Ming watched him, blushing. Please let it be over soon, she thought to herself.

'Come here, babe,' he signalled to Ming. 'Come and join us!'

'No, no, I don't do this.'

'I said, come over here! I'll pay you!' the man pulled out from *xiaojie* and stood pleading with her.

'No, no, I really can't do that,' Ming said, not knowing how to extricate herself from the situation.

'Now I'm not going to carry on with this session if you don't join us,' he said. 'I'll ask your boss for my money back.'

Xiaojie sat up, crossing her arms, as if expecting trouble. 'Ming, it's up to you – if you want to have a try, you can,' she said persuasively. 'He clearly likes you. *Shuang-fei* is always good for business – he'll pay double. It's really easy money. But it's up to you.'

Ming listened quietly, genuinely not knowing what to think. She had never imagined this scenario. Could it ever be possible? For her, sex had to be private, even if it was being paid for.

'No, no, I can't, I can't do this,' she repeated. 'I'm a maid here.'

'Come on, darling,' the man insisted. 'Other maids do it, why can't you? Have a bit of fun!'

Ming shook her head gently. 'I'm sorry.'

As she started to walk towards the bedroom door, the man grabbed her. 'Come on, sweetie, you'll like it!'

She tried to push him away.

'Listen, I'll pay you £100 per hour, on top of what she gets. All right? Come on, give it a go!' the man said, confirming what *xiaojie* had already told Ming: double pay for 'double-fly'.

For a second or two, Ming froze: £100 per hour; could this be real? She'd never earned so much in her life – in one single hour. Of course, whatever she made would have to be shared with Sarah, so she would in fact earn £50. Even so, that wasn't bad for an hour. More than she could ever dream of in any other job. But still, she wasn't quite sure that he meant it.

She turned to *xiaojie*, who seemed to have guessed her thoughts. 'Trust me. He's going to pay you £100, and pay me the same,' she said to Ming. 'Didn't I tell you?'

'What would I have to do, then?' Ming stood, hesitant. Even if she'd wanted to agree, she didn't have the slightest clue how to proceed.

'I can't tell you what to do,' *xiaojie* said, crossing her arms on her bare breasts again. 'If you want to do it, do it. It can be a one-off and I won't tell the boss. You can keep your money. Keep the whole £100.'

Ming tried to take it in. What they were asking her to do was unprecedented, distasteful, the man's stuck-up belly repugnant, but against that was the thought of all that much-needed cash so quickly earned. Even *xiaojie* was offering to help her keep the lot. How could she say no?

The man could see that Ming was wavering and repeated his offer. 'I'll pay £100 for an hour, darling,' he said, while *xiaojie* whispered gently to her in Chinese: 'It will all be finished before you even notice, Ming. Think of how you can use this money for your daughter. That's all that matters. That's why I'm doing it.'

Then the punter gently pulled Ming over to him and started to undress her. She found herself offering no resistance.

She tried to rationalise the situation. After all, she'd never said she would never sell sex. The idea of maiding was to give herself time to learn about the work environment before making a career choice. But in her heart of hearts she knew the money on offer left her with no choice at all. With £100, the equivalent of more than a month's wages back home, there was a lot she could do. What crossed her mind as she lay on the bed were the things that her earnings could bring to Ting Ting and her parents.

It all happened very quickly and before Ming knew it the punter was on top of her. She felt unable to move a muscle. This was the first time she'd had any physical contact with a Westerner and she was overwhelmed by the experience – and the weight. He was proactive and talkative, although Ming had no idea what he was mumbling. He was rough, and had his hands over her face and was rubbing her neck as if to bruise her. She could hardly breathe. And as if that wasn't bad enough, *xiaojie* was right next to them, watching intensely. Ming closed her eyes. She tried to imagine he was David Beckham. But even that didn't seem to bring the experience anywhere close to bearable. His right hand was now tightly round her neck, and when she fearfully opened her eyes, she could only see his sweating, wrinkled forehead and *xiaojie*'s curious black eyes.

When it was over, she had to admit that, although unpleasant, it was not as difficult as she'd expected.

'You feel OK?' *xiaojie* asked her over dinner. 'From what I could see, you did fine.'

'I didn't expect to be doing this so soon …'

'None of us did when we started out, you know,' *xiaojie*

said. 'The moment comes to you when you realise there is no alternative and no time to waste. None of us are young any more. If we don't make all the money we can now, we will lose the opportunity for ever.'

Ming nodded.

'And look on the bright side,' *xiaojie* carried on. 'You will learn some English in the process. Bonus to the job.'

'Well, it's certainly the only time and place in England where we'll ever have contact with the locals,' Ming replied. 'If you can call it that.'

That night, Ming went to sleep thinking about what had happened and how she felt about it. She thought hard about whether she was ready for a career in sex work. She felt she was strong enough, both physically and emotionally. She recalled the casual words of Ying, her flatmate in London, and thought how it all finally made sense.

The next day, however, the punter returned, asking to see Ming. Unfortunately, the person he asked was Sarah.

'She is our housekeeper,' said Sarah. 'She doesn't do sex.'

'Oh yes she does, and she does it well,' the man said to Sarah with a wink. He clearly had no idea of the trouble he was causing.

'Is it true? Ming?' Sarah questioned, shocked. 'Did he do it with you?'

Ming was totally taken aback by Sarah's interrogation. 'No, I didn't.'

'Speak up!' Sarah became angry. 'Did you or not?'

'No.' Ming looked down, not wanting to meet Sarah's fierce eyes. She couldn't pretend to look confident. But she didn't want to tell the truth, not only for herself but so as not to make trouble for *xiaojie*.

'Did you do it with this girl?' Sarah now turned to ask the punter, pointing at Ming.

'Er ... Yes, but what's the problem? I did it with both of them. They were good.'

'What? Both of them?' Sarah couldn't believe her ears. '*Both of them?*'

The man nodded timidly, and then decided that he didn't want to get involved in the dispute that he'd just stirred up and hurriedly left.

Sarah was livid. 'So you ganged up to cheat money out of me!' she screamed. 'Bitches!'

'*Xiaojie* did nothing. It was me,' Ming said. 'The customer asked for me to take part, so I did. And I kept the £100. *Xiaojie* took her £100 and gave you £50. You can check the accounts. She gave you the £50.'

Sarah turned to *xiaojie*. 'You know the rules, you bitch. How did you let her take the £100 without telling me it was a *shuang-fei* session?'

'I ... I ...' *xiaojie* stammered, knowing where this would soon lead to.

'She wasn't in a position to tell you anything,' Ming broke in. 'It was my job to keep the accounts ... and I forgot to tell you about the £100.'

'Bitches! Bitches!' Sarah said again, panting as if she was running out of breath as well as insults.

She went back into the lounge and started phoning her contacts in the trade. 'Have to look for new maid now!' she said to one of them. 'This one just stole £50 from me! You believe that? This bitch maid upgraded herself into a *xiaojie*, and dared to keep the money for herself. And I need a new *xiaojie* as well!'

Ming didn't expect to lose her job in Milton Keynes quite so soon. She didn't expect her co-worker to try to save it for her, either. Solidarity between workers is a rarity in this ruthless underground world where greed and profit rule. There are no unions here, and people become transformed by the trade and eventually see beating the competition as the only key to survival. That brief moment of solidarity shown by *xiaojie* in order to make it easy for Ming to earn her first fee had proved to be a double-edged sword, for Sarah was sure tell anyone who would listen that this particular *xiaojie* had helped a maid to deceive her. Such defamation spread fast and lasted long.

Ming knew she would have to find somewhere else to work. She still had the notepad in which she'd jotted down phone numbers during her previous job search. She could now see the path her future life in England would take – and she would have only that one straight line to follow. As she slowly dragged her suitcase through the lifeless streets of Milton Keynes, she looked back on her time there and found comfort in her conclusion. At the end of the day, she was willing to sacrifice both her soul and her reputation if doing so meant she could put food on the table and provide for her family. As *xiaojie* had said before the 'double-fly' session, that was all that mattered.

A Tale of Two Women

Sitting in her armchair against the window, Pam recalled the day she entered the sex trade. Beata listened quietly. Although it was no consolation to hear of Pam's miserable past, she was beginning to feel some empathy with her, this strange old lady. 'It turned out that it wasn't just a receptionist job. I was doing maiding, and that included opening the door to customers and cleaning the place up. And the girls I was working with … they were from all over. All over England, I mean. Not like you. In them days, it was all English girls doing this job.'

Pam lit up another Marlboro, and took one from the packet to offer Beata.

'This is my first in England,' Beata said, accepting the cigarette and lighting it up.

'Always a first time for everything,' said Pam.

'Tell me, Pam, are there many Polish women doing this work?'

'Your people didn't do this before, you know,' Pam said by way of reply. Her deep, warm voice reminded Beata of her grandmother. 'Neither did the Czechs. It wasn't until round about the millennium that foreign girls started to turn up in the massage parlours and working flats round 'ere. The Albanian girls came first. And then the Thai and Russian girls. Truly, I haven't met one who wasn't a bit upset on her first day.'

Beata looked down, remembering her first session. She tightened the belt on her dressing gown and sipped her coffee.

'And don't think only the Poles get treated like this. A lot of the Albanian and Russian girls I worked with all had smart-looking "boyfriends" like your Robert who brought them in,' Pam carried on.

'You think this makes me feel better?' Beata said. 'Just because you meet a lot of women like me?'

'No, I didn't mean it like that, sweet'eart. I just mean a lot of girls get pimped by their boyfriends. You're not the only one. When I first started out in the trade, one of the first girls I worked with was pimped by her boyfriend. Maria, her name was. Poor thing.'

'An English girl?'

'Yeah. We was working together in a place in Mayfair. It was over a butcher's in Shepherd Market. She was five foot two, really pretty. Such a good figure and a lovely character, laughing and joking all day long. She told me all about her life. She said she didn't know who her father was, only that he was a lorry driver from up north somewhere. Her mum told her that she'd come from a one-night stand. So she tried not to have sex with men from up north, because it might be her dad.'

'That's so sad.'

'Maria's mum was never really like a mum to her. When she was fifteen, her step-father tied her to a chair and raped her while her mum was out, but when she told her mum about it, she wouldn't believe her. In the end, she ran away from that hell place and made for London. Everyone she loved had let her down and she couldn't get out of the circle of abuse. When she got here, she met a young man she felt she could finally trust. He seemed kind and let her stay with him. But after two weeks he said she had to get some money. So he took her to the beat at Finsbury Park.'

Beata listened, picturing Robert in her mind as Pam talked of Maria's pimp. She was eager to understand it all.

'When Maria started out at Finsbury Park, her first punter was a man of about eighty and he didn't want to use a condom. He was kissing her and at the same time taking the piss out of her. Other girls working that beat told Maria what to do. They said don't do nothing without a condom. But worse things happened to her. Another man took her from the first ponce. He just took her away.'

'What is a ponce?' Beata had never heard of the word.

'A ponce? A ponce is a pimp, ain' it?' replied Pam, smiling, puffing away. 'Like your Robert.'

'Did you mean that this second man kidnapped her and became her pimp?' Beata was surprised such a thing could happen in England.

'Yeah. It was years and years ago. The new ponce used to beat her and send her on the streets to work day and night. She couldn't run away. She was too scared to. He was a lot worse than the first ponce. Maria tried to run away once. But he looked everywhere to find her and caught her at King's Cross. He ran after her ... and she hid in a dustbin. A dustbin! He found her eventually, and beat her up again. He hit her knees with a bottle and told her to run. "Run!" he said. "Come on, run, see how far you can run!" and she just fell on the floor. Then he put her straight back on the corner again.'

Beata felt frightened, hearing about what happened to Maria. She began to imagine a similar scenario with Robert. 'Did she stay with him?' she asked.

'Yeah, Maria stayed with that ponce for years. She worried so much about getting money for him. If she took £200, he would tear it up and say it wasn't enough – sweetie money, he called it. Maria carried on with her life of pleasing men in the flat he'd found for her and feeding the pimp at home. She used to get all sorts of men.'

Seeing that Beata looked like she was about to cry, Pam changed the subject and started to talk about some of the things punters wanted.

''Ere, this'll make you laugh. I remember one afternoon, she did schoolgirl fantasy in a school uniform for a middle-aged man. She charged him £100 to cane her. He acted as a school master and told her to bend down, then he caned her as hard as he could.' Pam put on a little girl's voice. '"Oh, teacher," she said, "I've been really naughty! I'm so sorry!" When that was over, he asked her for a blow job.'

Pam chuckled to herself. 'A lot of men like that service – Maria had around five each week. In fact, she was known for taking the cane or poddle, you know, a round leather thing with a handle. One day, a man came in and asked if she would take sixty strokes for £600. Well, she couldn't say no to that much money, and so she took the sixty strokes. She was in tears when she came out of the room. "My arse is bleeding!" she said. "I swear on my fucking life that I'll never do this again!" But later that afternoon when there weren't many punters, Maria was hoping he'd come back.'

'God …' Beata sighed in disbelief. She found no humour in these stories, despite Pam telling them with a laugh.

'Maria did any fantasy you can name, and was good at them. She had all the uniforms – policewoman, French maid, rubber, leather, all the kinky stuff. One day, she had to go to one punter's gaff. When she got back she looked pale, as if she was going to throw up. I asked her what happened. She said, "That sick fucker! He got me to lay in a coffin while he wanked himself. It took ages!" What a laugh that was.'

'I hope I don't ever have men like that here,' Beata said anxiously.

'The best ones was those who wanted to be a slave and clean all the flat up. There were plenty of 'em, too. Maria loved them, and so did I – I didn't have to do any tidying up then.'

At last, Beata smiled. The first smile since she'd been led into the flat by Robert, a smile that Pam was pleased to see. 'That's the ticket – it's my job to make you feel better, love.'

'I really want to know what happened to Maria since? Did she still stay with the man – the ponce?' Beata asked.

'She did, yeah, and he never laid off her. One day, she called me to say that she couldn't work. Well, she never took time off, so I asked her what the matter was. Maria said the ponce had cut her leg with a machete from her knee to her ankle, and pushed her down the stairs. She was in agony. Maria thought about running away every single day, but she never did. I actually advised her to tell the coppers about him. She'd always refused, but this was the last straw. She made up her mind to grass him up.'

'So you called the police?'

'We did. That day, two coppers came to the flat. They took photos of the canes and all the working gear. They set up to follow Maria and she told them that he would be waiting for her at a pub in Stoke Newington.

'The police, all plain clothes, went in the pub for a drink and watched it all. They filmed the whole process of the pimp meeting Maria and getting her to hand over the cash for the day. They had all the evidence that they needed to nick him and he got banged up.'

'Nick him? Banged up? What's that?'

'I mean he got arrested. But he only got three months inside. He was an evil bastard. He should have done more bird than that.'

'More bird?' Beata asked, mystified again.

'I mean a longer sentence, darlin'. You don't always know what I'm on about, do you? Anyway, while this was all going on, one of the coppers who'd come to the working flat said he fancied me.'

'Really?' Beata said, looking at Pam, trying to picture her as a stunning-looking blonde. 'I mean, I can see that. You have beautiful blue eyes, Pam.'

'Get away with you!' Pam waved her hand at Beata, laughing from her abdomen.

'And you have pretty, thick lips,' Beata carried on, giggling.

'Is that supposed to be a compliment? No, really, he did fancy me something rotten. He asked me, "Would you like to go out with me one evening?" I looked him up and down and thought he was quite handsome, and so I said yes. He took me for a meal after work – an Italian meal, it was – and then we went to a pub. It was funny really, because at closing time the landlord locked the door and he said we could have afters.'

'After what?' Beata wondered whether she was ever going to understand Pam's language.

'Oh, I mean, staying late. After hours. Anyway, there were a lot of people in the pub. And then there was a loud banging on the door, and when he opened it there was a policewoman standing there. What we didn't know was that it was the landlord's birthday and the policewoman was a strippergram that his wife had booked. Well, You should have seen the copper's face. He was terrified – a sergeant in a pub after hours with his car outside and him half cut. He would really have been for the high jump. When the policewoman started taking her clothes off, my copper realised she was a just a stripper and he was over the moon.'

'So you had a police boyfriend,' said Beata, grasping one of the few hard facts she had been able to gather from Pam's story.

'Yeah. I took him to meet my family once. But that went pear shaped when my younger sister, Sandra, turned up. Sandra was always on the wacky baccy – that's cannabis, dear. She would light a joint anywhere she wanted. When I saw her, I had to warn her: '*Hagees a cagopager!*'

'Is that English?'

'It's back slang; me and Sandra used to use it as kids. It means, "He's a copper!"' Pam couldn't help laughing as she recalled the scene. 'Everyone in the family understood and tried not to burst out laughing. My bloke was asking, "What's the matter? Are you all stoned or something?" which made us laugh even more. In the end Sandra, who wasn't the conforming type, turned and said to me, "Fuck him!" And then she took out her weed, rolled a spliff and lit up.'

'English people like to smoke cannabis, I know,' Beata said, half understanding what Pam has just told her.

'I was dead worried that my copper would nick her, but all he said to me was, "Do you think you could get me some?" I was well pleased but I thought to myself, I'm not doing that – Imagine getting nicked with a copper!

'Anyhow, at this point, Maria had some freedom for the first time in her life, now that her ponce was in prison. But the bizarre thing was that Maria had started to go out with the pimp's identical twin brother. When I asked her why, she said to me, "You don't understand what I've been through. I've never been given a chance in my life. Never really gone to school or anything like that. The only thing I'm really good at is this job.

And then his brother came along and he was really nice to me."
I knew then that Maria would probably never get out of the
vicious circle she was trapped in. She'd just go on replacing one
pimp with another.'

Beata shook her head as she listened and tried to imagine
what had led Maria to such desperation.

'When the ponce was released from prison after three
months, he tracked her down and locked her in his flat. His
brother, who apparently wasn't quite such a bastard, went
looking for her. Eventually he found her in his brother's flat,
but of course she couldn't open the door to let him in. She
hadn't eaten for two days, so he fetched her a bag of chips
and fed them to her through the letterbox. This went on for
a week. The ponce never once came back to the flat to check
on her.

'In the end, he went and stole the ponce's key from him. He
let her out and they set up together. "It's a bit like going out
with the same man with a different soul," she said. But it was
out of the frying pan and into the fire. Although the brother
wasn't violent, he was hopelessly hooked on crack and heroin
and permanently on the dole. The only thing what kept him
going was the drugs. So of course, just like his brother, he put
her to work, back on the streets. But Maria still couldn't see
she was being used: "He used to pity me and help me. Why
shouldn't I do the same when he needs me?"'

'I don't understand this girl,' Beata said. 'I just don't get it.'

'She'd never been given love, or a decent opportunity in her
life, you see. She just didn't know how to hope, or fight for the
better. Do you understand?'

Beata nodded sorrowfully.

'Anyhow, Maria was worse off on the street. He took all she
earned for his drugs, and he couldn't care less about her safety.

One time, five men raped her and took all her money. Another time she got in a van and someone in the back tried to strangle her. She jumped out while the van was still moving but her leg got caught in the seat belt and she was pulled down the road. She had to get a metal knee cap put in.

'After that, Maria said she'd only work indoors. She started to bring punters to the flat she shared with the pimp.'

'Was it better for her then?' Beata asked.

'It would have been, but as well as being a junkie, her ponce was a jealous psycho, too. One time she asked him to give her a couple of hours with one of her regulars and not stay in the flat like he usually did. Of course, he came back early, high as a kite, got jealous when he saw the punter and just plunged into him, beating him unconscious and robbing him. Lucky for him, the punter was married and apparently quite high-profile, so he didn't go to the police, but Maria never saw him again.'

Beata shook her head again. 'Did Maria leave the pimp in the end?'

'Well, no. Months later, when I met her again, she looked dreadful. She told me the ponce had got her on crack and heroin. In the end, she rented a cupboard in a crack house to sleep in. It was so sad that it broke my heart.'

Now it was Pam's turn to shake her head and look sad.

'One day, one of her mates called me and told me that Maria had been run over by a drunk driver in Clapton while she was on the streets one night. He just drove into her. She died instantly.'

Pam paused, lit up another cigarette and sighed, genuinely upset.

'A week later, I went to Maria's funeral with Trish. I needed a shoulder to cry on. I'd been close to Maria and I was very fond of her. There was an innocence and freshness about her that made her adorable. But good people never stay long, especially those good people around me. No one else at the funeral seemed particularly sad. In fact, there were only about ten turned up. It was a smashing send-off, though. One of Maria's regulars from years ago paid for everything. He read out a beautiful piece he'd written about her. "She was a truly lovely woman," he said. And she truly was.'

In the days that followed, Beata had to accommodate men of all sorts in the dreary Soho flat. The faces – so many different kinds of faces – flashed in front of her like the £20 notes she was counting. But there was one thing that she had stopped counting – time. Time dragged on, as if waiting for her pain to dissolve into numbness. Robert had arranged for her to work here three days a week, Sunday, Monday and Tuesday, the most shifts he could get.

One day, Beata arrived as usual at 11 a.m. and got changed into her lacy black underwear, one of four different outfits she wore during her working week. She checked her make-up in the bedroom mirror as the buzzer rang.

The first customer of the day was a white businessman in a suit. He politely asked for what he wanted and gave Beata the impression that he would be quiet and considerate and leave a big tip. But as Pam liked to say, you could never judge a book by its cover.

In the bedroom, Beata undressed with her back to the punter – she hadn't yet learned the game of teasing, but the man didn't appear to mind. As always, she kept her eyes shut during the session. There were flashbacks of a good time at home in Katowice: of her and her son at a noisy funfair. Tomasz had blue eyes and soft blonde hair, just like her.

But Beata's wandering thoughts were interrupted when the punter on top of her abruptly withdrew, reached under the pillow and took out a long belt he had hidden there, presumably while she was getting undressed. Now he was waving the belt high and trying to beat her with it.

'Stop! Stop! Help!' Beata screamed, wriggling out from under him and running for the door. The man seemed to enjoy her fright. He replaced his previously polite English with a stream of swearwords. Then he waved the belt even higher and harder, hitting her as she ran out of the room. When Pam finally managed to get the man to leave, Beata was still in shock. She couldn't hold back her tears. She could not understand why men could enjoy abusing her.

'You want a cuppa, love?' Pam asked with concern, putting on the kettle. She felt bad that the girl she was supposed to be looking after had just been treated so badly, but a chat with a cup of tea were all she could offer by way of consolation.

'Get it off your chest, love,' Pam carried on. 'If you want to cry, have a good cry. It helps.'

'I do many things wrong in my life, Pam.'

'So do I,' Pam said. 'But it's usually those bastards' fault, not ours.'

Beata looked at her and had to squeeze out a smile.

'Now wipe away your little tears, love!' Pam said, patting her on her shoulders. 'And drink your cuppa!'

Minutes later, Beata felt better and sat up. She took out a cigarette from Pam's packet of Marlboro and lit it.

'Listen, love, you wanna do this job better, don't you?' said Pam, looking concerned. 'What you need is a little training session. You need to learn how to deal with punters like him.'

As one of the oldest maids around, Pam seemed to enjoy acting as a mentor. Beata nodded and listened quietly.

'You remind me a bit of Ana, a lovely girl from Albania I looked after. She worked here for two years.'

'What was she like?'

'Pretty, like you. She had no papers and she used to date a bouncer who worked outside a strip club down the road. He used to buy her things and spoil her, you know. And she used to spoil me! She bought bracelets for me. We got on really well. Then there were Emily and Candy from Romania ... I trained them up, too.'

'And you can train me as well?' Beata asked curiously.

'Just like you was my daughter. Let's start you with some real basics, shall we?' Pam said with an impish grin.

'All right, mum,' Beata put on a warm smile, then she corrected herself. 'English mum.'

Pam laughed. 'The first thing you need to know about working in the trade is that you need to make sure the punters wear a condom, no matter what they say or how much they offer you.'

'Ah, I know that already.'

'Do you? Many girls don't when they first start. You've got to be aware that the punters would all try to take advantage of you because you're foreign. But you've got to know how to protect yourself. You understand?'

Beata nodded thankfully. Only that day, a punter had come in and asked for oral sex without a condom. Beata had said no, but he'd insisted. She hadn't known how to handle it, and had called Pam for help.

To Beata's surprise, Pam said straight to the man, 'Tell me, do you want a mouthful of filthy spunk yourself? I don't think so.' As the man stood there looking shocked, Pam pointed at the door and said, 'Now fuck off.'

Looking back, Beata realised that had been her first lesson.

It has been a 'good day'. Beata had served eighteen customers in all, ten of them for half an hour each – which had earned her £650 – and the other eight for ten minutes. All in all, she had earned £810 that day, out of which Pam would take £400 rent. That sum was payable by every woman daily, regardless of how much she made. Pam would keep £100 as her wages and pass the rest to Trish. Trish would then pay some of it – £110 per day, according to Pam – to the owner of the flat, whom no one seemed to know anything about other than that he was a local man who owned several working flats in Soho. He rarely showed up in person but sent someone to collect the money once a week.

To compensate for her small wage, Pam asked her girls for tips, the amount depending on how well she got on with them and how popular they were with the punters. Pam asked for a £10 tip from Beata for each hour she worked. Although Beata felt that this was quite a lot, as a new girl she didn't want to argue. Also, she liked Pam and didn't want to fall out with her over money.

That night, then, Beata had £340 to take home with her – a sum impossible to earn in a sandwich bar or a factory, even in a week. As she looked at the money, she admitted to herself that she had settled into the job. Being able to put that sort of sum in her pocket when she left the flat at 11 p.m. made the risks and the humiliation worthwhile.

Robert was waiting outside for her, as he'd done every day since she started work. And every day Beata feared the worst: that he would start ordering her to hand over the money she had earned.

But not tonight. She felt relieved but unsettled, wondering what was to come. Yet he cooked her dinner, as usual, and remained attentive towards her. For the entire evening, it looked as if he was trying to win back her trust and reassure her about her work. 'You see, many girls do this type of work and there's nothing shameful about it,' he said, holding her hands on the dining table. 'In Poland, maybe people frown about it, but here it is just another job.'

Was it true? Just another job? Beata wondered. Did he really have such different values from her? Did he really think he was acting in her best interests by finding work for her in that Soho flat? While Beata pondered, Robert carried on telling her how much she meant to him. 'I truly love you,' he said as he went to run a bath for her.

'But how can you feel love when I have sex with other men?'

'My love doesn't change. I feel like I am a special person because I can have you all the time when other men can't and have to pay for it,' he replied, kissing her on her forehead.

She laughed bitterly. Either he was lying or he was not in this world. She thought back to the day when she met him – how she had thought there was something unusual about him and the way he tried to please her. He'd tried to win her like a trophy. Perhaps they truly did live in completely different worlds.

'My little Beata, ask yourself – who can love you more than me? Who can accept you the way you are, whatever job you do?' he said.

Beata looked up and stared at him. He had such eagerly persuasive eyes. She wondered when she had so carelessly fallen for him, without even knowing it.

'No matter what happens, I will always look after you, you know that,' he reassured her, holding her hands in his once again. But as he looked at her intensely, she could see the dark shadow lurking behind those loving eyes. She froze.

The part of Beata that desperately wanted to believe in him had been shattered. Working in Soho had at least taught her about the ruthlessness of male desire. How could Robert want to expose her to that ruthlessness if he cared the slightest about her? Confused as she was, she was thinking clearly enough to know that Robert would do whatever was necessary to reach his desired aim. She had just happened to be in the wrong place at the wrong time. She felt as though he was playing a game with her mind, manipulating her fear and confusion, waiting for the final moment to strip her of her dignity. She knew, somehow, that the final nightmarish confrontation with his greedily ambitious project was yet to come.

Most sex workers need to adopt a hidden identity. Not only was Beata unable to tell her family about her situation, she also had to keep it secret from the Polish migrant communities and social networks with whom she shared both her native language and her religion. Her Polish friends and acquaintances in England, most of them Catholics, would surely judge her harshly, and how could she ever explain to her friends – even her best friend Anna in Poland – why she hadn't run away from either Robert or the work she was doing? After all, no one was physically forcing her to stay. She did not really understand it herself, so how could she expect anyone else to? The only option was to close herself up, to have no friends and lead a solitary life.

Isolation was one of the things that affected Beata most profoundly. She found herself fighting her battle alone, day in, day out. This isolation from everyday life kept her trapped in her situation and made it difficult for her to equip herself with the resources and knowledge with which to improve her lot. Her isolation fed her vulnerability.

For her, sex work blurred the boundary between the public and the private. Her body had become a battleground in her struggle to earn a wage, and she found it hard to think of her job as simply a twelve-hour shift. She wondered how the old hands made sense of it all. Might she one day manage to disengage her inner self from the work that she did with her outer one, to detach soul from corpus, to separate the physical being from the spiritual?

To make sense of her alienating existence, Beata needed to confide in someone who knew the truth about her – and at this moment, Pam was the only candidate, readily offering a sympathetic and willing ear. While receiving daily consolation from Pam, Beata also found her English improving, although she still didn't always understand Pam's Cockney slang.

As she serviced one man after another, Beata relived again and again the pain of losing her love for Robert, of being betrayed and discovering the truth about him. 'I can understand how painful it was for Maria not to have anyone to trust,' she said to Pam during a break. She had only empathy for Maria, a woman she'd never met. 'I feel I'm living the same life now.'

'I know, sweet'eart,' said Pam, pouring hot water into their tea mugs. 'Girls here have a hard time.'

'You know what it feels like, Pam? To trust someone totally and he takes away that trust. Maria believed all her men who turned out to be pimps, didn't she? I believed Robert very much.'

'Well, girls wouldn't end up 'ere if they weren't a bit gullible,' Pam said as she sipped her tea, not thinking that her casual remark might have hurt Beata's feelings. 'You've got to ask yourself—'

'But Pam,' Beata anxiously interrupted her for the first time. 'If you're in a foreign country, it's easy to lose your balance. If you don't know many people and don't speak the language well, you put your trust in the first person that comes along and says he wants to look after you. Don't you understand?'

'Of course I do, love. You're no different to the Albanian and Romanian girls I told you about that got sent 'ere. They all fell for the men who were pimping them. It ain't just you.'

Pam paused and looked up at Beata's sorrowful eyes. She recognised that the girl was probably still in the denial stage of the process – maybe she, like many other girls, was just pretending all this wasn't really happening. Pam had always been sceptical about denial, though, and she spoke her mind. 'I'll ask you, same as I asked Maria and all the other girls who've come here after being pimped by their boyfriends: why didn't you turn round and leave as soon as you got here, if you don't want to do this job? Robert might be a creep, but he isn't putting a gun on your head, is he? You could walk out now, if you wanted.'

Beata was taken aback by Pam's candour. Wounded, in fact. How could this Englishwoman really understand her desperate need to belong, to be accepted and loved? How could she appreciate how poor she'd been back in Poland? Her lack of choice? Beata struggled to convey her unspeakable pain. 'You have no idea, Pam. You don't know how shocked I was when he told me the first time about sex work. It was just outside this flat, when he brought me here. I only realised then what he meant by "special places" to make quick cash. I was so shocked that I didn't know how to speak to him. I was so destroyed, inside. He destroyed me.'

'I know, love,' Pam said, seeing the anxiety rising in Beata's eyes and not wanting to upset her more.

'I became very attached to him very quickly, within a few weeks of knowing him,' Beata carried on gloomily. 'Not because he paid for everything and always took me to expensive places. I'm not that type of girl. I fell for him because I was very lonely and depressed. I had a broken marriage, like you, and I was going to divorce. I thought working in England would bring me new opportunities, but it brought me a new set of problems. Jobs never lasted here. When I lost my job in the sandwich bar, I was just devastated. I know you had a hard time when you tried to make ends meet, Pam, but whatever happens, this is your country and you have your family here and your circle. You were never without social support. I was tired of fighting life alone, you know. I needed someone. I was in that situation and I easily fell in love with him. We were lovers and I really believed he cared for me.'

'Men can be such bastards,' Pam agreed.

Beata began to cry as she recalled the betrayal. 'But when I began to trust him with my heart, he began to lie. Little lies. But more and more. They warned me of trouble. But I didn't want to see the signs. I pretended it wasn't important – which man doesn't lie sometimes? I stayed with him and pretended it was OK, because I wanted to be with him. Now I feel so unloved. I don't understand it! I really don't. What's happening? I ask him. How can he love me and want me to do sex work? Half of me thinks that maybe he's had a hard time and has been changed into another person by his misfortunes. The other half of me thinks he has planned this all and has targeted me, to lie to me and maybe to profit from me. But he has lied to me so much that my life has become messed up in his lies.'

Beata sobbed again. 'And now he wants me to do even more sex work. He is taking me to many places in Soho – this one first, because he says it's good location and has many customers, and now he's going to take me to other flats in Bounds Green and book me for work there. So I'm going there to work this week, after this job. He wants to make me work every day of the week.'

'You do realise he's going to take all your wages, don't you?' Pam said, looking straight into Beata's eyes.

Beata nodded, disheartened, and lowered her head. She knew that day would come, but she dared not think much about it. The thought of having no money of her own and being entirely dependent on him frightened her.

'Make no mistake, love,' Pam warned. 'This man who calls himself your boyfriend will take every penny off you. He sent in a Russian girl last year when another maid was on duty. And he earned £1,000 a week from that poor girl. When the maid left the job, I started working with her … and she told me all about it.'

'Did Robert come up here, to this flat?' Beata asked, sensing a straw to clutch at.

'No, he didn't,' Pam replied. 'He told the girl to come up herself to ask for work while he sat waiting in the car. Why?'

'How can you be so sure, then, that it was him?' asked Beata, hoping against hope that she had been the first, that pimping girls from eastern Europe was not how Robert made a living.

'Listen, love, everyone knew it was him. The handsome Robert is well known in these parts. No mistake there. You know full well what he's done to you and I'm telling you, he's been doing it to a lot of other girls for a long time. If you don't want him to start using you as a money-making machine, it's not too late to end it with him.'

Beata sobbed again. The heartbreak felt as unbearable as on the day Robert sent her into this flat. The truth was that she still hadn't admitted – and now was afraid to admit – how completely he had deceived her. Deep down, she'd secretly clung to the last hope that Robert had been led astray by the temptation around him and had simply stumbled across sex work as an employment option for her.

How much did Beata actually know about the world in which she spent her time working? She had little control over how long she worked, or who she saw, and certainly had no say in what she was being paid. In the month that followed, Beata was taking home around £300 per day on average, after rent and tips. She constantly felt she needed to take home more.

Beata couldn't decide how she felt about Pam. On the one hand, she was like a friend, extremely sociable and sympathetic and good to work with. She was like Beata's gate to the local world: a readily accessible source of information for everything that went on in the trade, the neighbourhood and, indeed, in British society generally. Pam was always ready to offer emotional support. Many women here must have relied on her advice and entrusted her with their secrets.

On the other hand, both Pam and her sister Trish were instrumental in running the place. Not only did they take in women introduced by pimps like Robert, they also made a regular profit from their daily earnings – £400 a day in rent was a huge amount, even for Soho. Beata wondered whether Pam made as little as she said. Either way, Pam was hardly a neutral.

But Pam had her own theory, although she wouldn't say it so openly to Beata. 'No point in turning them [the pimps] away. They'll just keep coming,' she told me later. 'It's like years ago when I used to know those local girls who were groomed into prostitution. You'd have little chance of catching the men who sent in the girls and controlled their earnings. And if it's not 'ere, it'd be somewhere else.'

Pam seemed content with what she got from the job. Decades of experience meant that tasks such as receiving the punters, taking care of the money, cleaning and shopping were nothing but daily domestic chores which she handled with ease.

Here in this flat, each working girl was allocated a maid. Pam worked with two to three of them per week. She seemed to get along with everyone.

During her time with Beata, she often went out to buy food for her. She could only do so between sessions, otherwise Beata would be left on her own with the punters. If things got so busy that Pam wasn't able to leave the flat, Beata had to go through a day serving more than sixteen men without having anything to eat. After a while, Beata sensibly began to bring sandwiches, just in case.

Despite the high fees and maintenance costs, a steady flow of young migrant women arrived to inquire about work. The woman who'd rang the bell when Robert was introducing Beata to Pam was waiting outside for her the next morning.

'I look for job,' she told Pam, following her up the stairs.

'Come in, then,' Pam said. 'Not sure what I've got for you though.'

'Pardon?'

'I said I'm not sure we need more girls at the moment,' Pam repeated. 'But sit down anyway.'

The woman remained standing. Clearly, she spoke little English.

'So how long have you been doing this, then?' asked Pam.

'Pardon?'

'I said how long have you been doing this?'

The woman got the gist of the sentence. 'No, no, never did …' She struggled with the words.

Pam lit a cigarette. 'It don't matter if you've never done it before. We get a lot of new girls here and they're all doing well. Where you from, darlin'? You speak English?'

'Er, I from Thailand. I … speak a little,' the young woman stuttered.

'Less than a little, by the sound of it!' Pam said. 'How you gonna talk to the men? You're gonna have hell of a hard time working 'ere, darlin'.'

'You have work for me here, then?' the woman tried, again misunderstanding.

'I told ya, we don't need no more girls at the moment,' Pam sounded firmer this time, standing up and walking to the kitchen sink, starting to wash up the tea mugs. 'I got things to get on with now, love. Leave me your phone number, or you can drop by when you've learned some English. All right?'

I've continued to explore the idea of a growing British demand for 'eastern European femininity' and have found it most prominent in the stag-night phenomenon in central and eastern Europe.

I talked with Beata about this, and she said that, before coming to Britain, she had no idea what a 'stag night' was and what had turned cities like Krakow – and her home town Katowice, for that matter – into cheap sex resorts. After coming here, though, she began to see the trend clearly: 'eastern Europeans' are much sought after by Brits.

I tried looking at the 'demand side' by talking to experienced punters. I found that the attractions to British sex tourists of central and eastern Europe were clear: the cheap weekend flights and the promise of the new, the exotic and the more feminine in a country where their debauchery would have no social consequences.

All over central and eastern Europe, British men fill the strip clubs and brothels every weekend. They book their tours through operators like Stag Republic, a Europe-wide stag-weekend operator. Andrew is a regular stag-night tourist. He not only organised his own stag night abroad, but has also been on many similar trips with friends. He said, 'One of the attractions of doing a stag night abroad is that "what goes on stag, stays on stag".'

Andrew prefers the women abroad because 'the girls are nicer and slimmer over there than British girls, who have become obese in the past fifteen to twenty years'. He has been on stag nights in Prague, Riga and Budapest. 'I chose to go to central and eastern Europe for stag nights because there are many good strip clubs there – and believe me, Prague has the biggest stripping industry in Europe.' He recommended Darling, off the historical Wenceslas Square, and Gold Fingers as the two best clubs in Prague.

He recalls that there were over a hundred strippers at Darling when he and his mates visited. 'There was so much choice,' he said. 'To sleep with a stripper will cost £80 per half hour, although not every stripper will let you. Some of them don't do that.'

In Darling there are up to 150 dancers working at any one time. The women, referred to in English-language travel guides as 'legal, self-employed', are mostly in their early and mid twenties, and come mainly from the local area as well as Slovakia and Russia. Selling their labour voluntarily, young women perform on stage like animals in a circus, climbing up and down poles to entertain the customers. The relatively low cost of sex entertainment there is the great appeal to the Brits: £10.70 admission fee, plus £3.50 for the lowest priced drink per hour and, if a guest fancies, only £36 for a table dance and £53 for a private dance.

But the fun doesn't stop here. The climax, if you'll pardon the pun, of a good stag weekend is the so-called 'Prague Strip Boat' along the Vltava river, where men have their fun in groups. The activity begins on deck with a drink of beer, and then moves downstairs to the bar area for the Strip Boat show. Trip A, for a minimum of six, lasts one and a half hours and is accompanied by an English-speaking guide and one stripper, plus a champagne toast, for which the price ranges from £25.50 upwards per person. Trip B, which costs from £33.50 upwards, for a minimum of ten people, is designed to offer greater pleasure: it has two strippers on this trip, performing three shows. As part of the performance, a member of the stag group is chosen to join in the show, which boasts 'red hot lesbian action' at the end.

Andrew went to Budapest for his own stag night this summer. He said that the idea was 'to combine sightseeing activities with the idea of nice Hungarian girls'. Eight of them set out from Britain and were joined by others when arriving in Budapest. They spent the first two nights in a popular strip club, P1 Club, which cost £20 to get in. They spent the first three hours drinking free and watching the strip show. Women there come from the local area, as well as Russia and Poland.

One of Andrew's mates said, 'The women stripped half nude, for the men to pick. If you like any of the girls, you go up to tell them her number, which was written on her pants. Then she'll come over and lead you from your table to the room behind, where you'll have the private dance.'

Andrew did the picking, and he was led into a room for his private stripping session, that is, a ten-minute strip dance in a private room that cost him £83. 'I had to spend a lot to get the girl to drink with me. I paid for her drink, which was £50,' he said.

British men comprise the majority of the punters in the Hungarian sex entertainment scene, but Andrew said he enjoyed a stag night in Riga the most. Thirteen of them went on the trip to Latvia. 'I like the Baltic girls best. It's the Scandinavian look … the blondes.'

I witnessed the growing demand for the idea of 'eastern European femininity' during my next undercover job in the sex trade. To punters, 'eastern European' encompasses the entire former Soviet bloc, but there is a particular group of migrant sex workers who frequently suffer from racial stereotyping and ethnic discrimination within sex businesses: Romanian women.

I got a job as a housekeeper in a newly opened brothel in Stratford in June 2012. Again, it was Chinese run, and the manageress, Ah Qin, met me at the station and took me to the flat on Tennyson Road. She was from Shenyang, the same place as Ming. 'We have another premises in Marylebone and many Romanian girls work for us, a very popular place,' she told me. 'We thought it would be a good idea to open a new place here in Stratford, to take advantage of the Olympics tourism.'

Ah Qin said she would pay me £210 to work seven days per week. I would have two days off a month. 'I'm giving you one day more than the previous housekeeper,' she said, with a smile on her moon-like face.

I soon found that Ah Qin had provided next to nothing in the house she was taking me to: no gas, no hot water, no bedding. She told me my room would be used as a work room during busy periods. Then she gave me the keys and £30 to buy all the provisions I needed, including food, for a week.

The only room with bedding was the sex worker's room, lit up in red. Tina, a Romanian, was there when I arrived. She looked tiny, wrapped in a pink dressing gown, and was smoking silently in the lounge. She didn't seem to want to speak to Ah Qin. She just looked out of the window the whole time, avoiding Ah Qin's eyes.

I followed Tina into her room, where she smiled amicably, gestured for me to sit down on her bed and gave me a cigarette. She told me this was the first day they'd been open for business, and that there had only been five customers all day. 'I'm here only to sponsor my studies,' she said. 'I am a college student in Romania. I also have to support my twelve-year-old brother.'

She wasn't happy about handing over half her income to her employers, 'But in a Baker Street place where I worked, it was worse,' she said. 'I had to serve very wealthy men. They demanded difficult services – my boss even told me to give some of them oral sex without condoms, which most Romanian girls wouldn't do.'

How had she come into the business?

'My boyfriend encouraged me to take up sex work,' Tina told me. 'This is a common type of work for Romanian girls these days. There's little else we can do.'

Despite the lack of choice in Britain, young Romanian women like her feel they have to try to hide their identity in order to protect their reputation back home. For this reason, Tina always told her punters she was Bulgarian, in case any of them were Romanian like her.

After Tina left, I was alone in the semi-empty house. Ah Qin had told me to double lock the front door and never open it to anyone, in case of 'unwanted visitors'. Her warning had made me worried. (Later I heard that there were local gangs charging for protection from brothels.) Besides this, I had no bedding. It was cold, and I kept waking up through the night.

In the morning, Ah Qin sent two young Romanian women and a forty-something Chinese man to the flat. The man told me he was the housekeeper at Ah Qin's Marylebone premises, and she'd asked him to accompany the two women here, though he didn't know why. The women were open and friendly; one of them introduced herself as Jessica and said she was twenty. The girl who was sitting next to her, she said, was her sister-in-law and was eighteen. They both also worked in the Marylebone flat.

'Many Romanian women do this work because Britain has very harsh work restrictions on us,' Jessica said. 'We all have to support our families. If we can't be allowed to work in the factory because they say there are too many of us, or if the money is too bad doing cleaning, then we don't have much choice left.' Jessica now earns £1,200 per week on average, most of which she sends home.

The Chinese housekeeper, who was named Zhang, agreed that sex workers can earn up to £50,000 per year. 'I would do it myself if I were female,' he said.

Despite the talk of all this cash, there were no customers today. Jessica and her sister-in-law waited and waited. They looked out of the window every now and then, sighing. At noon, they took out a loaf of bread and spread tomato paste on it for lunch. Then Jessica spent an hour combing and styling her sister-in-law's long black hair. Still no customers arrived.

Zhang told me he was forty-six and used work on the state-run railway in Tianjin, in the north of China. If it hadn't been for supporting his son, he said, he wouldn't have come abroad. He had been living in Britain for ten years. He'd worked in a supply factory for Samsung in Hartlepool and also did restaurant work for years. Then he was introduced to a flatmate's girlfriend who has a half share in the working flat in Marylebone. 'Kitchen work is really rough; in comparison, housekeeping in a brothel is a breeze,' he said. Ah Qin pays him £280 a week.

At around 5 p.m., a local man turned up. The only customer of the day.

'How much do you charge?' he asked.

'Fifty per half hour, ninety for an hour,' Zhang replied before I could speak.

'How come?' Jessica protested. 'I thought the price was £60 per half hour and £100 per hour!'

'Ah Qin decided to change the price,' Zhang explained, 'because this is a poorer area.'

'That's not right!' Jessica got angry and raised her voice.

Seeing that there was a row brewing, the only punter of the day turned tail. Soon after that, Jessica and her sister-in-law decided that they'd waited long enough. They packed their bags and left.

Zhang called me late that night, sounding melancholic. 'We are all working hard in a foreign country. We have to look after each other.'

The following morning, I had Zhang's leftovers for breakfast. There was one more packet of noodles to last the day. Still no hot water – I'd told Ah Qin about it but she'd done nothing.

Alexandra, a twenty-one-year-old Romanian, arrived at noon. 'It's so quiet,' she said, frowning at the emptiness of the place. She probably sensed that business was poor here. When Ah Qin showed up an hour later, Alexandra said she had to go to the bank and never returned. Ah Qin then called Rose, another Romanian, to take her place. Rose looked in her late thirties, but said she was twenty-three and had been working in London for three years. 'My first job was in Soho,' she said. 'It was tough because the rent was so high over there. I had to leave in the end.'

For Rose, work seemed to be everything. She didn't like going out much in this country because she didn't drink. 'I'm a Catholic. I don't like the way people socialise here,' she said. Earning money and sending some home to her mother every two weeks was all she cared about.

A north-eastern Chinese man with black spectacles whom Ah Qin called 'brother' arrived. I realised that he was actually the owner of the business. He had an intimidating presence: he never smiled but frowned a lot. The men who came with him never even acknowledged me or Rose. It was as if we were another species – they perceived us as nothing but breathing tools. They exchanged noisy conversation around us, probably not even noticing our existence. The owner chatted to Ah Qin about his involvement with Shuifang (Water House: one of the biggest Chinese gangs in the UK). I wondered whether he was still a member.

In the afternoon, a Hong-Kong businessman from Canary Wharf visited and asked for unprotected oral sex. Ah Qin said he'd have to pay Rose a £10 tip. He went for a standard half-hour service at £50 instead. The second punter was a British Asian man who looked put out by the Chinese crowd. (The boss and his aggressive-looking entourage were still there.) He rushed out as soon as his half-hour session was over. In all, after a long day largely spent waiting around, Rose had earned £100, half of which was taken by Ah Qin.

The following day Ah Qin asked me to pick up a woman named Flory from Stratford station. 'She's from Lithuania,' Ah Qin told me. Flory was bottle blonde, and said she was twenty-one but looked in her thirties. She spoke little English and told me she was Spanish, but then quickly changed her nationality to French when I tried a few words of Spanish on her. She obviously wasn't French, or Lithuanian either, come to that. Her mobile ring tone was a Romanian tune and she spoke in Romanian with someone on the other end all the time. Whenever I asked her something she couldn't understand, she would pass me her phone so I could speak to her 'friend'.

We ended up speaking to each other quite often. He told me he was from Romania. He thought I was an experienced receptionist. 'Can you help, please?' he said to me. 'Can you introduce another Romanian friend of mine to work, please? She's twenty-four. She needs a job.' He seemed very keen, and gave me his friend's phone number.

Flory worked twelve hours a day, three days a week. Her Romanian friend called her regularly throughout the day. In the early evening when he called again, she seemed to be arguing with him, explaining something. Then she passed the phone to me.

'Can she go home, please?' he said to me. 'There is no customer.'

Was he her friend, her boyfriend or her pimp? He certainly seemed to be in control of her. As my undercover work continued, I was to see that same type of ambiguous relationship between other Romanian sex workers and their male acquaintances.

Taking the Plunge

Before returning to London after her dismissal from Sarah's brothel, Ming called Brother Li, the always-friendly kitchen fryer she knew from Elephant & Castle. She'd heard that his friend Sister Yan, like her an expat from Shenyang, used to work in the sex trade. Perhaps she would advise Ming about going into sex work.

By a happy coincidence, Sister Yan was also living in Milton Keynes. Brother Li arranged for Ming to visit her terraced house in a quiet residential estate. Ming had imagined her as shy and evasive, perhaps not easy to talk to. Within the closely knit Chinese communities, sex workers tend to keep their professional lives to themselves, for fear of discrimination and getting a bad name. But Sister Yan seemed open and hospitable. She welcomed Ming with a broad, warm smile on her face, as if she had just found a long-lost friend.

She sat Ming down in a lonely looking lounge. The room was so bare that Ming couldn't look anywhere but at the focal point hanging above the mantelpiece – a life-size, gold-framed wedding picture of Sister Yan and her English husband William. In it, Sister Yan was wearing an elegant high-collared bright red dress and had her hair in a bun. Her hands were in William's. His blue eyes, light brown hair and plump cheeks contrasted sharply with his bride. Behind them was Westminster Abbey.

'Oh! What a magnificent building!' Ming said. 'Did you marry there?'

'No, no!' Sister Yan explained with a chuckle. 'This picture was taken in a wedding-photo studio in Shenyang!'

Yes, of course! Now Ming remembered the fashionable photo studios that were becoming a must-have item of any wedding plan back home.

Sister Yan told her they'd been married for two years. 'He's such a romantic. He wanted to have a big red traditional wedding ceremony in China, with tens of feast tables and deafening firecrackers in the streets.' Ming had never met anyone who had married a Westerner, and couldn't help being curious. She asked how they met.

'He came to our massage parlour here in Milton Keynes one day, where I was a maid,' Sister Yan recalled. 'I had worked as a *xiaojie* before that, but I didn't do it for long. It drained my energy, working fourteen hours every single day. I was exhausted within a year and badly needed a break. Some of the *xiaojies* I worked with lasted longer, though.'

Ming sat up and listened.

'But I was used to the parlour, its pace of work, its rules and all that. The boss had got used to me as well, and he asked me to stay on as a housekeeper, so I said yes. The boss knew me well enough to trust me to run the place. If you have worked as a *xiaojie*, changing your job to be a housekeeper is like having a holiday! So I was earning some regular money without having to take ten showers a day! I was feeling so much better. More like a human, you know?'

Ming nodded sympathetically.

'And one day, William came to our parlour. He wasn't a great catch at first sight, as you can see. Forty-something, half bald. He was wearing a dark blue suit that made me think he must be a banker – and I was right. He looked so pale, almost like he was wearing powder on his face. His cheeks were pinky red, as if he was blushing. Which he was! I found out later that was his first time ever to *tou-xing* [steal raw meat: have an affair].'

Sister Yan announced it was time for lunch and went into the kitchen to fetch some steamed fish she had prepared. Ming sat at the dining table in the middle of the room, facing the giant, shrine-like image.

Ming's hostess continued her story as they ate. 'William kept staring at me when I led him to the *xiaojie*. That doesn't usually happen to the housekeepers, you know. I felt quite flattered. He asked me where I was from. He said he had no clue where Shenyang was, but that he'd like to visit China one day. He could have had that conversation with the *xiaojie*, don't you think? But he took his time talking to me. He was really eloquent. Anyway, a few minutes later he chose one of the *xiaojie* and had a session with her. I sat in the reception area thinking about how he had just chatted to me.'

Sister Yan blushed with joy as she recalled the past. 'When his session ended and he came out of the room, I felt too embarrassed to look him in the eye. But instead of leaving he began to ask me if I had a boyfriend and whether I'd like to go out sometime with him. I thought it was really odd, to be flirting with someone in a place like that! But I was polite to him, and said yes, I'd meet him outside the parlour on my day off, which was in two weeks' time.

'When the day came, William was waiting for me in his car. I really didn't think he'd show up. I felt like Cinderella, being taken away in his pumpkin carriage! He was kind and gentle, always asking, "Is it all right with you?" I thought maybe that's what an English gentleman is like. When we sat down to a lovely Italian meal, he told me he liked me much more than any of the *xiaojies*. I wasn't sure whether to thank him or feel insulted. Well, it wasn't exactly a conventional compliment, was it? I had an image in my head of me and a *xiaojie* both trying to please him in bed. Was he planning to pay me like an escort to spend the night with him? But his display of luxury and good intentions seemed too lavish for that.'

Ming felt as if she was listening to a film script. She held her breath and waited for Sister Yan to continue.

'Two weeks later, we were still going out and he hadn't tried to get me into bed or anything like that. Then, just as I was beginning to wonder where all this was leading to, he told me he wanted to marry me!' Sister Yan exclaimed.

'How amazing!' Ming responded with genuine surprise. She'd never heard a story like this. But she began to regret showing such enthusiasm when Sister Yan rushed upstairs and returned with what looked like a library of wedding photo albums. For the next hour, Ming had to sit looking through the photos with her, page by page.

'This was the most wonderful thing that could ever have happened to me,' Sister Yan said with conviction. 'To be saved from that world.'

Ming had never heard a more genuine sentiment. She nodded in appreciation.

'My daughter was thrilled. She was only thirteen but she understood how happy I was. She said I looked like an empress in these wedding costumes.' Sister Yan giggled. 'We did have lots of firecrackers that day. And a big feast on the street, just the way William planned it.'

'Getting married was definitely the best thing you ever did,'

Ming said. 'Now you don't have to worry about a thing – not finding a job or keeping a roof over your head.'

'I do love William, but our marriage certainly also brought me the one thing I've always wanted – legal status. As William's wife, I am able to work here in the open. What a difference that has made! To feel able to choose to stay or leave my employment. Of course, just because a job is legal doesn't mean you can put up your feet! I worked at KFC. Minimum wage, very tough! People said to me that it is a job that keeps you fed but gets you nowhere. You won't starve on their wages, but you won't live above subsistence level on them in this expensive country, either!'

Ming nodded, trying to imagine what it must be like working in the open – and in KFC.

'William asked me to give up that job after just a few months,' Sister Yan continued. 'He said I didn't really need to work so hard for so little money – I had him now.'

Ming couldn't help thinking that Sister Yan was one of the luckier women from the *da-gong* (manual labour) ranks. Working in a brothel seemed an unlikely way to find a life partner!

'How often did you meet nice men in your job at the parlour?' Ming probed. 'Aren't they rare?'

'As rare as winning the lottery,' Sister Yan replied. 'Usually you get the vile, the rough, the scum of the male species! But occasionally you get lucky and meet a few who are … How should I put it? Sad and a little pathetic, but not completely socially dysfunctional. And out of those, you might meet one who has a fairly decent job, and he might ask you out. William is a good man, but he isn't exactly a prince on a white horse.'

Ming couldn't help giggling at the comparison.

'It's always been at the back of my mind that William was

the one who chose and I was the one who was in that place to be chosen. But William never makes me feel that he picked me out of pity. He never even refers to my time at the parlour. I'm grateful for that. And one day, I'm going to give him a baby.'

Ming sighed at the thought, smiling.

'But I want to wait till my daughter comes over to live with us, so she doesn't feel jealous and left out, you know.'

Sister Yan had come to England to provide for her daughter. But once here, out of the most unlikely circumstances, she had formed a new family. Now she was frightened of losing her daughter if her new family grew.

Ming thought about her own situation and couldn't help sighing again.

Sister Yan looked at Ming knowingly and said, 'You know, life becomes a little purposeless when you don't have someone to look after, and to earn for!'

'What do you mean?'

'Now I have so much time on my hands,' Sister Yan continued, 'well, life must be pretty aimless if we can spend all our time betting on horses and racing dogs!'

'Is that what you do for fun these days, Sister Yan?'

'Yes, bad habit! I wasn't like this before. It's so dull in Milton Keynes. I often feel I'm living in the middle of nowhere. Nothing's happening and I feel like one day I might just go to sleep and not wake up and no one would know, except William when returned from work in the evening.'

'Don't say that, Sister Yan!'

'Don't worry, I'm not serious. But isn't it bizarre that when I was a *xiaojie*, I was too busy entertaining customers to worry about the terrible things that could have happened, such as being beaten up or robbed, which happens a lot. But now I'm a suburban housewife, life has become lifeless. I worry more, now there's nothing to worry about. Do you understand what I mean?'

Ming stared at Sister Yan's vacant gaze, and couldn't believe that this fortunate woman with her legal status could be so bored with her new-found comfort. It always irritated her when she heard well-off people complain.

'You are very lucky, Sister Yan, to have the leisure to be depressed. Give me a chance to be in your shoes ... and I'll prove that I can be happy!'

But Sister Yan carried on about how she had to gamble in order to cope with a life without ambition. 'I'd heard a lot about the casinos in London from Brother Li, so one day when I was bored I caught the train to Euston and I spent the day in a casino in Gerrard Street. There were many women there, just like me, having a lot of time to spare. And it's a comfortable place to hang around. I had a drink first, and a second drink and that was free. If you're a member, you can have free food there as well. I felt relaxed, and then I joined a few good games. There were quite a few *xiaojies* from the Chinese massage parlours there, too. I could tell them by the way they looked. They were all made up, and looked totally exhausted.'

'Why do they go to the casinos?' Ming wondered. 'Don't they just lose their hard-earned money?'

'They do, but some of them feel they don't earn enough in the brothels, because the bosses take too big a share. So the *xiaojies* go gambling in between their bookings, to try to make some extra cash. Also it gives them a chance to relax once in a while! After a week or two of non-stop sex, *xiaojies* need a little break, even just for a night, before they have to go on to the next booking.'

'I suppose they would,' Ming murmured, wondering about her own decision to go into sex work.

'Anyway, when I went, I won at first. But then I got greedy and lost control. I started losing, bit by bit, and then losing more. But I found it difficult to stop. The people around me were trying to win as badly as I was. We were like a team. I didn't feel alone any more. It was good fun. It didn't matter that I lost.'

'Did you go there a lot, then?' Ming stared at her again, amazed.

'Sure I did! It became a real hobby. It was the only thing that made me feel alive. When William went to work, I'd often just get on the next train to London. It was the only thing I ever kept secret from him. But secrets can't be kept for ever. He discovered my addiction when I lost big – £1,000 in one week!'

Ming became silent. It would take her at least five weeks working as a brothel maid to earn that much.

As Ming made to leave, Sister Yan took out a notepad and jotted down a list of numbers from it. 'There, take these, sister. These are the numbers of all the brothel owners that I know in England. You might want to give being a *xiaojie* a try sometime. You never know where life will take you, but some paths will get you there a lot more quickly!'

Ming thanked her wholeheartedly and left. Sister Yan had given her a lot to think about.

Ming's parents had called to say they were in urgent need of money. Ming knew she had to find work straight away; there was no time to waste. She called the first number on Sister Yan's list, a parlour run by a northern Chinese man based in Birmingham. He politely told Ming that his parlour was very busy and completely full. 'But I will need more women in two months' time,' he said, suggesting she call back in August.

She then dialled a number that Sister Yan had marked as located in 'zone one of London'. A Cantonese-speaking man answered. 'It's a very hectic place. We have a stream of young girls coming to work here, seeing both Chinese and Western customers. At this moment, we're all full. But I can book you for a later time, in September.' Ming eagerly accepted and received her first booking, for a week in mid September.

The next number, this one in Nottingham, was marked *furen-qu* (affluent area). A southern-sounding man answered.

'How old are you?'

'I'm twenty-five,' she lied.

'You sound older. Come on, tell me.' The man's voice was stern, intimidating. 'We have girls of all ages.'

Ming paused.

'Have you done this before?' he seemed to suspect that she was new.

'Yes, but only for a little while.'

'That's all right. If you aren't that experienced, my manager here will sort you out. You'll learn fast – everyone does.' He then told Ming she could start working the very next day. 'You'll be here for two weeks, and if it all goes well, then I'll send you to another place of mine. I'll pick you up from the station at lunchtime. Give me a call when you get there.'

The midday sun was glaring as Ming walked out of Nottingham station at noon the following day. The aroma of coffee drifted from a nearby store. She'd not had a sip of water for the whole morning, but she had spent the last of her money on a cheap hotel room in King's Cross, where she'd spent the previous night. (She hadn't wanted to return to the Elephant & Castle flat for fear of having to explain to Ying why she'd lost her last job.) Ming waited by the kerb for her lift. She was wearing a grey silk dress that she had brought from home – the only piece of clothing that Ying said didn't mark her as a 'rural woman'. But Ming felt exactly that, standing there as a dumb stranger waiting for a boss she'd never met.

Heavens, this mid June sun. Sweat ran down her forehead. Where was Mr Boss? Then she saw a man in a black suit waving at her from a shiny silver Mercedes – almost the same colour as her dress.

'Please, get in the back,' he said politely, nodding at her from the driver's seat. As Ming did so, he turned to get a proper look at her.

'OK, pretty.' He smiled, almost in relief, at another black-suited man sitting next to him. They set off. She felt as if she were in a movie, being driven into the unknown.

'Call me Lao Chen,' the well-mannered boss introduced himself. 'I have two parlours in this city. If you do well – which I think you will, by the look of you – I'll send you to work in the other parlour in a fortnight.'

'Thank you, Lao Chen.'

'This parlour we are going to is in an excellent location, not far from the Nottingham Trent University,' Lao Chen told her. 'I have good, regular customers from all backgrounds. Always busy. I'm planning to expand our business to other cities.'

They drove through a beautiful boulevard. So green! Ming had never seen anything like this in Shenyang. Shops and cafés were dotted along the way, shaded by the trees. And then there was another boulevard, with sunlight glittering through. Between the trees she could see a sign that read Han Chao (Han Dynasty) over the door to a karaoke bar, and a number of Chinese restaurants along the way.

'There are many Chinese people living in this city?' she asked.

'Yeah, quite a few. Many are students; there are two universities here,' Lao Chen replied.

A minute later they turned into a narrower, quieter street of pre-war red-brick terraced houses. Lao Chen double parked outside one of them. So this is the brothel, Ming thought – such an ordinary looking house, unremarkable, like the flat in Milton Keynes had been.

As they opened the front door, the place began to look a little less homely. The empty hallway led to a heavy metal door which Lao Chen opened with a large key. And then there was the final door to the parlour itself.

Inside, it was as though the place had just been burgled. There was nothing but a sofa, a table and a Chinese calendar on the bare wall. A young woman was sitting at the table having her lunch. She introduced herself as Ah Chun. 'The customer is still with Ah Ling,' she told Lao Chen. Her accent was southern, but Ming couldn't quite place the province.

Ah Chun must be one of the *xiaojies*, Ming thought. She looked at least five years younger than herself. Those thin fingers with polished nails. And those almond-shaped bright eyes! She must attract a lot of regulars.

Lao Chen's friend in the black suit took Ming's suitcase from her. 'Let me put this in your room, miss,' he said. 'The new housekeeper hasn't arrived yet.' Her 'room' was, of course, also her work room. Ming followed him to a bedroom at the end of a corridor. The pink curtains were tightly drawn, and pink wallpaper made the room look like a teenager's. There was a woollen mat with a cartoon piggy face on it. On top of a chest of drawers was an unopened box of tissues. So this was to be Ming's living space: one in which she would both work and sleep.

They heard keys turning and the entrance door opening. Ming was led back into the sitting area to meet a woman introduced as 'Sister Deng', Lao Chen's business partner who also managed the place.

Sister Deng was laden with bags of shopping. 'I'm exhausted! Take these into the kitchen!' she waved at Ming, mistaking her for the new housekeeper.

As Ming took over her plastic bags, Sister Deng looked fiercely at her up and down. 'Where did she come from?' she asked Lao Chen. 'She's too young for a *baomu* [housekeeper].'

Sister Deng sounded like she came from the north of China. Her voice contained an air of self-righteousness and cultural superiority. Even her tiny, slitted eyes exuded disdain and ruthless pride. Ming recognised those eyes. The eyes of the urban better-off that she remembered so well.

Ming tried to explain to her: 'I am the new *xiaojie*, Sister Deng, not *baomu*.'

'Ah, I am so sorry! I didn't know,' Sister Deng apologised profusely. She squeezed out her first smile and patronisingly patted Ming's shoulders. 'Welcome, welcome!'

In a Chinese brothel, the *xiaojies* are high above the *baomu* in the labour hierarchy. The *xiaojies* are the means of profits, the *yao-qian-shu* (money tree), while the maids are far more dispensable in the eyes of the owners. Some maids are encouraged to become *zhuangzhong* (stand-in sex workers during busy periods), and those who agree to fulfil such a dual role are highly sought after.

But neither *xiaojie*, *zhuangzhong* nor *baomu* has any say in the amount of her workload or the length of her day. There is no negotiation of working conditions in the sex businesses.

Sister Deng turned to Lao Chen. 'Where is that housekeeper? Is she late on her first day? We don't have time to wait around for some old grandma!'

Lao Chen explained that his associate had gone to fetch her from the bus station.

Then she said to Ming, 'The *baomu* will cook two meals a day for you, lunch and dinner. You can tell her what you like to eat. She's from Guangxi and I've no idea what they eat down there. I'm not even sure that she's Han [the majority ethnic group in China].' She raised her eyebrow to show her contempt.

'She will do all your cleaning, so you don't need to worry about that,' Sister Deng continued. 'And don't let her persuade you into giving her tips. You aren't obliged to, you understand? Housekeepers nowadays! They think they run the place! You can never give them an inch, these cheeky old aunties!'

Ming knew for a fact that some brothel owners refused to employ young housekeepers, for fear that they would rebel against their working conditions or leave the job rather than put up with them, but she held her tongue.

Lao Chen's associate arrived with the new housekeeper. As the fifty-something *baomu* walked into the house, limping and with a suitcase in her hand, Sister Deng scrutinised her closely, just as she had Ming, and said in her bitter voice, 'So did you walk all the way from China? Don't try to be too early, auntie. We were just about to play mah-jong and wait patiently for your majesty's arrival.'

The newcomer, not daring to put down her case, apologised humbly: 'I am very, very sorry, madam! It is the first time for me in this city. I could not find the right bus ... Please, forgive me!'

'But not next time, auntie,' warned Sister Deng. 'So you are from Guangxi? Are you Han?'

'Yes, madam, I'm of Han group.'

'Thank heavens for that! Now I won't need to educate you. You know what to do – what kind of food to cook and so on?' Sister Deng said, narrowing her eyes as she puffed out cigarette smoke. Ming thought she looked frighteningly similar to Sarah.

The housekeeper stood taking in the second-hand smoke, not daring to move.

'Now, as we've agreed on the phone, your money will be £180 per week. No bargaining about that. And remember the most important rule here: you are strictly forbidden to go out at any time during work hours, not even to collect the post outside the door. That is my job. Your duties are cleaning all the rooms and the toilet every morning, cooking two meals a day for the *xiaojies*. Keeping accounts properly. You are required to work from 7 a.m. to 1 a.m.'

The *baomu* kept nodding. Lao Chen and his friend left, uninterested in such domestic business.

Having done with the housekeeper, Sister Deng now turned to Ming and began to brief her about the job.

'I heard that you've done this work before, sweetie? So you aren't gonna think the sky has fallen on you!'

Ming prepared herself for a lecture.

'Remember, there are primarily four types of men who come to the parlours. The first are the desperate white men. The ugly bastards. These are men who don't even know how to talk to women. They can only get sex in the brothels. But they're scared of getting caught or seen by neighbours. They come into the parlour with their heads down and leave like that, too. Pity them!

'The second type is harder to please. They are the perverted white men who ask for extra service or make difficult demands. They might bring their girlfriends and ask you to do "couples". Then you'll have to satisfy her as well as him!'

Ming nodded – she knew this from her own experience.

'Most *xiaojies* find it objectionable to do "couples",' Sister Deng continued. 'But really, that's definitely not the worst kind of customers.

'The third type are the British-based Chinese men. They may be owners of restaurants or takeaways or other businesses. They come after work, to wind down and relax. This type always prefers younger girls. We don't have many of them around here – they tend to go to Chinese-only places, for really young girls. Some have white-collar jobs: lawyers and professionals who work nearby. Some of them aren't living with their wives: they may be working in different cities. You have to pay special attention to them, because they can choose to come back, or go somewhere else if you aren't good enough.'

Ming nodded her understanding.

'The fourth type are Chinese visitors – a small minority for our business, but they can be a good source of income because they're always in a mood to be generous. For example, Chinese officials on "business observation" missions who are travelling on expenses. Among them there are some businessmen as well. These customers are always looking for a great time and *xiaojies* are part of their holiday in England! Serve them well and you'll be rewarded – they are very good tippers.'

Ah Ling had just finished her session. As her customer slowly walked out of the bedroom, Sister Deng quickly stood up to see him out. He was a regular, white, looked in his late forties: a Type 1.

'Hope to see you soon again, darling!' simpered Sister Deng.

Ah Ling avoided Ming's eyes as she hurried into the bathroom for a shower. She came out with her hair up in a bundle. She was wearing a track suit, making her look like a teenager, and a noisy pair of plastic slippers that showed her polished toes. Click, click, each step she made.

As she came to sit with Ah Chun at the table, Ming could finally see her face properly. Ah Ling had long, thin eyes, with her eyelashes curled up. When she smiled, she showed her dimples, which again made her look adolescent. Despite her apparent youth, she tutted every time she looked at herself in the mirror on the table. 'Tse, these wrinkles! They keep growing at the end of my eyes!'

She noticed Ming staring at her. 'All right? Sorry, what's your name?' Ah Ling asked, in an accent that reminded Ming of home.

'Ming.'

'You want some lunch, Ming?' she asked. 'You must let the housekeeper know when you need to eat. Don't starve on this job! You need stamina.'

Ah Ling then took out her make-up and started to massage cream into her face. Then she powdered it. Layers of powder. Now she looked every one of her almost forty years.

'These sessions are exhausting, and yet we need to keep looking young, fresh and energetic. The only way to do it is to apply lots of cosmetics all the time,' she said to Ming.

'Ming! Come with me to your room; I've got something to show you,' said Sister Deng in her most endearing voice. She held Ming's hand, sister-like, leading her along the corridor. She sat Ming down on the bed in her work room. Then she opened a wardrobe and took out a red silk baby doll nightie.

'I got this for you, sweetie.'

She insisted that Ming try it on, watching as she stripped naked and carefully put on the flimsy piece of clothing and some matching panties. The nightie came to just below her crotch, and she could see the panties revealed when she looked at herself in the mirror.

'Perfect! Perfect!' gushed Sister Deng.

Having satisfied the manageress, Ming was given a few more instructions about how to greet the customers at her door and then told she had five minutes to get herself ready for the two who were on their way. She looked at her watch. She'd been in Nottingham for less than an hour!

Would she cope? She had no idea. There wasn't even time to panic.

The bell rang. 'Your customers are here!' Sister Deng shouted out to Ming, loud as a fire alarm.

Ming quickly adjusted the red silky work clothes and stood outside the door to her room, as she'd been told. Ah Chun was doing the same. They looked like workers in Amsterdam's red-light district.

The two men were led by Sister Deng through the lounge to the corridor. They were both white, in their early thirties. One had light brown hair and wore a white shirt and blue jeans. The other man had darker hair and a plump face, and he kept looking from Ming to Ah Chun and back, trying to figure out which one he fancied more. They were going to choose one girl each.

'Be very nice to them,' Sister Deng nervously whispered in Chinese. 'These two look like they're on a stag treat.'

'What?' Ming didn't understand what that meant.

Sister Deng explained but Ming could sense the madam's concern about her inexperience. She frowned anxiously, like a desperate shopkeeper trying to sell her exotic tea sets. Women new to the business can be a real bonus, but at the same time their naiveté may put some customers off. Sister Deng wanted to make sure that Ming would be an asset.

She whispered again, 'The light-hair *guilao* is getting married tomorrow. If he picks you, make sure that you do all he wants.'

Then the darker-haired man started whispering too, to his friend. They both laughed. The *xiaojies* had no idea what was said, but Sister Deng looked nervous.

'Listen, they might want *shuang-fei* with the pair of you. Be good and do what they ask,' she urged.

At last, after ten minutes' of hard thinking, the fair-haired man made his decision. 'I'll have her,' he said, pointing to Ming.

His companion went to Ah Chun. Ming felt tremendously relieved to be spared the trauma of a four-person session.

She welcomed the groom into her work room feeling almost grateful. As soon as the punter crossed the threshold, Sister Deng poked her head in and asked him, 'You want to do it for one hour? If you want a really good time, I recommend one hour – only £100.' She omitted mentioning the £60-per-half-hour and £40-for-fifteen-minutes-without-massage options.

The man was determined to have fun – he eagerly agreed to an hour.

'Have a good time!' said Sister Deng cheerfully as he handed her the cash. She shut the door behind them. Ming's new job had begun.

'Where are you from, darling?' the stag-night man asked. He smelled of lager, even though it was only lunchtime. 'Your boss said you're from Korea.'

'Yes, from Korea,' Ming replied, starting to help him take off his shirt. 'I give you massage first.'

He stripped naked within seconds. 'Undress yourself, darling,' he ordered. After the experience in Milton Keynes, Ming found this quite easy. She took off her thin silky garment and stood looking at him. He isn't bad-looking, she thought. No beer belly. I suppose that will make it easier.

'Hurry up, love, I've only paid for an hour!' he rushed her. 'Off with your pants.'

He waited for her in bed, face down. She straddled him, applied massage oil to his back, and got to work. As she gently massaged him, he turned his head on the pillow to look at her.

He's getting married tomorrow, Ming kept thinking to herself. There isn't such a custom in China that men go wild on the day before they walk up to the wedding altar. But perhaps this custom means Western men don't visit parlours once they're married.

The man seemed to have had enough of massage after just two minutes. He turned round and grabbed her. 'Come here, darling!' He clearly didn't need more warming up. Ming took out a condom from the drawer next to the bed, and asked him to put it on.

'Don't be so harsh with me, baby! Not today!' he was reluctant. 'Look, I'll pay you more!'

Ming shook her head. 'No, no! Everyone must use a condom!'

'I'll pay you £5 more,' he insisted. 'OK, £10 more. Let me have some fun here!' There was no way she could allow that. His type would have been everywhere and anywhere.

'I don't want to go home in a coffin,' Ming murmured in Chinese.

'I don't understand Korean! Speak English!' the man protested smilingly.

'No. You must use a condom!' Ming repeated.

He looked down at his now-flaccid penis. 'Now look what you've done. I need warming up all over again!'

'I curse eight generations of your ancestors,' she mumbled back in Chinese.

Eventually, he was persuaded, and by the time he was finished she had run out of strength to get up from the bed. She lay there exhausted.

'What's the matter, darling? I'm not done yet.'

With dismay, she realised he wanted another round. 'Thick-skinned pig,' she murmured, and was about to refuse when she remembered Sister Deng saying that the one-hour service allows *chu-shui* (outflow) twice, in other words, two bloody rounds!

This time, the punter didn't want to see her face. She could only hear the repulsive sound of plastic expanding as he put on another condom. That second round felt like five hours to Ming. She tried hard to divert her thoughts to the past and future, so that she could forget the present. But it was impossible. Time felt like a heavy stone, with so much weight, pushing her further into the ground. It felt as though time was trying to bury her.

At last the hour was up and the stag finally left. As Ming came out of her room, Ah Chun had also just finished her session. She looked pale and there was anguish in her eyes. Ming wondered what had happened behind those closed doors, but Ah Chun shook her head and ran into the bathroom.

At dinner, Ah Chun told Ming that her punter had taken off his condom half way through the session and pretended it was broken. Before Ah Chun could resist him, he'd entered her again. 'If it weren't for my son, I would stab that stinking bastard and send him to where he belongs: hell!'

Ah Chun was from Yunnan province in south-west China and had been working in the sex trade for six months. 'You know, I always try to turn my anger into strength, and more strength,' she said to Ming. But the experience had left her with no appetite. She had two mouthfuls of rice and retreated to her room.

Ah Ling broke the silence as they sat through the last part of their dinner. 'You feel OK?'

'I'm not too bad. It could be worse.'

'You got to be really careful with Sister Deng,' Ah Ling warned Ming. 'She always tries to tell the customers on the phone that they can have *chui-xiao* [flute blowing: oral sex] without condoms. So the customers will ask you for it. But you mustn't say yes if you don't want to risk your health. Do you understand?'

Ming nodded – now she understood why the stag man had thought he could ask her for unprotected sex.

'She tells the men that we do that too. Old fox, she is. She doesn't give a damn.' Ah Ling knew of other bosses like that.

She'd been in the trade for nearly a year.

'Business is doing well here, though, even without the extra service, no?' Ming asked.

'You're right. This place is the most prosperous in town,' Ah Ling said. 'Most parlours around are tiny, with only one *xiaojie*, and can only cater for the regulars in the neighbourhood. This one pulls in men from other cities.'

'But for us, it must be easier to work for the smaller places,' said Ming.

'Oh yeah, just less money. I've worked in one of those small parlours, like that one advertised all over town called A Mei. If you go there to find them in Standhill Road, you'll probably miss the place – it's hidden in between flats, and the punters have to climb up that narrow staircase and sneak around to look for 73a! With that sort of inferior location, they have to charge a lower price: £90 per hour and £50 per half hour. And you know, the manageress there told everyone that they have a twenty-one-year-old *xiaojie*! Do I look twenty-one to you? Only the real desperate locals would go there!'

Ah Ling had more to say. 'And there's another one in Carlton called Mei Ling – she tells everyone that she has a long-haired eighteen-year-old Chinese girl working for her! If you believe that! And then you got those located in more central areas – they can't compete with this parlour, either. Like that one called Siu Fung in a run-down backstreet near the city centre. It's so discreet that it's probably difficult for punters from outside the city to find on the map! Those on a stag night would never choose to go to Siu Fung! The place looks haunted from outside, with their blinds half broken and curtains tightly drawn. Last time I walked past there one evening, I saw their upstairs window opened, with the red curtains flying in the wind. Spooky. And they also say they've got a twenty-one-year-old *xiaojie* there!'

'Are there many *guilao*-run parlours around?' Ming asked.

'There are a few and they all claim they have Chinese and Korean girls – whichever nationality and age you're asking, they say yes, yes, they have that. Like the one in West Bridgford ...'

Two weeks later, Ming passed her 'probation'. Lao Chen gave her a day off at the end of the fortnight, and told her to come to work at his other brothel the day after. Ming's job looked secure.

Risks and Rewards

The flat in Soho was full and there was no shortage of workers. Business was good. Beata was taking turns with two other women to work on the first floor. Twenty-two-year-old Sabrina from Albania worked on Wednesday and Thursday, while Linda from Thailand worked on Friday and Saturday. Pam was maiding for both Beata and Linda, and occasionally for Sabrina when her regular maid was off.

The tall, dyed-blonde Sabrina was a likeable character – always making fun of her own broken English and acting the fool. It was as if she thought remaining in high spirits was part of the job description. Pam didn't get it – how could a woman like her, who'd suffered so much during her desperate working life, remain so cheerful? Her laughter and open-mindedness made her a very popular character.

Sabrina had been introduced by an Albanian man who, like Beata's Robert, said he was her boyfriend who 'looked after' her. Like many Albanian women sex workers, Sabrina passed herself off as Polish, because she had no work papers. She had come from a village where few jobs were available for young people. 'Every young man and woman wants to leave. We all want to go as far as possible, best to western Europe, where we can find work and a future,' Sabrina said to Pam.

Following the collapse of its communist government in 1990, poor Albanians began to migrate in large numbers, and by 2000 it was estimated that at least 600,000, that is one in five Albanians, had left the country – the largest rate of emigration among the Balkan and Baltic nations. (No surprise there, as Albania's per capita income is the lowest in the area, with privatisation and rampant corruption eroding people's livelihood.)

Facing such desperate economic circumstances and with little chance of entering western Europe legally, Sabrina and many young women like her became an easy target for Albania's opportunistic profiteers, who were among the few making money out of the country's poverty.

'When I met Jack, I was fifteen. We met at a party. He came up to me and his eyes never moved away from me,' Sabrina told Pam. 'We met a few times after that. Then he told me he was in love with me. He said he could take me to Italy and we could get married there. I thought I was getting lucky. Really lucky. We were going to have such a happy life together, far away from my village, far away from Albania.'

When Jack proposed, Sabrina said yes at once. 'My heart was flying when he said the words "marry me".'

'You poor thing,' Pam said, already guessing how her story would develop, for Pam knew well the pimp who'd sent her to this flat.

'Then Jack helped me with all the procedures. He got me the passport and everything. I had no idea how he did all that, but I never doubted him. He was very close to me and I believed every word he said. Besides, he didn't ask me for money at all. He paid for everything. My parents were very happy for me. I'd found a future, they thought.'

Sabrina travelled with Jack to Italy by boat. 'I started to think it was very strange. Why were there ten other Albanians travelling with us? All women. One of them told me her boyfriend had got her a bartending job in Italy. Jack was talking to some of the women. How did he know them, I asked myself. He became cold to me and I didn't know why. I didn't dare to ask him. It was when we arrived in Italy that he began to reveal who he wasn't – he wasn't my fiancé. "Shocked" doesn't describe how I felt. It was like a really bad dream. He said I must go on a van with the other women. I had no idea where we were heading, only that we were travelling for hours and hours on end.'

'Did it bring you to Dover?'

'No, not then. We were told to get off the van after a while, and days later, we boarded another boat. We still had no idea where we were or where we were going. By this time, I knew something was very, very wrong and I feared what might happen to me. Jack just wouldn't talk to me or tell me what was happening. We saw some land, and when we were near the shore, we were told to get off and swim.'

'What? Fucking bastard! Could you swim?' Pam asked.

'Luckily, yes. I had water up to my neck. We were swimming for what seemed like ages, and then when we reached the shore, we were told we were in England. Dover, I found out later.'

Sabrina and the other women walked up to the coast road, where they were passed on to a local man with a lorry. He dropped them in the middle of nowhere. Again, the women had no idea where they were. They could only walk, so they kept walking. All the way to London. Sabrina thought that no one back home would believe that she actually walked from the middle of Kent to the capital of England!

Soon after they arrived in London, Jack was arrested and jailed. Sabrina didn't know why.

'Well, that was lucky, wasn't it!' said Pam.

'I'm not finished yet. I was looking for work then. When he was released from prison, he found me. He knows too many Albanian people here. He just asked around and found me through his Albanian contacts.' Since then, Sabrina had been living with Jack. She couldn't choose not to. Most of her earnings also went to him. She didn't feel that she had any alternative. She believed that he would find her wherever she went.

Pam and Trish had heard it all before. Trish advised her to keep her money in a bank so Jack couldn't get to it, but Jack found out almost at once. It seemed that she couldn't hide anything from him. He forced her to give him the bank details, so that he could 'look after' her wages for her.

'And you let him?' Pam asked.

'Tell me what I should do, and where I should run to! Back to Albania? You have no idea what kind of life I had there. I can't go back.'

'But surely if you don't want him to control you and your earnings, you can run away! You can run away from this job!' said Pam.

'If you lose your job, your government will help you, Pam. You can receive money for your housing, too. If I lose my job, where do I go?' Without papers, like tens of thousands of Albanian migrants living in the UK, Sabrina wouldn't be entitled to any support. With only low-paid, casual work on offer, many Albanian women have been driven into the sex trade – some by force, others voluntarily. In the case of the latter, the money they send home has become a major factor in relieving poverty there. (Albania is one of the top twenty remittance-receiving countries in the world. From the mid 1990s to the early 2000s, Albania had the fastest growth of GDP among the Balkan and Baltic countries while it experienced the largest wave of emigration – by late 2005, 25 per cent of Albania's population had left to live and work abroad and the country relies for its survival on the remittances they send home.)

Between sessions, Sabrina liked to look out of the window, smoking. 'There is freedom out there, but the question is how to get it,' she said. For the moment, she was hopeful that the situation had improved because Jack no longer waited for her in the street outside like he had every night when she started the job.

'Now he begins to trust me. He knows I don't run away. And I'm not running away,' she told Pam. She was trying to make the best of things, and had begun to save the small part of her wages that Jack let her keep.

Apart from her pimp's control over her earnings, Sabrina also lived in the dark shadow of a more violent day-to-day danger: gang robbery. Once, when she was working with Pam, two young men came in and asked them if they were interested in buying some drugs.

'No thanks,' Pam replied.

To their horror, the two men then threatened them with hunting knives that they had concealed in their coats. It all happened within seconds. One of the men ripped off Sabrina's necklace and pushed her to the floor. Pam was terrified and froze, watching as they stole all the money Sabrina had earned that day. That was why the CCTV system had been installed, and why Pam was more careful now who she let in.

Safety was one of the basics that Pam tried to drum into Beata during her first few months at the flat. She told her about another frightening experience she'd had: 'In my last job, when I was doing maiding next to Harrods, we had this nice-looking man, all smartly dressed, who came in to have a session with Kris, the girl from Leeds I was working with. Kris had two kids, and had to rely on her relatives to look after them in turns while she worked a couple of days every week.

'Anyhow, that day, I'd shown the gentleman in and just put my feet up with the paper and a mug of tea when Kris ran in, screaming, and this lovely man was standing behind her with a gun. "Give us all the money or you'll die!" he shouted. Kris was shaking and crying with fear. I thought the best thing was to give him what he wanted. Let's face it, you can't argue with a bullet. We gave him £300 or so. Kris was too shook up to carry on working the rest of the day. After that, we hid the money behind a loose brick in the fireplace, all bar £100 or so, so's we'd have something to hand over if it happened again. Remember, dear, working flats can be just as dangerous as the streets.'

Pam told Beata about the time her younger sister, Sandra, had been considering working as a maid. 'I told her she'd have to be careful. You never can tell what a punter will be like. He could be a nutter on medication. Or he could be there just to rob you.'

In the end, Sandra thought better of it. A week later, a young American student came to work in the flat upstairs with Trish as her maid, intending to earn some money to support her while she studied in London. On her second day, a punter came in and not only paid her upfront but also gave a tip to Trish. When she went into the bedroom with him, he asked her to lie between the two pillows. 'I like to rest my arms on the pillows when I have sex,' he said.

'Sure, go ahead,' she replied without a second thought. While he was inside her, he suddenly put a hand under one of the pillows and pulled out a big knife. Before she could move, he'd cut her throat. Trish was still sitting outside the bedroom, reading. The first thing she knew about it was when the punter ran out with blood all over him.

Trish acted fast and called an ambulance and the police. Against all odds, the girl survived, though her attacker was never found.

Girls leaving work are also easy targets. At the end of one working day, close to midnight, Pam retrieved Beata's earnings from their hiding place in her armchair, counted out the rent and her tips and gave the rest to Beata. They locked up and went downstairs together with a Romanian woman who'd been working in the top flat.

The alley was dark and quiet as the cafés and restaurants had closed for the night. As they came out, they saw a shadowy figure lurking opposite the entrance to the flats, smoking a cigarette, looking as if he was waiting for someone. Apparently, he'd been waiting for them. The man grabbed Beata's handbag, and when she tried to grab it back, he hit her in the face. Despite the pain, the only thing she could think about was her passport in the handbag.

'Give it back to me! Give it back!' she screamed.

He became furious. He hit her on the head. Once, twice, three times. 'Shut up! Shut your mouth!'

Beata fell on the floor, still screaming, 'Help!'

The Romanian woman ran away without even looking back.

'Don't leave me here! Help!' Beata screamed again. Now she and Pam were on their own. They weren't sure what the robber was going to do next. They had no idea whether he was armed. Fortunately, their screams attracted the attention of a passer-by, who came over and scared the robber off.

Since then, Beata had always made sure the coast was clear before leaving work. 'The danger is always there and you never know when it's coming. We just need to be on alert. The way to prevent an attack or robbery is to trust your instinct.'

Robert had told Beata she'd need to find additional work, and on her first day off from the Soho flat he drove her to Bounds Green, in north London, and parked outside a terraced house in a run-down street. Beata had never felt so frightened. Frightened of what was to come.

'Go in yourself. You don't need me in there,' Robert instructed in a voice so casual that he might have been telling her what to pick up from the supermarket. Seeing her hesitation, he said, 'Just go in and ask them for work. It's like the place in Soho. They are all friendly.'

So he waited outside while Beata went in. The maid, who was English and in her thirties, seemed to be expecting her. She introduced her to the two women – one from Poland and the other local – working there. The Polish woman spoke quite good English, and seeing that Beata wasn't fluent, she volunteered to act as her interpreter. As they spoke, it became obvious that Robert had brought other women to work there. They all knew of him.

'I've been here for about six months, doing 10 a.m. to 10 p.m., five or six days a week,' the Polish woman told Beata. 'That's how I've picked up some English.'

The maid agreed that Beata could start work the next day. But here in Bounds Green, the women had to give half their wages to the boss, as well as paying the maid and the security man. To Beata, it felt like she was working for nothing.

When she started working in Bounds Green, the most unbearable thing was that she was told to offer oral sex without condoms. This didn't happen in the Soho flat, where Pam was strongly against it. 'I'm not going to do it,' Beata said to the maid when she passed on the demand from the manager.

'Everyone here does it,' the maid told her.

'I thought this kind of thing is not allowed in these places any more,' she complained, but the maid obviously had no control over the punters' constant requests and the manager's demands.

Beata wasn't happy and decided to tell Robert that she wouldn't work under those conditions.

He was far from pleased. 'I have tried very hard to find you work.' And then he dropped the pretence that their relationship was about anything other than money. 'I've loved you, looked after you and fed you when you were out of work, but you are letting me down. Is this something in your character, or you are turning down work deliberately to upset me? You need to pay me half of what you earn every day for my help with finding you work. I have already spent a lot of my time on this.'

Beata did not utter a word. He had revealed his true role as her pimp, but for some reason she did not feel that deep pain that she had expected when this moment arrived. In fact, it came as a relief to know where she stood. His deception had been ruthlessly confirmed and she now had no alternative but to confront it. She didn't even shed a tear. She went to sleep in the same double bed that she had shared with him since losing the sandwich-bar job in Stratford. But now, as Robert lay next to her, she was planning her escape rather than their future.

Early next morning, before Robert woke, Beata picked up her bag and quietly sneaked down the stairs. She was so frightened, she could hear her own heartbeat. But as she opened the front door and walked out of his place, she felt as though she had been released from prison. Like a slave unshackled, Beata simply ran and ran as far as she could, without once looking back.

She finally stopped and gasped for air. She found herself outside Stratford underground station, already busy with commuters. Why should she have to run? Why couldn't she just live a normal life like these people all around her? She took a slow, deep breath: she was inhaling the air of freedom! She felt liberated. The morning sunshine of London had never seemed so bright. She walked calmly into the station and boarded the first train that arrived.

Of course, he called her when he woke up and found her gone, but his power over her was lost. 'You are not going to get a penny from me,' she informed him. 'I am not selling myself for you!'

Robert was furious and tried his old tricks of threat and intimidation. 'I know where you work. You have no place to hide. You are nothing in this country. Wherever you are, I find you easy!'

But Beata was no longer a timid innocent, and his heartless cruelty only made her stronger. 'Listen, bastard, I am legal in this country. Don't think you can do anything to me, like you did with God knows how many women! You may think you are so clever to trick me into this situation. But don't forget you aren't legal and I have seen your passport. All my friends know about you. If anything happens to me, you will be the first person to have the police knocking on your door.'

He called her again that afternoon and changed his tactics – and his tone of voice.

'Oh, my little sweet love, Beata, I am so, so sorry for my mistakes. I don't know what got into me. You don't know how much I miss you. I really, really miss you. I need you in my life. You are the woman I truly love! I can't—'

Beata put the phone down.

She had discovered *Loot*, and from an ad there she found a bedsit in Finsbury Park, a tiny four-metre-square space, including a small cooking area and just enough room for a bed and a wardrobe. On moving in, she pulled up the window and breathed the air from the main street. This is where my new life will start, she said to herself. The bustling traffic noises and the sight of red buses outside all made her feel part of a happening town. She finally had her freedom.

As a sex worker, Beata resented the work regime, disliked many of her punters, worried about the safety risks and sacrificed her association with anyone from Poland for fear of discrimination and getting a bad name. Now, she could put an end to all this by simply leaving the working flat. She had no pimp. She was no longer under anyone's control. But as it turned out, Beata found it as difficult to leave the sex trade as she had to enter it.

Despite all its risks and disadvantages, sex work was probably, as she saw it, one of the best ways for someone like her, with poor English and unrecognised qualifications, to earn a living. The alternative was to return to the world of low-paid, casual employment: serving customers in a sandwich bar or hard labour picking lettuce on a farm. She would still be serving customers and giving her hard labour, but with much, much better rewards.

Clearly, there was no real incentive for Beata to give up sex work, now that she'd endured her 'apprenticeship'. And even had she wished to, her parents and Tomasz still needed her support. The need to provide for them largely determined her work choices and the course of her working life in Britain.

'I am a stronger person now,' she said to her best friend Anna on the phone, though, of course, she knew nothing about how Beata really earned her money. 'Sometimes you just have to close your eyes and do what you have to do.'

Pam was of a similar opinion. 'You're getting a regular stream of men coming to you now. You'll just need to keep on and do the right thing and you'll be fine,' she said.

'You think so?'

'Of course, love,' Pam smiled warmly. 'You'll just need to learn to work like the local girls round 'ere.'

'Local girls?'

'Yeah, if you learn the tricks, you won't have to work so hard, love. Look at the local girls, they don't just do straightforward sex work like you foreigners. They specialise, and that's why it's easier for them to make money.'

'What do you mean, "specialise"?'

'I mean things like doing domination games,' said Pam, winking as if she was sharing a secret. 'The fun stuff.'

'You're not serious, are you?' Beata giggled. 'Domination games?'

'I'm dead serious, love! When I first started out in this flat, Soho was full of dungeons. I tell you, the place was like a bleedin' zoo!'

'What?'

'It was like a Mecca for kinky sex back then, in the early 1990s. Working girls would set themselves up and go straight into it, no messing.'

'What is "kinky sex"?' Beata tried not to laugh. 'I haven't heard this word.'

'Oh, there's all sorts. Don't worry, I'll train you. Dressing up, for instance. One of my girls, Lyn, had a favourite regular punter who was a school teacher. He always came in looking all normal, but without any chit-chat he would take out his gear and get changed into a tight miniskirt and put on lipstick. Bright red lipstick that most women would never wear. As a rule, me and Lyn had to make him work. He asked to be called Suzi. Suzi with red lips.'

Now Beata couldn't help laughing. She'd never come across a punter in that league.

'It was the real stuff, believe me. He wanted Lyn to order him about. Lyn would shout, "Bend over and sweep the floor! Now!" He'd pretend to be upset, as part of the act. "Go on, sweep!" Lyn would shout out to him again. That was how he liked it, see? He was what you call a submissive. He'd have carried on sweeping that bloody floor all afternoon, if we'd let him.'

Beata laughed with both hands on her belly.

'And there was another punter,' Pam went on, enjoying her memories. 'He asked Lyn and me to lock him in the wardrobe, and so we did. Lyn didn't have to do anything but that. Can you imagine getting paid £150 per hour for locking someone up?'

'Oh, I wish!' said Beata, still laughing.

'And there was another girl I used to work with in Paddington, Tanya, from Wakefield. She had a punter who locked himself in the toilet. He wouldn't come out, not even with both Tanya and me laughing our heads off outside. Three hours he stayed in there, and paid us for the privilege.'

'I can't believe that ...'

'You've got a lot to learn. And you know, the cops used to come in 'ere, too. They weren't worried at all. They came in their uniforms and asked to be spanked.'

'Did the girls do it?'

'Well, you can't say no to the cops, can you?' Pam said, laughing herself now. 'But if you say yes, you've got to do the job right – they like to be spanked hard!'

Many celebrities, too, liked a bit of kinky sex. 'I was speechless when I saw one of the actors from a famous soap opera walking up the stairs. I was sure it was him. But I didn't dare point him out. Lyn didn't care about his reputation, though – she was telling all the other girls working upstairs who she'd just had.'

'So, if I learn to do funny things and speak funny, I'll make money quicker, will I?' Beata asked, still laughing, still unconvinced.

'Trust me, you will. But the most important thing is to learn how to speak to the punters properly. Not many foreign girls can do it like the locals, but really, it's not that hard. How hard is it to tell a punter, "Look what a piece of fucking rubbish you are" in one of those domination games?'

'Look what a piece of fucking rubbish you are,' Beata repeated after Pam, giggling.

'See? And don't feel insecure about your English! You got to be brash in this job, you know that.'

'Brash?'

'Yeah, brash, outspoken, hard. The punters like to feel you're in control. Take Tanya. She didn't look like she belonged in that place at all. She spoke quite posh and was always smart. Rented the flat herself and was her own boss. Looked like butter wouldn't melt, but Tanya had more kinky punters than anyone else. One liked to be dressed up like a baby. Tanya had all the baby clothes made to fit him. He used to crawl about on the carpet talking baby talk. She would put milk in a baby's bottle for him and talk to him as if she was talking to a kid about two years old. And he didn't mind when I laughed and called him a right stupid arsehole. Brash, see? They love it.'

'Right stupid arsehole,' Beata repeated, mimicking Pam's accent.

'Tanya also had a slave that she made clean the flat and wash her underwear. When he had finished his work, Tanya would inspect it. He did the job perfectly, but she deliberately found fault with it and sent him back to do it all over again. He enjoyed being told off and taught like a kid. Apparently, he was also a school teacher in a primary school.'

'You really think I have to play these games and speak the same way?' Beata still couldn't imagine herself doing what Tanya did.

'You'll learn! Plenty of others have.'

Beata looked doubtful.

Pam paused. 'Look, ten years ago I was meeting new faces all the time – young women of all nationalities came to my door to ask for work. Me and my sister found ourselves working with a new phenomenon! First it was the Albanian girls, then those from Russia, Romania, Latvia and the Czech Republic. They were all brought in by their "boyfriends" and they all knew nothing about how to do the work like locals. You had to train them up from scratch. Later on, the Thais started to come in. They don't even speak the language, let alone do the games. But see, the number of foreign girls has grown so fast. We have to add more exotic names onto the wall at the bottom of the staircase: Eva, Galina, Sabrina … My sister used to moan, but I'd say, "Let them learn! I wouldn't be able to talk sex in Latvian!" So don't you worry, love. You've got plenty of punters in the meantime. Just try to pick up the little tricks bit by bit. You'll be all right. The punters will keep coming back once they know you're here. You'll have a load of regulars in no time. You'll be coining it in.'

And the punters did come back – even without Beata doing anything kinky. Three of Beata's eighteen customers that day returned the next. One of them was in his early forties and from south-east Europe, though he wouldn't say where, and when Beata flattered him by asking where he'd got all his muscles from he said he was a builder. Beata couldn't ignore his slightly crooked nose when he was on top of her. He noticed that she was staring.

'You looking at my nose?' he asked.

'Oh! I'm sorry. I just …'

'I had an operation before. That's why it's like this now,' he said. 'No one is perfect, yes?'

She laughed. 'You are right. No one is perfect.'

When he returned the next day, he paid for an hour and lit a cigarette as soon as he got into the bedroom. She frowned, but hoping that he would become a regular, decided to let it pass. 'OK, just this once, OK? People don't smoke in here.'

He asked her to lie on the bed with her legs open and masturbate for him. 'I like to watch,' he said.

'You never saw nudity before?' Beata teased him. 'You are like a little boy.'

'Er … I saw naked women apart from my wife before, but only once, in a strip club,' he said. 'That was just after our totalitarian time finished. It was the first time in my country we saw such things like strippers.'

'Did you enjoy it?'

'No, not really. Too many people there, with their families. It was like in a zoo. But everyone must see it once, yes? If you never see it, you want it too much!'

'Where are you from?' Beata asked.

'I can't really tell you. Our community here is small in London and people know each other. You Poles are the same, I'm sure. So you should understand why I don't want to tell you where I'm from.'

'Yes, I understand,' she smiled.

But he gave himself away on another visit, when he carelessly spoke in his own language while they were in bed.

'So you're from Bulgaria, right?' Beata knew a few words of Bulgarian.

He began to visit her even more frequently. He demanded the same ritual every time he visited. The sex itself didn't last more than a few minutes, which was perfect for her. Then, he would take out a cigarette, smoke and talk. Despite his obsession (and despite his crooked nose), Beata found him an angel compared to many of her other punters. At least he never abused her.

'So how long you do this job for?' he asked after one session.

'Not very long.' Beata didn't really want to talk about herself. 'I bet you're married with children, right?'

'Who isn't?' he replied, puffing away. 'Look, I've been good already, for a long time. In the first year in England, I didn't have any woman. See my nose, it's not easy to find a woman!'

They both burst out laughing.

'So tell me something – something about your country,' said Beata, trying to kill time.

'What about my country?'

'Anything! Todor Zhivkov?' she giggled.

'Todor Zhivkov?' The man gave a bitter smile. 'I don't feel sexy when I think of him.'

Beata laughed. She teased him: 'Please, please tell me, something about Todor Zhivkov. I really want to know.'

'OK. You want to know. OK. Under Todor Zhivkov, life was tough … very, very tough, but quiet. We were poor. Everyone was poor.'

'Yes? You're old enough to remember?' she teased again.

'I'm not as young as you think,' the man smiled. 'Back then, people wanted better things. Choices. The choices that we didn't have. When Todor Zhivkov went down in 1989, we were all very, very happy. I was in my early twenties then. Time for change has come, I thought.'

'You were married then?' she asked, looking at the clock above the bed – still twenty minutes before the hour ended.

'Yes, just married. I had a lot of dreams at that time – to set up my own firm. But our economy began to go downhill, steadily, since 1992. It seemed to be getting worse all the time. The worst time was between late 1995 and 1996 … I can never forget that. The inflation was killing us. We experienced the inflation of sixty times, from 50 leva per dollar to something like 3,000 leva per dollar.'

'That is bad.'

'Imagine going to a shop and you couldn't buy bread because today's price has gone up to £5 or £6. Old people queued outside the bread shop in the early morning in case the bread will be gone in midday. You were still a kid – you don't know anything about that kind of life.'

'How do you know? You don't know me,' Beata replied, though smiling. She looked up at the clock – ten minutes to go. The man didn't seem to want another round today, though he was entitled.

'That was a rough time,' he went on. 'People's salaries stayed the same when prices rose from day to day. State salaries were always delayed. Some factories couldn't pay up all the wages and so they gave products to workers instead.'

'That sounds really terrible,' Beata responded quietly. 'Things were rough in Poland, too. I—'

He ignored what she was saying and carried on. 'People wanted only for the situation to stay as it was, and not get any worse. Some of us thought that when things got to the worst point, it would go up again. But it seems like things have stayed in the bottom. Banks failed. People couldn't take money back, and lost their life savings. They—'

'Well – time's up.' It was Beata's turn to interrupt. 'Your hour's finished. I'm sorry. I need to prepare for the next customer. I see you again soon, yes?'

The man left the flat reluctantly just as another of Beata's returning punters arrived. This one was a British Asian, and he seemed to regard their sessions as some kind of date. He soon became a regular, and would always bring with him a box of chocolates. Once, he brought Beata a bracelet in a wrapped gift box – that really cheered her up. It was the first time a customer had bought anything for her. Unlike the Bulgarian builder, this man hardly said a word – he would just communicate through his little presents.

As Pam had forecast, Beata soon had plenty of regulars and was beginning to see the real benefit of the job, despite the high fees she still had to pay. She felt compelled to earn as much as she could – and earn it fast. She didn't even take time to sit down for lunch, just a ten-minute break during which she'd shovel down some Polish instant noodles so as not to stay hungry.

Her first customer after one such hurried meal was a young man in his twenties. He smelled strongly of sweat – he had clearly not bothered to take a shower before setting out. He got undressed and Beata passed him a condom.

'Must I use this?' he asked.

'Yes,' she said, wondering, as usual, how this would end.

He grumbled again but put on the condom, and climaxed within a minute. Then he took off the condom and complained, 'This is no good! It's too small! It almost broke! Give me another one!'

'But you already finished,' Beata said.

'I said give me another condom. You understand English?' The man was becoming irritated.

'No, you can't have two rounds for the price of one. I can't give you another condom. I can't make sex with you again. You did your session. It's finished.'

'What the fuck are you talking about?'

Beata was worried that he might lose his temper. She quickly opened the door and called for Pam to intervene.

'He wants another condom, but he's already finished.'

Pam was instantly on the offensive. 'What's the matter with you? You paid for one and you'll get one. Understand?'

'That's not the way I understood it. You give me another fuck or you give me my money back!' He started to roll up his sleeves, waving his fists in front of them. Beata was frightened. She had never met such an aggressive punter and didn't know what to expect. Pam looked worried, too.

'You heard what I said. I'm not gonna ask you again.'

Pam decided to return his money.

The man took the £20 note, sneered and spat on the floor, then left. This was the first time Beata had worked for free.

'There's nothing else you can do with that kind of punter,' Pam said.

As to the less aggressive customers, there were better ways to deal with them.

'Just tell them, "Go away, you *lagittle cagunt*!"' Pam advised.

'What?' Beata was totally confused.

'That's back slang again. It means "little cunt".'

Beata couldn't help bursting into laughter. She always learned something from Pam! She put the Cockney back slang into use at the earliest opportunity. That afternoon, a fifty-something punter was insulting her, looking her up and down and making filthy comments.

'Go away, you *lagittle cagunt*!' She showed him the door. He thought it was a Polish term of endearment.

Pam also had a dislike for 'nuisance' punters who couldn't make up their minds, such as the two East Asian men who turned up one evening. They were walking around the flat and poking into the bedroom. They then had a five-minute conversation in a language that Pam couldn't understand. Impatiently, she told them, 'Look, you're renting the girl, not the flat.'

A few days later, Bulgarian builder was back again. 'How are you?' Beata asked. 'You haven't told me your name.'

'No need to know my name. I don't ask your name,' he

answered firmly. 'Names don't matter when you're a foreigner here.'

'I understand,' Beata nodded.

'I want the same time – one hour.' He took out his cash and gave it to Pam.

Then he and Beata went into her room and got down to business. The sex was as clinical as ever, after an usually long masturbation session. Beata didn't mind; he seemed to enjoy it and was otherwise undemanding.

During the 'fag time' afterwards, he seemed to enjoy being questioned by her – he loved the attention. 'So tell me, when did you come to England?'

'A few years ago. Since 1989, Bulgarian people have finally been allowed to move abroad freely. Many people started to dream about earning a livelihood in western Europe. I thought about going abroad for the first time in 1999, when things became really too difficult in my country. I was only earning 200 leva per month in a factory owned by the local mafia. How can I feed my family?'

'My parents were in a similar situation,' Beata said.

'Anyway, that time, people were talking about working in Germany. The wages there were good. But most people didn't have the cash to travel and leave the country.'

'And you had the money to leave?' she asked.

'No. But I thought I must go. I must do something with my life and not let the bad time defeat me. I borrowed a lot of money to come here. But I work hard, and I've paid back every leva, and now I work for myself.'

'You work for yourself? Really? That's very clever. You must be making very good money,' Beata complimented him.

'Well, many Bulgarian people here are working for themselves, but they're not really like the self-employed people in Britain,' he said, shaking his head. 'We Bulgarians are actually workers who can't choose which industries to work in.'

'So are you self-employed or not?' Beata was curious to discover how other migrants coped.

'Our work status is self-employed, but that's because we have not the same work rights like other Europeans here. Like myself, I've moved from one building job to the next, and as I'm called self-employed, I have no overtime pay, no sick pay, no annual leave, no nothing. And they dodge wages all the time.'

'I understand,' said Beata. 'I too have done all sorts of low-paid work in this country. Now I have really become what you might call self-employed!'

The man smiled. Beata asked his name once again.

'No,' he said firmly. 'I told you – you don't need to know.'

'But you come here so often. I know you now,' Beata persisted. 'Why don't you trust me? Why don't you let me even know your name?'

'I fear that words will spread! People from my country talk too much,' he replied, lowering his head.

'Yes, but how do you know you won't meet any Bulgarian girls in these flats?' Beata teased.

'Because I know Bulgarian girls don't work in this kind of place. Most Bulgarian girls work in Amsterdam if they want to do sex work.'

'Is that what you think? You'd be surprised,' Beata replied. 'I've heard about them working in London. Many are doing escort service from their own places, but there are some who are working in flats, just like me.'

The man frowned. She went on, 'So there's no point in keeping your name from me. Who knows, you might even bump into someone from your town one day, in this very flat! And she might pretend to *you* that she's from somewhere else.

How funny that would be.'

He stared intensely at her for a second, and then got up from the chair. 'I think that's enough for today,' he said.

Beata never saw him again.

I continued my undercover work in Stratford, working for Ah Qin. One day, a young Romanian woman called Sonia arrived at the house. She was twenty-six, from Constanta and, unusually, spoke very good English. She was open and articulate. 'I was studying in a university back in Romania. It was unfortunate that I couldn't complete my education because I had to start to make a living,' she told me. 'I had to support my family.'

Sonia left home and joined a friend who was working in Ireland. She was soon introduced into a job as a lap dancer and part-time sex worker. She was amazed to find that she was able to earn up to £400 per day there. Then she met her fiancé, who worked as a builder, and went with him to Barcelona, where she also did sex work. It was clear to her that there was a good demand there for 'women from the other side of Europe'. A year ago, Sonia and her fiancé had come to London as she'd heard there was a higher demand for sex work here.

Her first job had been in a South Asian massage parlour. Soon she was introduced to Ah Qin and started working in her parlour in Marylebone. She had been busy ever since.

Given her history and experience, I'd expected Sonia to want to carry on working for as long as possible, but she had other ideas. 'I'm planning to quit sex work,' she told me. 'I am applying for a worker registration number so I can be eligible for other work. They are going to inform me of their decision in two weeks. I really hope I'll get it. You can't find any decent work without a worker registration number, which

means women can get a purple card and men a yellow card.'
(The UK rules of work restrictions are so complex and stratified
for Romanian and Bulgarian nationals that Sonia had become
confused by them. In fact, purple work cards are issued to
Romanian and Bulgarian migrants seeking specific jobs, such
as domestic work or employment in the service of a diplomat.
For jobs not specified by the authorities, not only do Romanian
and Bulgarian migrants have to apply for a purple card, their
employer must also apply for a work permit on their behalf.
The yellow registration card is issued to students, the self-
employed and 'self-sufficient' people. There is also a so-called
'blue' registration card, issued only to highly skilled Romanian
and Bulgarian migrants and spouses of UK nationals. Only
blue card holders have unrestricted access to Britain's labour
market.)

'Romanian working people are much discriminated against
and Romania's entry into the EU has not benefited us,' she
said, confirming what I had heard from so many Romanian
and Bulgarian migrants in Britain. 'The lack of work rights is
the main reason why so many Romanian women enter the sex
trade.' It appears to be a 'choice' at least partly determined by
government policies throughout much of the EU.

As a result, many Romanian women are victimised and
callously exploited. Some of them are so eager to find work
that they rely on unscrupulous agents to arrange employment
for them. Sonia told me, 'Many Romanian girls end up having
pimps looking over their earnings. Some of these girls are
willing to accept this kind of arrangement. Some are even in
a relationship with their pimps.' I thought back to Flory, and
her constant phone calls to her 'friend'. It was something I saw
often among Romanian women. Their communication often
seemed friendly and entirely voluntary. And, as Sonia said,

some of them seemed to be in genuine romantic relationships.

Sonia was planning to get married in a year's time. She was saving what she earned to pay for her wedding. 'We're going to have a ceremony here and then in Romania,' she said, showing me pictures of her fiancé.

'I'm also going to give my parents a holiday in the UK,' she told me. 'They will come to my wedding and I want them to have a good time.'

But the Stratford flat didn't seem like the ideal place for her to achieve those aims, as business remained poor. Sonia waited from 12.30 p.m. to 10 p.m., but only one customer visited, for a half-hour service costing £60 (of which Sonia received only £30, of course). He was from Finland and nervous because this was his first time visiting a working girl. He couldn't go through with it, so she gave him a hand job. 'At least it isn't strenuous work,' she said, trying to look on the bright side. But how optimistic can you be, waiting the whole day for just £30? Sonia never came back to the flat.

A Taiwanese woman called Mia took her place the following day. She said she was thirty-six (though when we got to know each other better I found out she was forty-two). The previous week she'd worked at a brothel owned by a man called Ah Li, from the north-east of China, who had promised her more work in 'a place in outer London' where business was doing well. He'd put her on an underground train with instructions to get off at Stratford. Ah Qin had collected her from the station.

Too late, Mia realised she'd been sent to a half-empty flat in the run-down east of the city and a business that had just been set up. She was infuriated by the arrangement and called Ah Li, shouting at him on the phone. 'You promised to give me work in a good part of London. This is an empty flat with no customers! Do you take me as a fool?'

Ah Li seemed to be apologising on the other end of the line, but had no intention of changing the arrangement. Mia was stuck here.

'There's no hot water here! No gas, no heating! Not even clean towels! How do you expect me to survive here?' Mia carried on berating Ah Li. 'I worked hard for you, and this is all you can do for me?'

Although Ah Li kept telling Mia that the place in Stratford was nothing to do with him, Mia suspected that he had a share. Ah Qin listened to Mia's angry complaints on the phone as she smoked quietly in the lounge. Then she got up and went out to shop. It seemed that it took an angry *xiaojie* to make the bosses provide basic facilities. They couldn't afford to lose Mia now.

While Ah Qin was out, a customer rang the bell. I could see from the window that it was a well-built middle-aged white man. I didn't admit him immediately because of Ah Qin's previous warning about not opening the door to strangers. She had made a point about calling her first, to check whether the punter had booked.

'Wait, please,' I said through the closed door. 'Let me call my manager first.'

He was impatient and kept knocking on the door. By the time Ah Qin answered her mobile phone a few seconds later, he'd stormed off.

'Why did you do that? Why didn't you open the door to him?' Ah Qin was furious when she returned.

'Because you told me not to do so before checking with you,' I replied.

She shook her head, looking frustrated, and said, 'I don't think you are suitable for this job. Looks like it's too tough for you and you don't know how to deal with the customers.'

At first, she said she'd move me to their Marylebone parlour. But half an hour later she said they were going to relocate to Stratford and close down the Marylebone business. Zhang, the housekeeper in Marylebone, would take my job. 'You can stay here tonight,' Ah Qin said. 'But tomorrow you'll have to go. Zhang will move into your room.'

Ah Qin said I had to cook for Mia, but refused me money to buy food. 'I already gave you £30 last week. That should be enough,' she said.

Then the boss arrived, the man Ah Qin called 'brother'. He and Ah Qin were talking downstairs, and she sent me to my room. Later, Ah Qin told me it had been decided I'd be paid only £100 for the previous week's work rather than the originally agreed £210, because I 'wasn't suited to the job'.

Mia was sympathetic about my sudden unemployment. She felt somehow responsible for it, because the dispute had been over a punter I hadn't admitted. She said she'd ring round and try to get me another job.

Throughout the day, Mia continued to bemoan the lack of facilities in the flat. She smoked a lot, and then took out from the fridge two cans of beer she'd brought with her and offered me one. We sat in the lounge for a 'sip'.

Mia told me she had had her work trip arranged by an agency in Taipei, to which she'd paid £600. Back home, she used to do bar work, drinking with customers. She had only a high school education and few skills to get herself a 'white-collar job', she said. But apart from her grim career prospects, she was also in a relationship with a married man that was never going to develop into anything meaningful. 'He used to at least pay for my upkeep,' she said. 'But now, that's all stopped.' She'd tried to do something with her life by investing all the money she had in a café of her own. But the business made a loss and she decided that she must do something drastic to change the course of her life. After a blazing row with her married boyfriend, she switched off her mobile phone and got straight in touch with the agency.

Like many Chinese migrant women working in the trade, Mia had a very clear aim: she wanted to earn £20,000 in four months. So far, she was on target; she'd been here two months and had earned half that amount. On an average day, she worked sixteen hours. During her busiest week, she'd served, on average, fourteen men a day. She had worked non-stop, literally.

At Ah Li's premises the previous week, Mia had earned £1,500, the highest this month, she said. 'There's a limit to what you can do though, what your body can do,' she told me, swallowing a mouthful of beer. 'The job ads boast of £3,000 to £4,000 per week, but it is impossible for a normal human being. You would completely wreck your body if you worked to that level.'

Because she worked so hard, she resented those bosses who showed no respect for their workers. According to Mia, the band of Ah Li, Ah Qin and co. owned four places in all: in Marylebone, Stratford, Leyton and Heathrow. 'It's not as if they can't afford to provide facilities here,' she sneered.

Mia seemed like a strong woman who knew exactly what she wanted. She wasn't willing to tolerate second-class conditions in order to keep work, though many other women were. But despite her strength, one thing that saddened me about Mia was the sacrifice she was willing to make in order to earn money: she had been having unprotected sex throughout her time in England.

Initially, her employers did not inform her about the need for protection. She heard that some *xiaojies* were offering unprotected oral sex for tips. She misunderstood and thought it was the norm to have unprotected intercourse with customers. None of her employers explained to her that this wasn't the case, especially after they saw that punters were returning to Mia again and again, and how good it was for business. Such greedy and ruthless selfishness ensured that Mia continued to offer this 'special service', which brought her a much greater income but increased her risks even more.

On the day I met her, she had a punter who paid a £40 tip for unprotected oral sex. Mia cheered up instantly. 'Tips are so important to us, you know,' she said to me. 'I can keep tips for myself without having to share it half way with the boss ... and some punters can be generous.'

As a way of maintaining a good relationship with her best customers and ensuring their return, Mia tended to keep in contact with them outside work, frequently sending texts to her favourite punters. She asked me to help her with her English. At this point, she particularly liked one man who 'once drove for one hour' to see her. They couldn't really communicate at all. When he called, she could only giggle and say the few words of English she knew, like 'thank you', and 'see you soon', and then a stream of 'Japanese' flattery to keep him happy. (Japanese women are much prized in the business, having a reputation for providing 'good service' to punters. Many brothel owners pass off their Chinese workers as Japanese.) 'Although he doesn't understand a word I'm saying, he likes me to put on a girly voice to make him think of a young Japanese girl doing whatever he fancies to him,' Mia told me with a giggle.

Opportunities Knock

In Nottingham, it was supposed to be Ming's day off, but Lao Chen had made arrangements for her to join him for dinner and then karaoke at Han Chao, on Mansfield Road. Since she depended on him for a livelihood, it was an invitation she couldn't possibly turn down.

Mansfield Road was bright with neon lights as Ming walked up the narrow staircase to the restaurant. She was led by a waiter to a table where Lao Chen and a dozen young-looking Chinese were sitting. 'Come and meet some folk from your home town, Ming,' Lao Chen urged. One of the young men raised his glass at her, slurring, 'Long live the people of Shenyang!' The wine glass and his designer watch were both shining above everyone's shoulders. A teenage-looking girl was leaning on him. Her alcohol-blushed face stood out against the white pearl necklace she was wearing for the occasion.

To Ming, these 'home-town folk' didn't look in the slightest like the *da-gong* class to which she belonged. She noticed the half-empty bottles of ridiculously expensive wine that the youngsters were consuming.

Ming politely greeted everyone and sat down. Many delicious

dishes were already on the table, and more bottles of wine were sent for. The waiters seemed to be well acquainted with the party and were all paying obsequious attention to Lao Chen. It was just what you'd expect from a feast with a local crime boss or government official back home, Ming thought.

'This is Xiao Quan, from Shenyang,' said Lao Chen as he introduced one of the young men to her. 'He's from the university.'

'Nottingham Trent University, I'm afraid,' Xiao Quan said, smiling at Ming. 'I couldn't get into the University of Nottingham.'

'But that's still excellent,' Ming answered politely. 'A degree will surely serve you well back home.' If you also have good connections and know someone in high office, she added silently.

Xiao Quan didn't ask about Ming's line of work. Did he know already? He must do: Lao Chen had surely briefed everyone about her. Still, Ming decided it would be prudent to keep quiet about it for now.

She looked silently at each of the young strangers around her. Where had they all come from? How were they funding this playboy lifestyle? If they were really from Shenyang, they certainly weren't from her neighbourhood. And even if their parents were all rich as emperors, what were they doing hanging out with a brothel owner? How on earth had their paths crossed? They'd probably never have done so back in Shenyang: she couldn't imagine a glorified pimp drinking and dining with university undergraduates there.

'You are very quiet for a north-eastern girl,' Xiao Quan said suddenly. 'Are you new to England? How are you finding life here?'

'I'm getting by,' she struggled with the words, careful not to reveal any dissatisfaction with her working life under Lao Chen.

She added, 'Unlike you, my English is poor. I'm always feeling new to this country.'

'My English isn't all that good. I'm learning as I go along. Our college in China has a joint programme with the university here and we all came over for two years' study. My dad's the head of a joint venture back home. He's very keen on me studying in England, especially since I'm the only child.'

'That must have been pressuring for you,' said Ming. Here was another of the single-child generation, one whose father was a successful entrepreneur. This was no normal student. This innocent face masked a well-to-do young man with boundless wealth and all-round connections. The modesty in his looks was simply there to disguise the deep division between them. He'd been brought up to know how to use his resources. Look at how he was speaking now to Lao Chen, flattering him with such grace. And he was clearly at ease with his female compatriots.

Ming was growing dizzy. She felt completely out of place at this feast. She had to leave. She stood up, and put her hands on the table for support. 'Lao Chen, I'm sorry, I'm not feeling very well …'

'That's a great pity, Ming,' Lao Chen looked up curiously at her. 'We thought you might like to join us for karaoke. It's just upstairs. It'll be fun!'

'Honestly, I can't. I'm feeling quite sick. I need to sleep.'

'Let me take you home,' Xiao Quan offered, also standing. 'I'll drive you.'

He has a car? she thought. He's barely nineteen. Very few youngsters of his age could dream of owning a car back home. His dad must have made a lot of money, one way or another. And here he was in England, living it up with Daddy's cash. What a generation.

Xiao Quan's car was parked outside. Chivalrously, he opened the door for her. He didn't ask where she lived – he clearly already knew, and seemed to be familiar with each turn of the road.

'You have a car in China, too?' Ming asked.

'Yeah. My dad's got two cars. And he's just bought me this one for my birthday,' he said, patting his hand on the windscreen.

'You'd better put your hand back on the wheel,' Ming said. He looked too young and careless to be a trustworthy chauffeur. 'How often do you have these parties?' Even to herself, it sounded as if she was interrogating the young man.

'Er, every week. We get together every week,' he replied. 'You are always very welcome to join us.'

'I'm afraid I don't have the money to spend like you and your friends.'

'Oh, I see. I can understand that. The others have more money than I do. Their dads are all government officials who use their kids' bank accounts abroad to wash their money, you know what I'm talking about. Each of them has at least bought a house here and as you can see, they're only in their teens. My dad isn't nearly as wealthy and he doesn't send large sums of money to me all the time.'

'Ah, I see … So how do you manage to keep up with your rich friends, then?'

'Hey, I work.'

'You work?' Ming was surprised.

'Yes, I work now and then, when my money's run out. I work for your boss.'

'Who? Lao Chen?'

'Yes. I work for Lao Chen.' He lowered his head and lit a cigarette. Ming was confused. What work could he possibly do for her boss? But Xiao Quan wouldn't elaborate.

The following week, Ming was sent to work in Lao Chen's second premises on the other side of town. The housekeeper, a man with a northern Chinese accent, looked to be in his forties.

'Call me Old Horse,' he said amicably as he welcomed her in. His surname meant 'horse' in Chinese and his friends all called him Old Horse back home. He looked familiar, but she couldn't place him.

'Why are you looking at me like that? I get shy!' he smiled. He openly looked her up and down, touching his bald head.

'I'm just wondering if I've met you before … but I know it's not possible,' she said.

'I'm an old Beijinger, and you know, you might be right – you might well have met me before. I was a taxi driver. Did you ever visit the capital? If so, you might have sat in my cab,' he said, laughing.

'I have been to the capital, as a matter of fact,' Ming replied, thinking how funny it would be if she really had met this man before.

'Anyway, we are here, working together, that's the main thing. It's *yuan-fen* [a Buddhist concept that destiny is predetermined and that some people are bound to meet] that has brought us together,' said Old Horse. 'Let's make a pot of green tea.'

But this was not a job for green-tea breaks. Two men in their late twenties had just arrived. An exception to the 'punters must never meet' rule could be made in their case, because they were regulars and friends with each other. Old Horse knew them well.

'You get yourself ready. I'll talk to the guys first,' Old Horse said to Ming. He then led the two men into the front room. As she undressed, Ming could hear the conversation.

'She change clothes. You sit, two minutes.'

'No problem, Horse,' said one, who worked in the kebab shop just down the road.

'You good guy,' Old Horse flattered him. The man came every week, spending a quarter of his £250 weekly wages there.

'Yes, I like Orientals.'

'Why you not get girlfriend? You young, and strong!' Old Horse joked.

'Girlfriends? No, no!' the punter protested. 'No hassle if it's a woman in a place like this. My job is stressful already, believe me; I don't want the extra stress of having a girlfriend, you know what I mean.'

Old Horse laughed. 'You're right! You're right!'

Ming saw both men – one after the other – and emerged from her room with the second man to find the flat was empty. Where was Old Horse? Then, as she became worried, she saw the housekeeper rushing back into the flat with sweat on his forehead. She looked down and saw that he was wearing roller skates.

'What are you doing? Where have you been?'

'Sorry, miss, sorry …' Old Horse panted. 'I just went out for a break. I thought you'd be a while with these two, and I knew you were safe with them. Oh heavens, it was great fun.'

'You went skating outside?' Ming still couldn't believe it. She'd never met such a carefree housekeeper.

'Yeah, I got to keep myself fit, you know. Or I try, anyway!' he said, gasping for air. Then he turned to Ming's punter. 'You've had a good time, my friend?'

The man nodded, gave an embarrassed smile and left.

Old Horse noticed the surprise on Ming's face. 'Hey, don't make a fuss with me, all right? Lao Chen knows my hobbies. I work hard. It's just that I need my exercise as well.'

'I'm not making a fuss,' Ming explained. 'I couldn't care less if you want to spend all day skating round the neighbourhood. I'm just curious.'

'The roads are good here – they're quite flat. Good for skating.'

'You have to be careful with traffic!'

'No worries. I make them stop – I just wave my hand and they all stop.'

'You are a comedian, Old Horse.'

'You have to be, otherwise life would be very dull here,' he said, taking off his skates. 'Let's make some green tea.'

Ming felt relaxed with Old Horse. He seemed so naturally open and empathetic.

'All the girls who come here like me. I don't mean to sound big headed, but they do.'

'Am I the only one working here?'

'Yeah, now you are. But it used to be two girls when the business first opened. This was like an extended part of Lao Chen's business. He was hoping for it to be popular, but there aren't many customers around here. It's a very quiet residential area, you see. Only regulars come. And only local men who haven't really got that much to spend. So Lao Chen cut it down to one girl at a time.'

'I see,' said Ming.

'But also,' Old Horse carried on, 'as you can see, many parlours prefer to keep the number of girls down to one at a time, so that it's not illegal. It's the law of this country: one working girl, no problem! Anyway, one girl is still good enough – Lao Chen's making £1,500 pure profits per week. He's moaning about it, but it really isn't that bad, considering the area.'

'You seem to know the trade very well.'

'I learn fast, that's all. I used to wash dishes in a restaurant when I first arrived. I learned fast in that job, too. But hey, my luck came, and one day a friend told me about a job as a housekeeper in Essex. He said I would never have to swallow my pride with the stingy restaurant boss again. Later, he introduced me to Lao Chen as well.'

'But you really like it here?'

'For you it would be different. But when I first started this job, I thought to myself, Old Horse, there's not such an easy job anywhere else in this world! Compared with the stinky kitchen work that I had before, miss, this is a holiday for me.'

'I can see that – you're skating during work hours!' Ming teased him. 'I bet no one else in England is having such an easy time.'

'You may be right, although I'm not looking for an easy time. I just prefer to be in this job than elsewhere. I've seen more than you can imagine and I've had it hard since I came here six years ago. But during these two years housekeeping in the parlours, I've been learning … and now I know the sex trade well. I know it inside out. So I've been thinking …'

'What about?'

'I'm thinking about setting up my own business.'

'Really?'

'Yes, really. Now I'm telling this to you in confidence. Don't go blabbing to Lao Chen, OK?'

'Of course not. But you still have no status and no papers. How are you going to rent a flat?'

'I'm not as stupid as I look, miss!' Old Horse said. 'I've planned it all out. You've got to find someone you really trust to do the business with. It's a big commitment and you can't just go with second best. I got to know a Malaysian Chinese woman when I was working in Essex. She's a citizen here and she's the most lovely person – I mean, really generous and kind. I didn't meet her through the sex trade; I just bumped into her in a local shop. We used to go to places together on my day off every fortnight. Once she drove me to Dover … We spent the whole day there, just watching the sea. It was the best day of my time in England.

'She took all these pictures of me, look.' Old Horse produced a wad of photographs: there were pictures of him wearing a vest and showing his muscles, pictures of him jogging, others of him posing in various outfits.

'Don't I look like an executive in this suit?' he said to Ming, pointing to one of the pictures.

'She must like you a lot, to take all these shots of you …'

'Ay, those good times! How rare they are. When the parlour in Essex was raided, my boss didn't care. I couldn't get in touch with any of my so-called friends. They all vanished. But this woman came to the police station, helped me get a solicitor and bailed me out.'

'That was lucky.'

'Well, I've been a good person all my life, so maybe the heavens were pitying me! I'm a big man, but I was crying like a baby in that police station, I'm not ashamed to tell you. Do you know why? I was so frightened that I'd be sent back to China and be in debt for a very, very long time. My friend saved me from that. She saved my life, really.'

'She's obviously someone you can trust, then,' said Ming. 'Are you sure you want to set up in this business with her, though?'

'What choice is there? Times are hard; Chinese restaurants and takeaways aren't doing well as they are short of legal workers, and no boss wants to pay a heavy penalty of £10,000 for employing illegals, which are all you can get nowadays. The sex trade is where the money is, but I'm not going to make a lot cleaning and cooking like I do now, and I haven't got a body to sell! So, yes, I want to set up in this business, and I put the idea

to my Malaysian Chinese friend and she said yes! She's willing
to help me again!'

'Is she going to take a share?' asked Ming.

'I am going to ask her to split the profits half way with me.
All she has to do is rent a house like this and advertise the service
in the local papers, which I couldn't do because of my English.
I'll be looking after the day-to-day running of the place and
keeping the girls and the customers happy.'

Ming looked at Old Horse and tried to imagine what he
would be like as a boss.

'I'd be happy if you'd come to work for me,' he said
enthusiastically.

'And are you going to take half my wages, like all the other
bosses in the trade?'

Old Horse's warm smile disappeared. 'Of course, I will have
to, miss, if I want to make a profit at all,' he answered.

One morning, just after Ming had shown a customer out, Old
Horse told her merrily, 'You had a visitor! Xiao Quan from the
college just came to see you.'

'Xiao Quan?'

'Yeah. He didn't say much. Just left his number here and
asked you to give him a call,' said Old Horse, noting Ming's
response curiously. 'What's going on between you two?'

'Nothing. Lao Chen introduced us at a meal. He was with
some other students.'

'Ah! I know those kids! Spoiled brats,' Old Horse sneered.

'You know them?'

'All of them are children of corrupt officials back home,
cheating and extracting money out of people and laundering
their black cash through their kids. They think I have no clue

about their dirty bottoms.'

'You know them well?'

'I don't need to hang out with them, thank heaven, if that's what you mean. I know I'm not exactly an angel, but at least I'm not flaunting my wealth in front of those who don't have any. Look at how they live! Have you seen them driving round in their sports cars? They didn't earn that money, you know.'

'I could guess as much, just from the look of them,' said Ming.

'Xiao Quan isn't so bad, though,' admitted Old Horse. 'At least, he's not so stinking rich as the others. He knows his *fen-cun* [inches: limitations and boundaries].'

Ming wondered what Xiao Quan could want from her as she dialled his number.

He surprised her. 'I was just wondering if you'd like to meet up on your next day off?' Xiao Quan's voice was kind. 'You might like to go somewhere – maybe take a trip outside the city?'

Ming was puzzled. What would a middle-class youngster like Xiao Quan see in a middle-aged sex worker like her? Not only were their lives in China worlds apart, their lives here were, too. Did he have a thing for older women, or for women in the sex trade? Or perhaps he had something altogether different in mind, though she couldn't imagine what.

Meanwhile, Lao Chen had been extremely happy with Ming's work, as punters were returning to the parlour she'd just left and asking when she would be back. He made her an unusual offer: to work exclusively for him for the next two months, alternating between his two parlours, instead of making bookings anywhere else.

Ming realised it would be much easier to switch between two places in Nottingham than to travel up and down the country every week. It would also provide her with stability during her 'transition' period as she got used to the trade. Without hesitation, she said yes.

Ming began to see Xiao Quan regularly on her Sundays off, and being with him seemed to bring back some normality to her life. She particularly enjoyed walking through town with him, watching children playing and splashing water at the fountain in the market square on a sunny day. At times like this she felt human again, able to enjoy the small pleasures in life and put aside for a while the heavy burden of having to provide for her family back home. 'I think this is what they call in England a weekend break,' she said to Xiao Quan.

Xiao Quan pointed out the flats where he and his student friends lived, a few minutes' walk from the main shopping centre. Ming thought they must cost a lot to rent. 'A lot of parties going on there in the evenings,' said Xiao Quan. 'You'll have to come and join us sometimes.'

Xiao Quan never referred to Ming's work, but he talked frequently about Lao Chen, clearly an important person in his life in England. 'I met him in that karaoke restaurant, Han Chao, you know, where I met you. That's where we all hang out. Lao Chen was with his people and I was in my group with the students. As we got louder over the drinks, he came over and said hello. He was very sociable.'

'I suppose you know him well now?'

'He does look after me,' he told Ming, with genuine gratitude in his eyes. 'In the first few months when I knew him, he used to call me regularly to ask how I was getting on with my studies and whether I needed any help. He's like an uncle to me.'

'I tend to think that when people are kind, it isn't always for altruistic reasons,' Ming said, looking at Xiao Quan to see how he would respond.

'Sure. But I don't blame Lao Chen for putting himself first. We all have to, trying to survive in a foreign country. He's come a long way to do what he's doing.'

Ming wasn't too surprised by Xiao Quan's respect for her boss. Patronage and networking were a major part of anyone's success back home. Without these, it was hard to get anywhere. She quite understood Xiao Quan's attitude. Besides, in an isolated community such as that of the new Chinese migrants in Nottingham (and in Britain in general), seeking such patronage was a means not only of securing one's livelihood but also of fostering a sense of belonging.

'I am willing to help him and do odd jobs for him when I can, in return for his kindness,' Xiao Quan said.

'Does he pay you at all for the "odd jobs", then?' asked Ming.

Xiao Quan looked at her for a second, then said, 'We'll leave that till another occasion.'

On the surface, it seemed as if Xiao Quan was keen to get to know Ming better. He called her almost every day, talking to her about what was happening at university, but still he never asked a single question about Ming's work. It was as if Ming's work did not exist. In return, Xiao Quan seemed to want to keep his own work for Lao Chen equally private. Ming thought this meant he didn't trust her.

One Sunday, he offered to drive her to Sheffield.

'Have you ever been north of Nottingham?' he asked.

'No, never. I spend all my time working. Never had a chance to do sightseeing yet.'

'Sheffield's quite an interesting city. A lot of old industry around, like steel,' said Xiao Quan. 'I really like the look of it … Bleak and beautiful.'

Xiao Quan seemed to know his way to Sheffield well and never needed to look at a map or switch on his satnav.

'You've been this way often, haven't you?' Ming observed. 'It looks like you travel a lot.'

'Yes, I have,' he replied, looking ahead. 'I travel frequently from Nottingham to the north, and all the way to Scotland.'

'Scotland … I'd love to go there.'

'I also travel to Birmingham and London a lot. I've taken more train trips than bus trips in England!'

'You mean you don't drive there? Why not?'

'I think I can tell you this now, Ming … Wherever Lao Chen sends me, I can only travel by train.'

'What do you mean?' Ming looked at him, puzzled.

'Well …' Xiao Quan paused, then said, 'Ming, please try to understand. It's no worse than what you're doing, really.' It was the first time Xiao Quan had ever mentioned Ming's work.

'What are you talking about? What do you mean?' Since they'd first met, Ming had had the feeling that Xiao Quan had been hiding a secret from her. A secret between him and Lao Chen.

'What does he get you to do for him, Quan?' she pressed.

'Nothing as bad as you're imagining. It started when I first became cash-strapped, you know – Lao Chen offered me a job, and since then it's become my source of income. I need the money, you see; it's expensive, trying to keep up with my wealthy friends, and living costs are quite high in this country.'

'What do you do for him, Quan?' Ming asked again.

'The job is to transport some stuff … from city to city.'

'Stuff? What stuff?'

'Look, Ming, it's not as bad as it might sound, OK? We're all doing all sorts of *laobianmen* [side business] to survive. That's all. When I've earned enough, I go back to my studies and stop working for Lao Chen for a while.'

'Until you run out of cash again?' Ming began to raise her

voice like a scolding mother. 'So are you going to tell me what "stuff" you're transporting, or not?'

'It's cannabis. Just cannabis.'

'What!'

'I'm carrying cannabis with me on the trains, several kilos each time, in a suitcase, from Nottingham to other cities. I take the train because passengers on trains are never checked.'

'I can't believe what I'm hearing, Quan! I don't know what to say to you!' Ming sounded as if she was talking to a badly behaved teenager. 'Do you know what kind of trouble you are getting yourself into? I didn't even know that Lao Chen dealt in cannabis.'

'Oh yes, he does, and it's a big business, too. I am just a tiny, replaceable cog in the chain, not worth a mention, really – and I'm not getting myself into trouble. Quite a few students are doing this to bring in some income. It's nothing unusual.'

Ming stared at him, shocked.

Xiao Quan carried on about Lao Chen's business: 'He can harvest the plants within two to three months of growing them ... and the profit on each batch is around £100,000! Much bigger business than running a few brothels.' This was the first time Xiao Quan had used the term 'brothel' in front of Ming. The word's weight seemed to seal Ming's lips.

'Just imagine the amount of stuff he got me to carry. He paid me £700 per delivery. I think it's quite well paid, but the trip was always full of risks and I was petrified each time that I'd be caught.'

'And you say there's no trouble involved!' Ming resumed her matriarchal tone, shaking her head. 'You are a fool. I can't believe you're willing to do this, Quan. You are going to ruin your own chance of securing a better future for yourself. How would your parents feel if they found out? Wouldn't they be shocked and ashamed?'

'Listen to yourself, Ming!' Xiao Quan became annoyed and defensive. 'Do you think your family would be pleased to hear what line of work you're in? Come on, we're all trying to earn enough to get by.'

'No, no, no! I'm struggling to earn enough for my family. To put food on their table and to provide for their basic needs. You? You are earning pocket money for your luxurious lifestyle to keep up with your university friends! I'm a mother, only here for my daughter and my parents. You? What are you here for, Quan? You'll have a good career waiting for you, all planned out by your father, but you're throwing it away!'

Xiao Quan kept quiet, listening. Then he suddenly parked the car at the side of the road and started to chain-smoke. Ming coughed and wound down the window. 'You've been used, you know that, Quan,' she carried on. 'Tell me, how many of you are involved in this business of Lao Chen's?'

'I've no idea,' Xiao Quan said. (In fact, an older student named Ah Chuan was also helping Lao Chen with his cannabis production. Ah Chuan worked as the 'technician' of a cannabis farm located in the basement of a Nottingham restaurant, ensuring the plants received sufficient water, food and light. Ah Chuan was being paid £500 per week. This was one of a number of cannabis farms Lao Chen had in the town. One had been raided two months earlier after the authorities detected unusually high electricity usage at the property – keeping the plants adequately lit consumes a great deal of power. In that case his technician had been arrested and was currently awaiting deportation, but Lao Chen went unpunished and his cannabis enterprise lived on.)

According to Ming, Xiao Quan found her response to his revelations unsettling and hurtful. He also became increasingly concerned about the consequences of getting caught. He started looking for an alternative. Then, at university, he heard about another possibility.

Many female Chinese students take up sex work as a summer job, to help pay their tuition fees and living expenses in England. Some male Chinese students have followed suit, offering their services to women. They share the view of their female colleagues that low-paid part-time jobs in the service industries simply aren't worthwhile.

Xiao Quan was seriously considering doing the same. He'd heard that a number of male Chinese students in a nearby university were working in Soho as escorts during the summer break. Apparently, there were only a few dozen such men in the entire country; their rarity made them a valuable commodity.

I was intrigued, and keen to learn how such a Chinese male sex worker might view his circumstances. I scoured the Chinese newspapers, and in between the ads of women offering sex to men I spotted one or two aimed at a female clientele. They were rare, but stood out: 'Are you feeling lonely? Special service for Chinese women. Just one call, I'll be with you.'

I called the number, and a Malaysian Chinese man answered. (He told me he was the receptionist, but later I discovered that he ran the business.) He directed me to a web site, the title of which translated as *Stylish Asian Men*. 'We have men from everywhere. You can choose one you like from there,' he told me.

On the web site, he said, I would find pictures of men from north-eastern China, Hong Kong and Malaysia. 'The north-eastern Chinese boys are very good,' he told me. 'They are stronger.' He took my number and said he'd call me back after I'd been online.

Half an hour later, the phone rang. 'Have you made up your mind?' he asked. 'If you haven't, I'd recommend Xing. Most first-timers book him.'

'All right,' I said, 'I'll book for half an hour.'

'Why don't you try an hour? Most people book for an hour,' he tried to persuade me, sounding like an automatic answering machine. 'Half an hour won't be enough time for real fun. You'll get oral sex and will have time to use toys if you have the full hour.'

He then told me I'd have to see Xing in his own place. Apparently, first-timers often prefer to have their session at the main premises, where they feel safer. However, it wouldn't be possible on this occasion, he said, because 'the premises are under refurbishment'.

He was very chatty, continuing the fiction that he was just a receptionist and that this was his second job. 'In the main, I work as a chef in a restaurant.'

'Why do you need to do this as well, then? Aren't you earning enough as a chef?' I asked.

'Oh, I'm just doing it because I'm bored,' he said. 'I'm helping out my friend with his business.'

Later, my escort, Xing, sent me a text, introducing himself and telling me his address. 'I have a lot of customers coming to the place I rent in East Dulwich,' he wrote.

When I arrived, he led me to his room upstairs. Then I explained to him that I wasn't here for sex, but to learn more about his experiences. 'Would you be willing to talk?' I asked. He was both surprised and amused by my request, and politely agreed, as long as I didn't tell his boss.

'I saw an ad for male escorts placed by a student from Henan province,' Xing told me. 'I was running out of money and I had to pay my rent. My parents couldn't send me any more, so I decided to start working for him. It really wasn't very hard to do this job. All I had to do to keep myself fit was to eat a lot of ginger. It keeps my skin nice and pink, like a teenage boy! And I take a lot of Chinese medicine for nutrition. I did well. Then later, through agencies, I started working for four different employers, the only four parlours in the whole of London offering our kind of service.'

Xing said that one of the massage parlours was located in Elephant & Castle, not far from where he lives. 'My boss is a clever businessman. He's the largest employer in the sex trade in Kent.'

He paused, and said confidently, 'There are probably just twenty or so Chinese students doing this work in London. I met quite a few students at Stylish Asian Men. One of them was studying politics. He worked as a kitchen hand and as a waiter previously, but the money was crap. Another was doing a degree in banking investment. They needed more cash to enable them to live here, just like me. The good thing about the job is that I can work part-time, and it's perfect for my studies. And I can stop whenever I like.'

Xing seemed content with the work. 'I like this job more than any other job I could find in this country. It's good money. The company charges customers £60 per half hour, £100 per hour and £800 for overnight. If the work is done at the premises in Soho, then I have to give half of my earnings to the boss. But if the customers come here, then I only have to give one-sixth of my earnings as commission. I have about ten customers on average in a week. Out of ten, around three would book me overnight.'

'It sounds like you've easily covered your rent and all your living expenses,' I said.

'Definitely, yes,' he smiled. 'I hope I can carry on earning this amount. This is why I'd prefer the customers to come to my place, you see. Not only because then I won't have to share too much of my wages with the boss, but also because the customers won't have ten other men to choose from. There are three handsome boys from the north-east of China on the books apart from me, and some customers also like Malaysian Chinese men.'

I asked him about his clientele and whether work had always been pleasant.

'I meet all walks of life in this job, as you can imagine,' Xing said. 'Most of them are lonely women, aged between thirty and fifty – they could be wealthy divorcees, or perhaps their partners are often away, or they have difficulty finding men because of their careers. Quite a few work in finance and live in expensive areas in west London. Most women ask a lot of questions when they do it the first time. They have concerns about safety. They want to be reassured before they book their first session with us. The rich women prefer to meet in their own homes or in hotel rooms.'

Xing told me that he had developed close relationships with a few of his regular customers. 'I say four must be my lucky number – I usually began to develop some kind of a closer relationship with the women after the fourth session, the fourth time of contact ... How strange.'

One such customer was a woman from Zhejiang. 'She's in her early forties. She has a lover who works as a state banker back in China and he is very corrupt. She helped him with his money laundering. She bought a number of properties in the south here with his black money, and used the properties to run her brothels. Of course, her lover isn't the only corrupt official using dirty money to make even more money through the brothels here. During those six months when she visited me regularly, she kept trying to get me involved in her sex business in Southampton.'

'She must have trusted you,' I commented.

'More than that. She wanted to keep me for herself, and I

hated the idea of that,' Xing said. 'I was trying to make a living for myself. I didn't want to be controlled like that. She thought she could just buy me. She was a good customer – she spent around £10,000 on me altogether. But her domination became quite intimidating, with all her little threats about my other customers. In the end, I had to stop seeing her. I had to stop answering her calls.'

Xing said he was very popular. 'They all keep coming back. I've had six or seven customers with whom I've developed a relationship. They are middle-aged, but still fit to have a good sex life. The only problem is that they all try to interfere with my own life.'

Did he have any younger customers? 'The young ones are rare, for obvious reasons. But there was one, in her twenties, from Shandong. She wasn't bad-looking – made me wonder why the hell she wanted to pay for sex. But as the saying goes, one kind of rice breeds all kinds of people. She just had an unusually strong sex drive. Luckily for her, she was a very wealthy student and Daddy could pay for anything she wanted, including sex. I found out later that she was the daughter of a factory boss in Jinan [the capital of Shandong province] and owned a posh flat in Shepherds Bush bought for her by her dad. The flat is where we would have wild sex.' He smiled. 'It is unbelievable, isn't it? Some of us students are so in need of cash that we're taking up sex work, while other students are so wealthy that they can afford to hire us as escorts in their luxurious flats.'

Love and Money

A month after Beata left Robert, two new women began work in the upstairs flat with Trish. One was from Russia, the other from Romania. The Romanian, who was in her early twenties, had been smuggled into Britain and then sold by her first pimp for £2,000 to her current one.

Pam was unhappy about the way the business had changed over the decades. She felt that she and Trish had become reluctant participants in a system of forced labour over which they had no control.

'I was saying to Trish just the other day, they [the pimps] never stop coming, do they?' Pam told me one afternoon. Of all the flats in London, Robert had chosen hers for its excellent location, and over the years it had attracted a stream of pimps putting migrant women to work.

Romanians, both pimps and workers, seemed to be the most numerous, Pam revealed. An extensive network had been built up to exploit impoverished Romanian women wanting to migrate to western Europe for work, and Britain's ongoing imposition of work restrictions on Romanian migrants was continuing to sustain it.

Pam recalled how, back in October 2008, a Romanian man had knocked on her door. 'My niece is looking for work,' he said.

'Why doesn't she come up herself, then?'

'She's shy,' the man answered.

Of course, the 'niece' downstairs was a young woman who'd been smuggled into Britain for sex work. Pam later found out that the man not only pimped women but also sent them out to steal and shoplift. But during his first few visits, Pam didn't know all that. All she knew was that he would pick up his 'nieces' after work and 'look after' their cash for them. Later, some of the girls he ran told Pam about the full extent of his Fagin-like activities. She thought that was taking things too far. When he visited the flat with yet another 'niece', Pam told him, 'I can't help you. There'll be no more jobs.'

He was soon back, though, with another tale: 'Help me, Pam, my relatives need work. They come all the way to London. You must help them!'

'I told you, there's no jobs 'ere,' she replied. But he wouldn't take no for an answer. He thrust a piece of paper at her with his phone number scribbled on it. 'Help me, Pam. Call me when you have jobs here,' he pleaded again. But she never did.

Beata considered herself lucky. At least she had no one to take her earnings from her, no longer dreaded the end of the day, when she would have had to return to her lover-cum-pimp. And now she had a growing number of regular punters queuing to pay her for sex.

Two regulars had just brought flowers and left a £5 tip each. The experience was at least more pleasant than being verbally or physically abused.

Then a young Egyptian man came to the flat. He was good-looking and gentle with her, which made the hour-long session a lot more bearable. In the end he gave her a tip of £20 on top of the £120 fee. It was a nice change for Beata, and she showed her gratitude by telling him, 'Come back soon!'

He returned the following day, leaving an equally generous tip. 'He's such a nice guy!' Beata enthused, but Pam wasn't convinced: 'Don't think he's Prince Charming just because he gives you good tips.'

'At least he's good-looking and pleasant. What more can I ask?'

'Well, why do you think a nice-looking young man like that needs to pay for sex?' Pam poured more cold water on her. 'It's because paid sex is straightforward and hassle-free. Blokes don't want commitment – it's trouble for them, see? So don't be taken in so easily. You trust people too quickly and that's your weakness.'

Two days later, the Egyptian man returned with a present for Beata: a teddy bear with a message reading 'Every moment I think of you'.

'Getting romantic? Give me a break,' Pam sneered again. 'You get a lot of sad sods who come here for a bit of love. Has he forgotten that he's paying you to sleep with him? Is he paying you to love him now? For fuck's sake.'

Whatever his motives, the Egyptian man was soon forgotten when a new, handsome punter came to the flat. He looked to be his forties and had beautiful dark brown eyes. The first thing that he inquired about was Beata's age.

'She's twenty,' Pam lied without a blink. 'She's the youngest you can get around 'ere.'

He seemed pleased. He said he just travelled down from Luton and was meeting some people in an hour. Not too much time to spare. He went for a half-hour session and paid Beata £65, leaving a tip of £10.

'Nice and simple,' Beata said to Pam afterwards.

'I reckon you've got the most handsome punter around,' Pam commented. 'He seems civilised, too …'

'Where is Luton, Pam?'

'Above London, love. I call it the arsehole of the earth.'

'What?'

'I'm sure there's a lot of nice blokes there, though,' Pam said, laughing sarcastically.

The Luton man returned the next day.

'Beata's working at the moment,' Pam told him at the door. 'Would you like to go upstairs? There are girls up there, too.'

'Er … No. I'll wait,' he replied.

'All right. Why don't you come back in half an hour or so? She should be finished by then.'

'I'd sit here and wait,' he pointed to the stairs.

'All right, suit yourself.'

So he sat on the stairs, right next to the 'sexy models' sign. Exactly thirty minutes later, he rang the bell again.

'Nice to see you again!' Beata welcomed him.

'Nice to see you, too!' he said. He noticed that Pam was looking him up and down. 'I'll have an hour, this time.' He handed the cash to Pam.

'You've come from Luton, yes?' Beata asked as she took off her wrap.

'Yeah.'

'It's a long way to here, no?' She was wondering why he chose to pay for sex in London when there must be places closer to home.

'No, it's only forty-five minutes on the train. I come here a lot, to see my mates.'

'Oh, I see.'

'And I like Polish girls.' The man clearly meant it as a compliment, but Beata immediately became annoyed.

'Yeah, sure, your mates tell you about Polish girls? We fuck good, yes?'

'Oh no, I didn't mean that. I meant I think Polish girls are beautiful.'

So her handsome punter was just another sad Englishman with a teenage mind, Beata thought to herself while he was on top of her. 'I like Polish girls,' as though they were a make of car or a brand of cigarettes. When would they stop looking at her as a foreign exotic object? She cursed him silently. He was soon finished, and she quickly got up and went to put on her clothes.

'Wait, it's not over yet. I paid for an hour,' the Luton man said. 'Please, leave your clothes off.'

Beata had to do as he said. There was still fifty minutes to go.

He spent the time groping her, and she felt nothing but relief when the session finally ended. She let Pam see him to the door.

'He's obsessed! He's got a thing about women's body parts … I thought he was going to mutilate me!' she told Pam. 'He's not as civilised as you thought.'

A few days later, Beata had a new visitor – an Ecuadorean in his early thirties. He was swarthy and handsome, with a small beard around his chin. He couldn't take his eyes off her. They had a one-hour session, and he was back again the next day, and on several occasions after that.

He soon grew very affectionate. The sex was always followed by a long conversation in which he let her talk about herself. None of her punters had ever done that. She thought secretly that there might be something special about him. And he began to see her even more regularly – every day she worked, in fact.

'I think that man is becoming obsessed with you,' Pam said. 'I've got to tell you – that's not always a good thing in this job. You don't want obsessive punters making trouble for you.'

'He's just lonely,' Beata responded.

'As if you know him!'

The Ecuadorean man became the flat's number one regular.

'You got family?' Pam asked him, thinking he must be single if he could visit every evening.

'No. No family. Not here, not back home.'

'What do you do?' she probed.

'Some business,' was all he would reveal.

'You go home much?'

'No.'

But although he was uncommunicative with Pam, he chatted to Beata as if she were his best friend.

Sometimes, he paid just to talk to her. He would talk about life and religion – about how hard it was to connect with people and how Catholicism had sustained him through the years. Like her, he was a hypocritical Catholic who wasn't practising what the preachers had preached. She could relate to what he was saying. It was as if their common weakness – the one thing they shared – had led them both here, albeit along very different pathways. She would listen quietly as he spoke, passing an occasional remark to make him feel better about himself.

'I've stopped going to church now,' he told her. 'There's no point. I don't really live by those rules now ... Here, everything's about greed. And I've become a very weak man. No principles. No faith.'

'We are all the same,' she responded sympathetically, looking into his eyes. 'We put aside our faith and principles because we need to survive. You are not alone.'

He looked at her intensely, trying to hold back his tears. 'No one ever tells me that. No one else understands.'

Behind her genuine empathy, Beata was at the same time aware that she was being paid to listen, 'to caress a wounded soul', as she put it. She didn't want to read too much into their emotional encounters. After all, as Pam never ceased to remind her, 'A punter's a punter.'

But he seemed genuinely interested in her. He asked her to open up and give him the chance to know her properly. Beata was moved. No one in England had ever cared in the least about what she thought or how she felt. Her existence seemed to matter to no one. She could find meaning in her life only in her quest to support her son and her parents. She often woke up feeling that her disappearance from the world would not be noticed. The man from Ecuador made her feel human again. He made her feel appreciated and needed. His daily visits reinforced her self-belief, and she began to look forward to them. This was something she'd never expected.

His visits had been going on for four months, and as time passed, Beata grew closer and closer to him. One day he said, 'You know, you are too beautiful for this job.' He looked into her eyes, unintentionally exacerbating the guilt she was already feeling. He was the only Catholic she knew who was aware of her occupation and he was now challenging her.

'Are you telling me that what I do for a living disgusts you?' she asked. Before he could answer her, she burst into tears, and she couldn't stop. It was the first time her work had inflamed in her such a level of shame and self-loathing.

When he had left, Beata sought comfort from Pam. 'Why is he doing this to me? Why is he trying to make me feel bad about myself?'

'Never mind what he says to you, love! He should look at himself in the mirror. Isn't he coming here and paying for sex? Does that make him a good Catholic, then? He's the last person to take the moral high ground!'

'But Pam, he was only thinking of me. He wouldn't say these things if he didn't care for me. No other man has ever said this to me here. What he said made me feel small, but I know he's thinking of my welfare. He is not paying me to just have sex with me. He talks to me and tries to—'

'Listen to yourself! You're starting to like him now!' Pam said, shaking her head in despair.

'No, Pam, but he's not a bad guy deep down. He's got a good heart. He leads a simple life, working as a chef and earning a living with his own hands. He is a kind person. He doesn't care too much about material things, and for sure he doesn't want my money. But he doesn't want to see me carry on doing this.'

'It's all very well for men to say women shouldn't be on the game. Who do they think's going to give them a blow job when they turn up here, otherwise?' Pam sneered.

'Pam! Don't say that! He's not that sort of punter!' Beata had tears in her eyes.

'Look, if you got half a brain, you don't look for a boyfriend in this kind of place,' Pam said, frowning, getting annoyed.

'Are you saying you never meet nice guys in these places? Never?'

'Very rarely, young lady.' Pam knocked the ash from her cigarette. 'You might get a few sad weirdos who treat you like a therapist, you know what I mean? I met one of them on that last maiding job I told you about, with that girl Kris from Leeds. When the casino turned out, the men would go looking for sex, and those men were all nuisances. But there was this one regular – he always came to the flat bringing steak or lamb chops and all the trimmings to go with it. He would say hello and then get straight to cooking dinner for himself and me and Kris. He would tell us about his family and his past. He said he had two children, and his wife had passed away a year ago. Then he'd dish up dinner, as though Kris and me were his family. I think that's what he was trying to create in his mind. We would have this beautiful dinner together, drink wine and chat. Once the meal was over, Kris would take him into the room for sex. He'd pay Kris £140 and give me a £20 tip when all I'd done was just relax and watch TV, well full after the big dinner and the wine!'

'So you did meet a nice punter after all.'

'Once in a blue moon! Those were good times, though. On a really good day, Kris earned £1,400 or more. I was on 10 per cent of that plus £40, and there were plenty of good tips in that flat, too. Me and Kris had loads of chocolates and flowers brought up for us ... all the bloody time! And you know, one punter had a clothes shop, and he asked our sizes and gave us some really nice gear.'

'And what's your point, Pam?'

'My point is, don't get carried away by all this nice treatment from a few decent-looking punters,' Pam said. 'That's just part of their games. And remember, you're always playing a game when you're on the job. Don't give them your heart!'

But the Ecuadorean man continued to visit, and Beata continued to relish their long talks.

Secretly, Beata believed there was a relationship cycle between herself and 'the male race' that was destined always to be repeated. She believed herself weak and feared her weakness. The cycle would begin with affection fuelled by physical attraction. Men would win her trust with their emotional support and understanding until she began to fall in love with them. Then they would reveal their true selves, mocking her weakness, humiliating her. And then they would leave her.

Beata knew she was becoming emotionally dependent on her punter from Ecuador. He was the only man who both knew what she did and accepted her as a normal human being. Isolated as she was, she felt fortunate to have met someone like him, someone who was not contemptuous of her profession.

Against all advice, she was falling for him, and his words of condemnation were becoming unbearable. Despite her anguished justifications, he never stopped trying to persuade her to stop. She wondered what motivated him. Could it be anything other than his affections and deep concern for her? Did he have a hidden agenda?

'He just wants you for himself, that's all,' was Pam's opinion. 'It's all selfishness talking.'

'But what he said really hurt me … that I'm no good if I do this work. I was so upset that I couldn't focus on my other customers.' It was as if he was trying to love her and belittle her at the same time.

Beata went into work depressed the next day. The first punter who came into the flat depressed her further by asking for anal sex. By now, though, Beata knew just what to say. 'I wouldn't do it even if you pay me £100 for one minute – that's how much most places would charge you, no matter how long it takes you!'

Pam thought Beata was right to refuse, although not everyone was so choosy. 'I worked with this girl called Lucy. She just didn't care. Short, fat, skinny, ugly – didn't matter how the men looked, as long as they paid. She offered them anything they wanted. Straight sex, oral sex, anal sex. She let them cane her, too.

'And as a result, that place got too popular and caught the attention of a bloody journalist from the *Sunday People*, who did a big story about our flat with pictures of one of the girls and her maid going in and out of the place! That morning, as soon as the newspaper came out, the flat was raided. Thank God I wasn't there that day. What a show-up that would have been. I never went near that place again.'

After her latest refusal to leave the trade, the Ecuadorean man told Beata he wouldn't be seeing her again. He was convinced that there was no future for them – and now she believed the same. She knew she needed to get her priorities right and carry on earning for her family. Her own happiness would have to wait. As they said at home, she couldn't worry about roses without bread.

The economic downturn was affecting her own business as much as everyone else's, and today had been another bad one. Was it because of the rain? Whatever, she'd earned just £100 by the end of the evening, but she still had to pay £400 for the room. She'd need to earn fast the next day, if she was to avoid getting into debt.

Despite the sometimes astronomical earnings, debt was not uncommon among sex workers in Soho. A rental of £400 per day soon built up if it wasn't paid. One of Trish's girls had run away after her debt had become so large that it would have taken her months and months of working for nothing to pay back.

The drop-off in trade seemed to have coincided with the Ecuadorean man's departure. Beata knew she had disillusioned him with the realisation that he wouldn't be the one to save her, and now he'd given up trying. For a while, she missed him terribly. And, of course, apart from the emotional vacuum he'd left, her income had suffered, too. She thought about calling him many times, but her pride stopped her from dialling his number.

As the slack period dragged on, she tried to think of ways to make the punters return. Self-doubt began to creep in. 'Do you think I'm ugly?' she would ask Pam. 'Is that why no one comes to me?'

At such times Beata thought about leaving the trade and getting a steady job with regular pay. Perhaps the Ecuadorean man had been right all along. Uncertainty regarding what (or if) she would earn each day had become a major source of stress and anxiety. Why hadn't she listened to him? As her debt to Pam mounted, relations became strained. They spoke less and less often, and even if they avoided the subject of money, the knowledge of her debt was sufficient to make them both uncomfortable and weary. Additionally, there was the rent to pay back home in Katowice, and increasingly urgent demands from Beata's parents. Then she learned that Mariusz, her husband, had now decided to try his luck in England. He'd finally given up alcohol and turned over a new leaf; now, he wanted to help her support the family.

He called her as soon as he arrived in London. It was the first time they'd spoken in three years and it was comforting to hear his voice. At least now she had a relative here, some support. Via a Polish friend, Mariusz found work in a bakery in Wembley. It was low-paid, but regular, and his wages helped pay for Tomasz's education and English lessons, which cost £10 per hour.

Beata's mother was on the phone again. 'I got paid. I'm sending money tomorrow,' she reassured her. Her parents thought she was a waitress in a central London restaurant. She'd told the same lie to Mariusz. They never seemed to question why she could send home more some weeks than others.

'Take it easy on the work,' Mariusz cautioned. He was sharing the burden of supporting the family now. 'You're not alone any more.'

They remained estranged, but when their days off coincided they would meet and talk for hours. Beata showed him round Finsbury, and they would take long walks in Finsbury Park. He told her he liked the bakery job, which brought him a regular weekly wage of £200. Although it was meagre, especially considering the high living costs in London, he was happy that he could now at least help a little to take care of the family back home. What satisfied him most was to see their son enjoying his childhood – at last he was fulfilling his duties as a father. They were now saving up to give Tomasz a holiday in London during his school break.

Although he hadn't said as much, it was obvious to Beata that Mariusz wanted to rebuild their marriage. He seemed a different man now. Perhaps their time apart had given him time to re-evaluate their relationship. It had certainly changed him. He called her often to share with her his plans to work and live in England. In return, he asked her about her life here – he wanted to be part of it. Beata knew that it would be much easier for them to 'fight life' abroad as a married couple. She'd learned from experience how precious companionship is when you're struggling to find your place in a foreign country. She hadn't exactly coped well on her own. But at the same time she knew beyond doubt she couldn't go back to the past. She cared for Mariusz, but the days of his alcoholism, during which he had completely ceased to care for her and their son, had killed her love for him. He'd broken her trust. Now it was too late. Just as there was no turning away from the new life that she was leading, there would be no turning back to the old one. Although she hadn't told him, she'd made up her mind. She was going to ask for a divorce.

The bell rang. It was the sticker boy, Tom, a frail-looking lad in his mid twenties. His job was to put out flyers in the local phone boxes. He came in to pick up some more and have a tea break. Pam would always put on the kettle and chat with him.

Pam seemed to have a soft spot for Tom, in her eyes a young man with no prospects. 'I know your job can't be easy, Tom,' she often sympathised.

'Yeah, you're bloody right! We get arrested all the time for criminal damage – that's what the police call sticking a small bit of paper up,' Tom said. 'It's not as if we're making anything more than fag money!' But Tom couldn't seem to find any other type of work.

On her day off, Pam sometimes hung round with the sticker boys. Tom lived just a few doors down from her and she sometimes bought him a drink or two in the pub. He couldn't even afford to buy her one back. She felt fortunate that her children were doing better than Tom. She wondered if his mum worried about him.

Pam chatted with Tom about the old days, and another sticker boy she'd known called Pete. 'Pete worked quite hard, and so a lot of men called. The flat got so busy that we always had to work till three or four in the morning.' When Kris made money, so did Pam and Pete. 'We were on the same boat,' as Pam put it.

'And when I was maiding for Tanya, things got wilder. One time, Tanya made a mistake and had the stickers printed with the phone number of the man who owned flat. He chucked the lot of us out when he discovered that his phone number was all over Paddington, Marylebone and Great Portland Street.' Pam couldn't help laughing at the recollection. '"It's such a shame," Tanya kept saying to me. "His phone rang all day and we would have made a fortune."

'So me and Tanya had to pack up and leave again just after moving in. We didn't seem able to settle anywhere for long. I was beginning to feel like a nomad, betting on luck every day and getting nowhere. If I hadn't been given this Soho job, I'd probably have left the trade altogether.'

A month after that chat in the pub, Tom was arrested for fly-posting stickers for four different women from the Soho flats, and this time he got twelve months in prison. Pam was very upset. She didn't like to see youngsters getting a bad deal. She went to visit him.

'I wasn't doin' no 'arm to no one,' Tom told her. 'Just trying to make some money.'

'How did you get twelve months? It's so unfair!' Pam said.

'Because I used to sleep at this Polish girl's flat and she was one of the girls on the ads,' Tom explained. 'So I got done for living off immoral earnings, because I was staying with a prostitute. It ain't my fault whatever she was doing for a living. I was just unlucky because I had £900 on me when they arrested me. It was money I'd saved from the sticker job, but they assumed I was pimping her.'

'I know you've been unlucky, but you've got to think about getting a proper job, Tom, you've really got to.'

'Yeah, well, it's easy to say …' Tom lowered his head, whispering.

'If you was working straight, you'd be OK, wouldn't you?'

'I suppose so, yeah.'

'So while you're inside, I'll put your money in my bank until you come out. But when you get out, make sure you work straight, all right?'

As fewer punters came to the flat, Beata began to pay special attention to her regulars. It was as if she had to ensure their return. One of them, a local middle-aged man, seemed particularly interested in her. He visited her twice weekly. Before long, Beata had fallen for him. This time, Pam kept her opinions to herself, fully aware that Beata needed as many customers as she could get in order to pay off the fees she owed. If that meant developing an emotional connection with her regular punters, so be it.

Beata's latest admirer was a pilot and a romantic. His name was Karl and he had broken up with his partner the previous year. She believed that it was the pattern of his work that led him to pay for sex – just like her, he simply had no time to develop a relationship outside his job. He always brought her flowers, as if they were on a date. He made her feel special. And he told her that she was the only working girl he'd ever visited.

Beata was smitten. When she went home to Poland to spend a few days with her family, she asked Tomasz if he'd like to meet her new man. 'Of course,' Tomasz said.

'You really don't mind that I'm with a man who's not your dad?' she asked anxiously.

Tomasz looked up at her and said, adult-like, 'You need someone. If you are happy with him, I'm happy with him.'

Tomasz's reassurance gave Beata the confidence to develop the relationship further. She began to meet him outside work. Being part of a normal couple was such a liberating experience for her. For the first time, she felt she was with him as a woman rather than a purchase. They dined together, went to the cinema and strolled down the streets like young lovers. She held Karl's hands, caressed his hair and simply felt joyful to be with him. When his schedule permitted, they would spend the night together at her Finsbury bedsit. Free of charge, naturally.

It all seemed like a dream. She had fallen so deeply in love with Karl that every absence from him was like a wound. Finally, she had found happiness. And he seemed equally eager to please her. He took her and Tomasz on holiday to Majorca. Tomasz, of course, had no clue as to the circumstances leading to their meeting; he just thought it was wonderful to see his mother so happy. This was, quite simply, the best time he'd ever had. And Tomasz liked Karl. He was attentive, always careful to include the boy in their plans. Every morning, while Beata was still asleep in the hotel room, they went for a swim together. For Tomasz, it was like having his dad back.

After that, Beata found it impossible to focus on her work. She could only think of the better life she could have with Karl, a fulfilled life, a life in which she no longer sold her body, but gave it only to the man she loved. He seemed just as keen to share his life with her and Tomasz. They started planning a future together.

It was all happening so fast. Beata found the pace of the relationship thrilling, although sometimes she felt as though she was on a roller coaster that was about to fly off the rails. One day she brought up the subject of children. For her, having a baby was the way two people demonstrated their commitment to a shared existence – although perhaps psychologically she also thought that it would tie him irrevocably to her. Either way, he seemed to think it was a good idea. They talked about where they would move to, where they would begin their new life. 'Somewhere beautiful,' she said to him.

Beata clung on as the roller coaster sped forward, feeling almost dizzy at the prospect of the good times ahead. And then, a day before Christmas Eve, she realised that the dizziness was in fact morning sickness. She called him to share the good news.

'I have something to tell you,' she said.

'I have something to tell you, too,' Karl replied.

'OK. Why don't you go first?' she said.

'It's difficult … really difficult to explain,' he said, struggling for words.

'Try,' she said, not liking the sound of this at all.

'You remember that I told you about my ex?' he said. 'The woman I broke up with last year?'

'Yes …'

'Well, I've just found out that … I was just told that she's pregnant. With my child. And I've decided to get back with her. I'm so sorry, Beata. I'm so, so sorry!'

The roller coaster had finally derailed – just as she feared it might. She was both devastated and bewildered. How could the woman be pregnant with his child if they had split up the previous year? Had he been seeing them both at the same time? She couldn't get it straight in her head. But one thing was certain: there was no choice but for her to have an abortion. Now that Karl had gone, she couldn't afford to take time off work to have a baby. She went to a private clinic for the procedure, which cost her a day's earnings.

Beata felt emotionally battered. She hadn't the strength to return to work just yet. What was she going to tell Tomasz, who'd grown so close to Karl? Tomasz had no idea what had depressed his mother so much, but urged her to come home to Poland for a break. She thought that was a very sensible idea.

In the end, she spent two months back in Katowice. During that time, Beata reflected on the relationship that had been so suddenly cut short. Pam had been right all along. How naïve of her to have fallen for a man she'd met in her bed at work. The Egyptian, the man from Luton, the Ecuadorean and, finally, Karl. Each of these relationships had failed, first pathetically, now catastrophically. She should have focused entirely on work, and not allowed her emotional needs to cloud her judgment. She also thought about how much her work in England had cost her, and how much she had gained in return. Had it been worthwhile?

Leaving Tomasz to return to work in London was always painful. Beata wanted more than anything for him to accompany her. Theoretically, there was nothing to prevent it. He could move to England and go to school there. They could settle.

'Do you like the idea of going to school in England?' she asked him.

'I don't think so, Mama,' he replied, adult-like again. 'A boy in my class told me it's no good. He's been to school in England and he said you can't learn much there.' Tomasz was the best student in his class in Katowice.

Beata thought about the option of leaving England and returning to Poland to live. Would it really be so bad? But in Katowice it would take her a month to earn what she could in a day in England. She would have her peace of mind, but she would no longer be able to afford a good life for her son and her parents. No more after-school education. No more computers. No chance of ever owning a house. No more holidays with Tomasz ...

'I want him to have good time, like other children. I want him to enjoy being a kid,' she'd always told her parents on the phone.

So, for Tomasz's sake, Beata rang the airline and booked a flight back to Heathrow.

Mariusz had finally agreed to a divorce. He had become a caring husband and father since he'd come to London. He'd seen the hardship and loneliness that Beata had endured in order to provide for the family. He'd seen her strength and admired her for it. Now he had accepted Beata's assertion that they'd grown apart and were no longer suited as a couple. He respected her decision, volunteering to share childminding duties when Tomasz came to visit. Mariusz still had no idea about Beata's real job, still believing that she was a well-paid waitress. When Beata was working, Mariusz would book a few days off from the bakery and take their son on trips all over England.

Tomasz loved best the boat trip they took along the Thames, all the way from Embankment to Greenwich and back. Tomasz found the architecture along the river fascinating.

'What is that round tower over there?' Tomasz pointed to the London Assembly on the opposite side.

'I've no idea,' said Mariusz, who was still new to the city. He asked the elderly guide on the boat to explain to his son. Although neither of them really understood the guide's formal English, Mariusz heard the words 'Lord Mayor' and got the point.

Tomasz missed Beata. Although he always listened to her and respected her as if he were an understanding adult, he was still an eleven-year-old child who needed his mother. 'I don't like to be without you,' he complained one day as she left for the flat. 'Can I come with you to work?'

Beata shook her head.

'Why, Mama?'

'Because I'm working in an expensive restaurant and the boss won't like it if I bring a child with me.'

'I want to see your restaurant,' he said. 'They let in children who are customers, don't they?'

Beata clearly couldn't carry on with that particular fiction. She changed her story a few days later and told Tomasz that she had a new, well-paid job looking after an old lady in a care home where no visitors were allowed.

Despite the secrets and lies, Beata was making enough money to provide for everything Tomasz wanted or needed. She constantly reminded herself that wouldn't be possible if she returned to Poland or worked as a leek-picker or sandwich-bar assistant in England.

When Mariusz couldn't get time off and Beata had to work, she left Tomasz in the care of her good friend Jane, whom she'd met during a stroll round Finsbury Park. Beata had never met such an outgoing English person. In her experience, the locals kept themselves to themselves and showed little interest in the cultures of 'the others'. She felt lucky to have found Jane. 'She is so different from the rest of them!'

Jane's sensitivity stemmed from years of parental abuse. The pain had led her into an addiction to drugs which took her years to get free of. With no skills and no CV, Jane became addicted to something almost as risky: shoplifting. She would do it, get caught, stop for a while, and then go back to it again.

But somehow meeting Beata had begun to change her. Beata's struggle saddened her, and made her see that she wasn't alone in the world of abuse and victimisation. Beata's devotion to her son made Jane feel more positive about life. She was much moved by the bond between mother and son. She felt the urge to help them. She offered to look after Tomasz when Beata was at work, taking him for long walks in the great parks of London – complete with lots of ice cream. She'd spend all the babysitting wages Beata paid her on sweets and toys for Tomasz. By giving her affections to Beata's son, she felt she was regaining the love she'd lost as a child.

By summer 2010, Beata had managed to save enough to achieve one of the major goals she had set herself: to purchase an apartment for her family. That summer, she took a few days away from work and returned to Katowice to buy the place. It was a furnished, one-bedroom second-floor flat situated not far from the centre of town. Beata burst into tears when she saw it. She and her parents were thrilled to bits by the modern apartment with its small balcony looking out on the busy street below. That summer day, they stood watching the shopping crowds and talking about how best to decorate it.

The apartment cost £45,000. 'It's from my sweat and blood in England,' she told her best friend Anna in Katowice. But even Anna didn't have a clue that she meant it literally.

As Beata returned to London to work, her mother decided that it would be too extravagant to move into the new apartment and so rented it out and spent the rent on Tomasz's living expenses and education. Her mother wanted to relieve Beata's pressure to earn.

For Beata, being able to buy the apartment was a dream beyond words – to be able to make such a difference to the life of her family. She decided to carry on with the job for one more year. Just one more year. Then things would have improved enough at home for her to quit.

Back in Soho, Beata dragged herself into work every morning. She realised that she had returned to an unexpectedly hostile environment. Trish said she thought it was irresponsible of Beata to take time off to buy an apartment in Poland. 'We had to find someone to cover for you, you know,' she complained bitterly. 'And when your customers came to look for you, we could only tell them that you were away on holiday.'

Things started to go downhill from there. For some reason, if there was any other reason apart from simple jealousy, Trish has increased the rent, just for Beata. She said that the women there all had different levels of fees and tips to pay. The increase almost looked like a punishment for Beata's time away. It was as if she was entitled to nothing but hard work and misery, and going home to buy an apartment was too much of an achievement for Trish to bear.

Beata could now earn only about £250 per day after paying rent to Trish. And even on a really good day, when she might earn £400–600, she would have to use most of it to pay off what she owed from the previous day.

And where was the Pam she used to know? The talkative, warm woman had turned into a controlling assistant manager acting only on behalf of her sister. No more well-meaning advice, only harsh demands. What had happened while she'd been away? Why couldn't they be happy that she'd managed to help her family back home? Beata was much saddened by this change. Week after week she had to endure this new regime, the insidious pressure that Pam was exercising on her. She was now compelled to work harder – even during her periods. But one bad day would put her back in debt to Pam and Trish. Clearly, they were determined to have their money, and there was to be no negotiating about it.

Pam seemed to be sulking all day long, and Beata believed it was all about money. The women upstairs had told Beata that business wasn't doing too well. These days, Pam's attitude towards her had changed, too. She was rude, even entering Beata's room without knocking when she was with punters. Any respect Pam had shown her had disappeared. For the first time, Beata felt genuinely insecure about her position in the flat.

Her sense of insecurity grew day by day, especially when she saw that many women were leaving the trade because money had become harder to earn in the recession. She heard of brothels closing down and pimps moving women around in search of profit. She might lose her job at any moment. She had to look elsewhere for work.

Beata started looking for a second job. She searched Soho and booked herself into another working flat there. She was told that her daily fee would be £290 – a lot lower than at Trish and Pam's place.

In the new flat, Beata worked from 10.30 a.m. to 9 p.m. She got along well with the sixty-something maid from Scotland, whose sister managed the place – a not uncommon family set-up. The money wasn't as good – Beata was making only around £130 a day after rent – but she needed the extra work in order to reduce her debt.

One night, as Beata was about to leave the flat, she bumped into Paul, the boss of the flats managed by Trish and Pam. She realised that he was here to collect rent. She wondered just how many flats he owned.

'What are you doing here?' Paul asked.

'Oh, I have to find more work.'

'Why is that? I thought you were working fine with Pam.'

She decided to be frank. 'Yes, but Trish charges me too much, £400 per day, and it's difficult for me to afford the fees.'

'Really?' His voice betrayed no emotion.

'Do you think … Do you think you could lower the charge?' she pleaded.

'Look, there's nothing I can do about it,' he said firmly, without a trace of sympathy for her situation. 'Because Trish is the manager and Trish should decide.'

Soon enough, Paul picked up the phone and told Trish everything that Beata had said about the fees. Since then, she and Pam had made Beata's time working at the flat utterly unbearable.

In the following days and months, depression filled her life. Until it was cleared, her debt to Pam and Trish tied her to their flat, and every morning she woke up in her bedsit in Finsbury Park wondering whether she had the strength to last the day. She sobbed in bed before she finally sat up and got herself ready for work. Work! It had become intolerably painful, and the hours interminably long. The dreadful tension between her and those in charge was worsened by the fact that she had nowhere to turn for consolation or advice. Her work in the sex trade over the past few years had isolated her totally from society – and now she had no one. Even Mariusz, whom she met and talked to almost every week, hadn't the slightest idea about her working life in England. She felt she'd come to the end of her double life and she wanted desperately to leave the trade as soon as she could. Finally, she wanted to find a 'normal' job.

A Room with no View

As the months went by, Ming began to feel increasingly uneasy about working under Lao Chen. She kept her knowledge of his drug dealing quiet, but became more and more worried about the increased risk of police raids it entailed. Old Horse often talked about his own experience of a raid in Essex, and he'd heard about dozens of others in parlours all over the country. In more than half the cases, the arrested maids and *xiaojies* had been deported. The thought of suddenly losing work or, worse, being arrested and sent back to China, kept her awake many nights.

Ming decided to try to book herself into another parlour. She didn't tell Xiao Quan, fearful that Lao Chen might find out. Old Horse introduced her to a woman known as Ms Liu, a well-connected Leeds-based pimp originally from Yunnan in south-west China. She'd come a long way to do what she was doing – making a good profit running two brothels, both of which were full when Ming spoke to her. 'But I have many contacts with parlours in Manchester,' she told Ming. 'I can put you in touch with them. At the moment there are two places you might like to go: one is a parlour run by a Chinese man, safe and quite popular; the other is run by an Englishman called

Roger, who has two premises in town, and maybe he'll have work for you in both of them.'

Ming decided to try the Chinese-run place. She'd never worked for a Westerner and felt insecure about doing so. That turned out to be a wise choice.

I'd read about Roger in the *Manchester Evening News*; apparently he was a 'massage parlour baron' in Manchester's sex industry. He sounded like someone I should meet. I called him, requesting an interview as part of my research into the city's sex trade. He agreed, on the understanding that I wouldn't use his full name.

That evening, Roger showed up in his eye-catching purple Rolls-Royce. (Naturally, it had a personalised number plate.) The vehicle looked entirely out of place in humble Prince Street, where we had arranged to meet. Roger looked to me like a stereotypical pimp who would show little sympathy for his workers. In his mid fifties, he was overweight, balding and sported a small moustache. His inquisitive eyes were shielded by a pair of tinted glasses.

Roger was driving himself. He opened the passenger door to let me in. 'I have to say I have never seen a car like this in real life – only in the movies,' I said.

He took that as a compliment and smiled. He said he'd like to drive a little way out of town, so it would be easier to talk. He drove to the north of the city, to an area well lit by colourful neon restaurant signs. 'This is the Indian town,' he said. 'This city was once called Cottonopolis, you see, built up by the cotton mills, and the Indian people used to work there. That's why there's a large Asian population here.'

I nodded and thanked him for the background information, though I wasn't sure where the conversation was leading.

He turned on the CD player. 'You like this? It's the Gypsy Kings' version of "Hotel California".'

'Nice,' I said.

'I have a lot of good music here,' he said, flicking open the storage box. 'All from my friends.'

After a brief silence, Roger began to talk about the city's sex trade. He clearly assumed my interest would be in Chinese-run businesses. 'There are quite a few popular massage parlours run by the Chinese in Manchester. One of them is not far from my place at Shudehill. Two brothers run it. They're doing well and are even advertising online.'

He was warming to his subject. 'And there's another in Eccles – we call that Manchester's Chelsea. They charge Chelsea prices, too – £60 per half hour, £100 per hour – and they're still very popular. Open till four o'clock in the morning! They have around six Chinese girls there, aged between twenty and twenty-five. There's also the Manchester Darling in Prestwich. A two-floor business. They have seven Chinese girls, the youngest one is nineteen. They charge different prices for different punters. For the locals, they charge £100 per hour and £60 per half hour. For the Chinese, they charge £110 per hour, £70 per half hour. The manager, who's from Hong Kong, told me that the premises were registered as a guest house.'

'You certainly seem to know everyone,' I said.

'I've been around for quite some time, you see,' he said. 'I used to be in property. But this is much more fun.'

Over a glass of wine in a bar a few miles from the city centre, Roger talked about the changes that had taken place in Manchester's sex industry during the past few years. 'It's all different, now,' he said. 'The landscape of sex work has changed. Ten years ago, women from Scotland, Wales and a few from abroad got the jobs in our massage parlours through adverts and through word of mouth. In those days, you had only a few Chinese pimps bringing women in from overseas. But that was about it. Business was all quite straightforward. But now ...'

I waited for him to carry on, but he paused, and simply said, 'Now it's all quite complicated ... The market is dominated by real criminals.'

I've spoken to Roger on a number of occasions since then, and each time he's repeated what he implied during that first interview: that the city's sex trade now operated in a shadow cast by outside 'criminal elements'. 'Legitimate' sex businessmen like him, he said, are the 'victims' of this development rather than accomplices in it.

Nottingham and Lao Chen were now far behind, but Ming did not feel any less insecure. She'd let the stranger Liu pass her onto another stranger in Manchester. This is how things operated in her line of work. On her arrival at the coach station, she was met by her new boss, Ah Hui. 'The parlour's just ten minutes' walk away,' he told her. 'Very busy, but no rough punters.'

Ming found herself working with two women from China who, like her, were ex-restaurant workers, and one from Malaysia who was looking for a way to earn fast for her family. None of them had much previous experience. Between them, they were just about able to cope with the number of customers the parlour attracted. The clientele was mainly young local men looking for fun after the pubs closed, especially during weekends. Ming saw ten men on her first day, and around fourteen on average after that. There seemed little time for a break and she was rarely available to speak to me if I called after 11 p.m.

One day, Roger invited me for lunch with his business associate from Leeds. Sensing a good opportunity to find out more about his world, I readily agreed. We met at the Chinatown Gate. While we were waiting for his guest to arrive, Roger talked casually about his social circle, and I had the impression that all his female friends were in the sex trade, and mostly pimps. Coincidentally, Roger's business associate from Leeds turned out to be Old Horse's friend Ms Liu, who had put Ming in touch with Ah Hui. I decided to keep that piece of information to myself.

Liu was slim and tiny. As introductions were made, she scrutinised me closely. Her untrusting eyes said a lot more than her politely exchanged greeting. 'So how long have you known Roger?' she asked, still staring.

Liu seemed to worship Roger. As soon as we sat down in his favourite Malaysian Chinese buffet restaurant, she started to compliment him, telling me proudly that he was a 'former surveyor'. 'Roger's a reliable man and I sometimes send girls to work for him,' she said. But the admiration was mostly one way; for him, Liu was simply one of many Chinese associates.

Roger laid out a local newspaper that he had brought with him to show Liu. The headline read, 'A self-confessed pimp walked free from court after a judge was told police had "turned a blind eye" to organised prostitution.'

Liu had obviously already read the article. 'You're bloody famous!' she said. 'Calling yourself a pimp, openly, in front of a judge!'

'Look, Liu, the thing is that I admitted living off the earnings of prostitution. But the police had always been fine about it before. Like my solicitor said, the whole case was full of hypocrisy! Do you know who my solicitor is? He's close to someone up there ...' Roger pointed upwards.

'Oh, Roger, stop that,' Liu giggled. 'You told me this already on the phone. You don't want to make a public announcement here!'

'Look, the thing is, they can't tell me I'm a bad guy when they knew what I was doing all along and just let me get on with it,' Roger said, laughing with pride. 'There are over a hundred brothels in Manchester, with at least eight in the city centre. All of them are known to the police, and some owners, like myself, have regular meetings with the prostitution liaison officer of the Greater Manchester Police. Organisations like the Manchester Sauna Owners' Forum were sometimes there, too. I have witnesses.'

'All right, I know,' Liu said, stirring the rice noodles on her plate, eager to start the meal.

Roger carried on authoritatively, pushing up his thick black-framed glasses: 'The police made it quite clear that they were monitoring the activities. Their position has been that prostitution has to be managed so as to minimise the harm to women caught up in it. They said their policy is in line with government guidelines, that massage parlours would not be targeted unless there were complaints, drugs or under-age girls.' He was referring to the recommendations of a 2000 Home Office report called 'For Love or Money: Pimps and the management of sex work'.

Liu nodded, nibbling at the food on her plate.

'It was "police management" that enabled me to run two massage parlours for three bloody years!' Roger said, smiling bitterly, raising his voice. 'And there were never complaints from members of the public ...'

'Well, someone must have made a complaint,' said Liu, shrugging her shoulders. 'Why else would you have got raided?'

Roger turned to me and explained that he had been arrested following intelligence reports that some of the women working in Manchester could be victims of people-trafficking gangs. Since then, his name had been all over the local news. As he walked away from court with his eight-month jail sentence suspended owing to the 'exceptional circumstances' of the case, he began to be seen as the shrewd, unsinkable Mr Bad. His two premises in town, Foreign Touch in Cheetham Hill and Dolly Mixtures in Shudehill, became well known overnight.

Roger recalled, 'Someone gave a tip-off that one girl who had been trafficked was working at my parlour. But the police knew what I was up to ... And, as their inquiries revealed, I hadn't known about the girl's background and had never been involved in any trafficking activity. That's why the judge suspended my sentence. The judge said I'd gone into the business with my eyes wide open to make money.'

'You are a hero, aren't you?' Liu teased.

'Hero? But I still ended up having to pay the £2,000 prosecution costs.' Roger shook his head. 'All because I prefer to have foreign girls working for me.'

'So what's so wrong with the local girls, then?' I asked.

'Well, I used to take them on,' he said. 'Young single mums from the council estate, willingly selling cheap sex for a living. You think that'd bring you no trouble. But no. Nine out of ten were drug addicts. I need reliable workers, you know. And I've found foreign girls more reliable.'

'Is that so?' Liu responded absent-mindedly, still nibbling her food.

'Of course!' Roger said with conviction. 'They work much harder. They don't drink. They don't take drugs. They don't claim benefits. They just send money home, and they have no family ties here to affect their work, unlike the local girls, many of whom have kids to worry about.'

One day, without telling Roger, I went to visit Foreign Touch. Despite the exotic name, it was a shabby-looking first-floor flat. The paint on the wall of the narrow staircase was flaking and the air inside was suffocatingly stale. The women I saw there were mostly from eastern Europe and Russia. The only local was a heavily made-up receptionist with false eyelashes. She was in her early twenties and, she told me, had a young child to feed. She said she would be on the dole if she weren't working there.

Roger told me later that a twenty-one-year-old woman from Lithuania named Galina had been sent there to work by her 'boyfriend'. 'She's very young and innocent,' he said. Her pictures had been posted on a sex-for-sale web site, along with those of his other workers.

I ask where Galina was now. Roger wouldn't tell me at first. He was cautious because of police suspicion of his involvement in sex trafficking. But I was eager to understand her background and her choice of migration, and after a month of pestering he agreed to let me meet her, but only if Diane, another business partner of his, agreed. Diane was 'looking after' Galina at the moment.

Roger told me a bit about Diane's own sad past. 'She was a neglected child and an uncared-for teenager. Her mother died when she was ten and her father became an alcoholic. Diane has been working as a madam in Manchester for nearly twenty years. I trust her completely.'

I called Diane several times and tried to explain why I'd like to meet Galina. She was reluctant, but eventually agreed to see me at a brothel in Salford. Roger drove me there, and we chatted on the way. Although Roger had escaped jail, the business he was in was still illegal, and I soon found out that, to distance himself from it, Roger had effectively turned over the running of his sex businesses to Diane. Even so, they seemed to be attracting an increasing amount of attention from the authorities. Every month would see the police knocking on the door for a surprise inspection following intelligence reports. Roger was well aware that his businesses, even under new management, were still suspected of working with the trafficking networks.

As well as installing Diane as front woman, Roger had given his two premises new names: Foreign Touch, where Galina had been working, was now known as Caroline while Dolly Mixtures was rechristened Intercity.

In the Salford brothel, Roger and Diane left me in the living room with a Russian acquaintance of Roger's who was going to act as interpreter. A short while later, Galina entered. She looked even younger than her twenty-one years – thin, frail and, most of all, exhausted. She had shiny blonde hair to her shoulders and was wearing a tracksuit with white trainers. She looked like an innocent adolescent. She nodded at me without a word, biting a fingernail.

I introduced myself and asked her where she came from in Lithuania.

'A village, Viennes,' she answered nervously.

During the next three hours, Galina gradually opened up and shared her story with me. 'My parents were very, very poor. I lived with them and my grandparents in the village ... all three generations under one roof. I had a job in a food factory in the village. It paid something like £120 a month. Life is dead there.'

As a young and optimistic teenager, Galina felt suffocated by village life. She'd always wanted to leave home, to lead an independent life, emotionally and economically. 'At a Christmas party in the village three years ago, I met a girl of my age called Wioleta. I didn't find her all that interesting to talk to, but a friend of mine happened to take her phone number.' That exchange proved to be life-changing for Galina.

It transpired that Wioleta was a Lithuanian agent for a number of Albanian traffickers. Her role was to befriend young women and teenage girls, usually from impoverished villages, and send them into the fire pit of forced prostitution abroad, mostly in western Europe. Of course, Galina didn't find that out until it was too late.

'Very soon I heard from Wioleta,' Galina recalled. 'I thought: why is she calling me? I hardly knew her. But she seemed to like me. She invited me and my friend to come to the capital, Vilnius, for a visit. I thought, all right, why not? It would be good to visit new places. My friend couldn't make it, so I decided to go alone. Wioleta took me to a disco and we had a really good time. She seemed to really like me as a friend.

'One day, Wioleta called me, asking if I'd be interested in working away. She said she was going abroad and was looking for someone to go with her. Someone between the ages of seventeen and twenty-five. I didn't think it was strange. I thought she just needed some company. I was quite excited about the idea because I wanted to get out of my village and do something with my life. And then she asked me for my photos and said she'd find work for me on the internet. I started to look forward to it.

'A few days later, Wioleta said she'd found two types of jobs for me: one was babysitting, the other was sleeping with men, in the UK or Germany. I was surprised that she gave me the option of sex work. I immediately told her I only wanted to do babysitting. Then Wioleta asked me to pay £400 for the work arrangement. She was calling many other girls to help them get work abroad, so I didn't doubt her. I just thought she had many friends. And many young people wanted to leave the villages.'

Galina was full of hope as she happily left Lithuania with Wioleta one bright October morning. Wioleta had arranged for them to stop off in Tirana, in Albania, first. 'I had no idea why Tirana. But I didn't ask questions because Wioleta seemed very capable of arranging everything for us.'

In Tirana, Wioleta took Galina to the flat of a man she knew, an Albanian in his late twenties. This was not part of the plan, but Galina didn't think much about it. She trusted Wioleta. But then she overheard a conversation between them about sex work in Britain, following which Wioleta asked her again to consider doing it.

'I became really worried and told Wioleta that I was a virgin and wouldn't be able to do the work,' Galina recalled. She'd finally understood the true nature of the stopover when Wioleta asked the man to bring a friend to 'break her virginity'. The man decided to 'do the job' himself.

'I wanted to run away, but it was impossible,' Galina said, holding back her tears. She paused, sighing, then carried on. 'They were always around. They told me that I would have a "boyfriend" to look after me once I arrived in England – he would send me to work and be in charge of me. I was really, really frightened.'

Galina couldn't bring herself to tell me the details of her ordeal in that flat in the three weeks she spent there. All she could say was that she'd been repeatedly raped. That there had been no possibility of escape from that place.

When Galina and Wioleta arrived in London three weeks later, two Albanian men came to pick them up at the airport. Galina saw a return ticket to Tirana in Wioleta's hand, and when the two men took her away, Wioleta left alone in a bus, presumably heading back to Lithuania to recruit more village girls.

Galina was taken to live with the two Albanian men and another Lithuanian woman in her thirties named Gabriella. The door to her room had no lock, and she was warned not to open the front door herself and never to answer the phone. From the first day she was 'given' to one of the two men and he began to act as her 'boyfriend', not only using her for sex but selling her into brothels. She was told to hand over half her wages to him.

'When all this was going on, I still couldn't make sense of it. How could all this be happening to me?' Galina said, finally breaking into tears. I noticed that her eyes looked red and swollen and thought she probably cried a lot.

In the days that followed, Galina was made to 'self-train' by watching porn videos supplied by Gabriella, who was pimped by the other man in the house. She also instructed Galina 'how to have sex with customers during periods'. When Galina was sent to work in a massage parlour in central London, Gabriella was the person who initially approached the owner. He didn't seem to realise she was being forced to work. Or if he did, he made no acknowledgement of it.

Sex work is a business full of secrets. 'In our workplaces, me and other girls were told not to talk about our background or how we'd got into England. All the girls have "boyfriends" to control them. Then I heard about a girl who managed to run away, leaving a note to her pimp: "Don't try to find me, or I will put you in jail." I was really tempted by the idea. But I was too frightened.'

After a few days, Galina's handler started to demand all her wages. She tried to bargain, but it was hopeless. 'You're not in a position to make demands,' he said to her. Galina handled six to seven customers a day, earning £25 per half hour, £175 at best for a long exhausting day, and handed over all she made. If she brought home less than this, he would hit her.

'After a while, they said there was more business in Birmingham, and they moved me up there.' Gabriella arranged for her to work in a parlour, where a Latvian girl warned her that her pimp was someone extremely dangerous, 'whose name you should never know'. '"Pretend you are stupid," she said to me. I began to fear for my life. Yet I was living in the same house with this man, who was making profits from me. I never knew his name. He was just the boss. When he had to make contact himself with the massage parlours in town, he just used a different name each time.'

While she was working, Galina never shared with anyone the painful secret that she was being controlled, for fear of what might happen both to herself and to her family back home, whom she was sure Wioleta could get to.

A few months later, Galina was moved to Manchester to work in Foreign Touch. Galina was popular there, and soon had a number of regular customers. One of them, Joe, liked to chat after sex. He told her about the 'Albanian ladies' in Crumpsall. 'I work in a garage not far from this Albanian café on Lansdowne Road … A nice little place,' he said. 'Sometimes I'd stop for a coffee and I'd always be served by the lovely Albanian lady who apparently owns the café.'

Joe, a fifty-something divorcee, had a liking for 'eastern European' women. He had no clear idea of what 'eastern Europe' meant and imagined Albania to be part of it. 'I do stand out a bit in that café – the customers are 99 per cent Albanian,' he said. 'And frankly, I'm a bit wary of the men in there. They make me feel uncomfortable, you know?'

Galina nodded, saying nothing.

'Some of the men who go in and out of that café, they look a bit odd. They're always looking around, as if they're watching out for something. And then I heard that an Albanian was arrested near there on suspicion of people trafficking or something. Apparently there'd been a lot of raids in that area. My boss at the garage told me he'd seen police vans there … and that my favourite café had been raided, too.'

'And what happened?' Galina asked, speaking for the first time.

'The police suspected that the Albanian bloke was forcing women to work in the sex trade all over the country,' Joe said excitedly, waving his hand around. 'And apparently they'd found a woman in Birmingham who was being forced into prostitution.'

Galina looked down. She knew who he meant: a nineteen-year-old Latvian girl called Inga. She was alleged to have been kept in a house owned by the proprietor of the Albanian café (who was known to his associates as Aleksander), and sold into the sex trade. Just as she had been herself.

For a second, Galina thought of telling Joe everything. But as she looked at him, she knew there was no point. What could he do for her? What could anyone do for her?

In most brothels where migrant girls are forced to work, the managers must have a good idea what is going on, but they do nothing. In one brothel in Manchester, the manager told her to use the back door to avoid attention. At Foreign Touch, Roger had had Albanian pimps knocking on the door for years. How could he not be aware of the coercion involved?

The Albanians had arrived at Foreign Touch in the summer of 2003, though not directly. An Estonian woman named Rosie turned up, offering a girl on behalf of her boyfriend. Her boyfriend lived in Birmingham and was called Alex. The girl was called Inga – the very girl that Galina's punter Joe had told her about.

It turned out that both Rosie and Inga were doing sex work under Alex's control, though Roger continued to maintain his ignorance. 'Men like Alex always asked me if I would like to have their girlfriends working for me,' he said. 'This is how they've always approached businesses like mine.'

Like Galina, Inga felt trapped and longed to escape, but with little English, she could not even begin to know where to turn. She hardly ever spoke to anyone at the work, and had a reputation as a quiet one. While she was working for him, Roger put together her story: Inga had been sold for £4,000 to Alex, who had told her she was going to work in a café in Manchester. A while later, Alex sold Inga on to another Albanian known as Benny, who lived in Crumpsall. He kept her in the house owned by the Albanian café owner, Aleksander.

Roger said that Aleksander used to send young women from the Czech Republic to work at Foreign Touch, too. There was a twenty-year-old called Eva. 'She's the type of girl the businesses are looking for,' said Roger. She worked for £25 per half hour, £45 per hour, twelve hours a day, five days a week, for ten customers in the daytime and forty per night at the weekends.

'When Inga was at Foreign Touch, everyone was happy with her because she always said yes to continuous double shifts. Later, I heard from the receptionist that Inga wanted nothing more than to run away, but other girls warned her not to. They said she would be disfigured or murdered if she tried.'

When questioned, Roger would say that he did not know the man who sent Inga in – not directly. But I'm sure he must at least have had his suspicions about Inga's circumstances. He even used the word 'trafficking' when talking about her. He seemed to see trafficking as a growing problem in the city's sex trade. He said to me, 'Trafficking was outside of the rules in the sex trade in Manchester until 2003. Before then, I'd never even heard the term. Trafficking wasn't recognised as a problem in this city before then.'

Roger's theory was that the growing number of women forced into sex work was the result of an increase in demand among British men for both paid sex and a variety of nationalities. 'And seeing the trend, businesses want good and cheap workers, so are getting more and more foreign girls in,' he said. 'This was how the Albanian pimps found their way into the British sex industry. Where there's the demand, there's supply. And once they're in, they want to expand their business, to move outwards from London, to other cities in England. They are expanding to Birmingham and then Manchester, and I think they see Manchester as a stepping stone for cities like Liverpool and Leeds.'

As for Inga, her desire for freedom finally overcame her fear. She plucked up her courage and ran out into the street. Just like that. She realised it was easier than she ever imagined. She managed to run away and even to get one of her pimps prosecuted.

However, Roger said, since Inga's arrival in Manchester, there had been a growing number of women from Lithuania, Latvia, Estonia, the Czech Republic, Albania and Thailand coerced into working in nearly half of the city's sex businesses. Young migrant women working under duress could be found in the city centre as well as the outskirts of town. He alleged that the famous Shangri-La had Lithuanian, Thai and Chinese girls as young as sixteen or seventeen, working for pimps. He said Belle Air on Oldham Street and Cleopatra's in Bury, which had the same owner as Shangri-La, also had young migrant women who were being made to work. And the Georgian in Oldham. They'd all been approached by the Albanian pimps. Now even the escort agencies were being contacted by them.

Forced labour was no longer unusual. In fact, it was a growing trend, one Roger seemed to think he was under no obligation to do anything about.

I asked Galina whether she had thought about breaking free herself.

'Yes ... I've been feeling very depressed, for months,' she said. 'I've thought about running away many times, but they're everywhere.'

Her fear kept her compliant.

Galina had told me she had been sent to the newly renamed Intercity to provide variety for the local punters, and I decided to see for myself where she worked. It was an even more depressing location than Roger's other parlour. There in Shudehill, the brothel sat on the first floor, next to a run-down tattoo shop with posters of models on the windows, looking deserted from outside. Galina spent her shift in her tiny work room. Her pimp was always in touch and came to collect her money every day. He would park across the road, waiting for her to walk over to him with the cash.

The receptionist, Lillian, seemed to take all this lightly. She was a local woman of twenty. Despite her young age, she said she'd done and seen it all in the sex trade. She told me she'd been working in the business for over five years, three of them as an escort. Here at Intercity, Lillian worked from 10 a.m. to 10 p.m. as a receptionist for £50 a day, four or five days a week. After 10 p.m., her pay would depend on the number of punters they had. 'I used to work in Cloudnight, a massage parlour in the city centre. That was a really filthy place and the girls there took drugs. I left after two months. I picked up two jobs after that – one in a massage parlour in Oldham Street, where I get paid £25 per half hour for sex and work a couple of shifts a week, and the other as a receptionist here. I still do the sex work to supplement my wages from here. I've been doing these two jobs for two years now.'

Lillian said it was just a dirty business, that's all. At Oldham Street she'd worked with Russian women who were also controlled by pimps, just like Galina. To her, Galina was simply one of many.

Intercity pulled in ten to fifteen punters in the daytime, mostly between twenty and forty years of age, and up to thirty at night during weekends, shared between Galina and a Russian newcomer called Natalie. There were more younger men of between nineteen and thirty, mostly pubbers and clubbers, at night, especially at weekends. The most frightening time for Galina was when they arrived in groups, sometimes five or six at once. Then Galina and Natalie would have to work like dogs, having a session with two to three men at a time. Some of these younger men wanted sessions lasting up to four hours.

Intercity, now purportedly being run by Diane, continued to be contacted by traffickers from Birmingham and Nottingham. Many young women from Lithuania seemed to end up there, coerced into sex work. Rita, from Lithuania, was one, sent to Intercity by two Albanian men. Another Lithuanian woman, Daniela, soon followed. Later, Eleanor, also from Lithuania, arrived, accompanied by an English-speaking woman. All had been coerced in ways similar to Galina. And all gave their wages to their pimps.

Eleanor tried to escape once. Her pimp came to Intercity to look for her, searching every room, calling out her name. The other women workers there feared for their safety as he rampaged through the rooms, but they feared for Eleanor more. Luckily for her, she'd run far enough for her pimp not to find her, a story that brought some hope to the women she'd left behind.

A young Russian woman called Toma was less fortunate. Her attempted escape failed when her pimps captured her not far from the brothel and forced her into a car. Roger happened to be driving past at the time. He said there was no way he could have stopped them, three well-built men. Roger didn't call the police, either, believing that they would do nothing. 'Diane had already told the police about Toma being pushed around by those men, because she was worried that the problems would escalate and affect the businesses,' Roger said. 'The police went round there, but said Toma was all smiles and there was no evidence she was being forced into prostitution. So they weren't willing to pursue her case. God knows what happened to her after she was bundled away in that car.'

He continued, 'Soon after that, a young Thai woman was brought in by some London-based traffickers, and was earning her wages to pay back the £12,000 debt to the people who'd transported her into Britain. They sometimes appeared outside the parlour, too, to take her wages off her.'

Despite such episodes, Diane would later maintain she had no knowledge of the true relationship between these girls and the men who introduced them to her.

Galina's depression worsened as she continued to work at Intercity, not only living with her own slavery but watching the young lives of those around her being ruined. She had trouble sleeping and often worked with dark bags under her blue eyes.

One day, a Russian man came in. Galina had never had a Russian punter before. Galina spoke a little of the language and learned that his name was Sergiev and that he was working as a labourer on a building site in town. She couldn't say she was glad to meet him, but their shared language at least allowed her to feel some affinity towards him. And Sergiev seemed incredibly lonely: he spent two-thirds of his paid time with her talking about his isolated life in Manchester.

'I am a divorcee,' he told her. 'But I'd never have paid for sex back home.'

'And I'd never have made a living by selling my body,' she told him. And then she added, 'I'm still not making money from it, either.'

'What do you mean, not making money?'

'Someone else is making money from me,' Galina lowered her head, and all of a sudden it felt natural to reveal everything to him. She told him about Wioleta and how she'd been duped into coming to Britain.

Sergiev was shocked and indignant. 'I've heard of criminal organisations like that, but, truly, I've never really thought about the women who get caught up in it. I can hardly believe it … Such a normal massage parlour in town. I'd never imagined it could be possible that someone like you, working here, would be totally controlled by criminals.'

'Too many things have happened that I'd never imagined before in my life,' said Galina, and burst into tears. 'I have no idea how to get out of it. None at all!'

'Why don't you call the police?' Sergiev said. 'You can't live like this. You need to free yourself.'

Galina shook her head hopelessly, sobbing. 'No, no. I can't do that. They will come after me, and then my family. I'm sure they will hurt me before they can be punished.'

'But are you going to do this for the rest of your life? You are still young!'

'What do you care?' Galina turned her gaze to Sergiev. 'You come here for sex. You pay me for sex. I'm just a tool for you to ease your frustration. Why does it matter to you what happens to me?'

'I thought you wanted to do sex work. For me, that's different – if you want to exchange sex for money. Everyone sells their labour somewhere, don't they? But if you are forced into doing this job, for me that's a crime. No one has the right to put you in that situation. It's easy to do something about it. You must believe that you can escape from this.'

'My life is already ruined,' Galina said, weeping, her voice becoming weaker.

Galina's revelation had had a profound effect on Sergiev. As a migrant himself, he could relate to her wish to leave home,

even with so little knowledge of her destination country. The
desire to change and improve a poor life is so strong that it can
surpass all fear of the unknown. And certainly in Galina's case,
she thought she was to be accompanied by a friend, Wioleta.

Sergiev couldn't shake the images of Galina's imprisonment
and isolation. In fact, he felt guilty for adding to her misery
by paying for sex with her. He wouldn't have done so if he'd
known. He thought about his ex-wife, who'd left him to find a
new life. She was working on the railway back home now, as a
waitress in the restaurant car. She'd been working almost every
waking hour, but when he called her on the phone, she sounded
much happier than she used to. She'd become accustomed
to spending days and nights on the trains and was earning a
regular wage, enough to support their daughter, an ambitious
young woman with dreams of becoming a famous singer.

Galina had no dreams left. Before leaving her village she had
dreamt of giving a good life to her parents, of making the family
proud. Those dreams were all gone now. Sergiev understood
why Galina said she felt like a corpse. A person without dreams
might as well be dead. Sergiev desperately wanted to give her
some hope.

He decided to report Galina's case and ask the police to help
her. Sergiev had never been in a police station, and felt uneasy
telling the detective there how he met Galina and how she had
told him her story. But the police listened, and soon Intercity
was raided on suspicion of collusion with trafficking networks.

Galina was taken to Bootle Street police station, where she
was interviewed by a female officer with an interpreter present.
Galina tried her best to provide the details they wanted: her
background and the way she was brought into Britain. She
wasn't convinced the officer was asking the right questions,
or whether the interpreter believed her, but she carried on

answering as best she could. This was her chance to be free. She definitely remembered telling the officer that she had been 'coerced and threatened' into prostitution, and that her wages were being taken from her. She described how she was beaten by the man who controlled her.

Galina was incredulous when the police said they didn't believe she was being forced into sex work because she hadn't said specifically that she was being held against her will, or that she was being victimised, but she refused to give up. She asked for a second interview, desperate to convince them that she was being coerced. She said to the officer, 'I am frightened that the man you think is my boyfriend might find me and hurt me. He is dangerous.'

The officer promised her claim would be investigated, but Galina could tell they were fobbing her off. They were too busy trying to catch another Albanian man they were after at the time. All the questions the officer asked her were about him.

'They were not interested in me,' Galina told Sergiev after the second interview. It was clear that she wasn't going to receive any protection from the police.

'What are you going to do now?' he asked, worried for her safety. Galina's pimps had been looking for her since the raid. There was no way she could continue to work at Intercity. Where should she go? 'Come and stay with me for a while,' he offered.

But Galina suspected that Sergiev was just as much a target for the pimps as she was, and that they would soon trace him. She had to seek shelter somewhere safe. Unexpectedly, Roger offered a way out, though, as always, there would be a price to pay.

'Why don't you come to work at my new place? It's miles and miles away from Manchester. If you really want to get away from them, you can stay there for as long as you like.' Roger knew that Galina was a good worker, able to attract punters and keep them. He'd thought about moving her to his new business even before the raids.

Galina accepted the offer without hesitation. Where else could she possibly go? She had no cash of her own. She couldn't even afford a plane ticket back home. And she had no other job to go to. Penniless, homeless and with nowhere to turn, Galina remained trapped in a trade she would never have chosen to enter.

Roger's new business was in Bury, a depressed town not exactly 'miles and miles' away from Manchester. But Galina felt a little safer there. She changed her name and her SIM card. She was now able to keep some of her wages for herself and she started to save up for a plane ticket home.

Still the pimps came to Roger's businesses from all over the country. As more profits were being made – the brothels were estimated to have turned over more than £2.5 million within two and a half years – more attention was being drawn to Roger himself. The ruse of transferring the businesses to Diane didn't seem to be working. Soon after Galina had found her temporary shelter in Bury, Roger was arrested again. This time he was sentenced to three years and eight months after pleading guilty to keeping brothels and controlling prostitution in relation to a young Lithuanian woman who had been sent by traffickers to work at his premises. Roger's wife, Charlotte, was given a six-month jail sentence for laundering more than £9,000 from the brothels by using it to pay off the mortgage on their family home in Salford, a lushly decorated house with a shining marble-floored lounge. Diane, the manageress who allegedly dealt directly with the traffickers, was given a nine-month jail sentence, suspended for two years, and a three-month curfew between 10 p.m. and 7 a.m.

With Roger's sex businesses splashed all over the local newspapers, Galina knew she was no longer safe. She had to get out of Bury before the pimps found her. I hadn't been able to reach her by phone, even before Roger's arrest (he'd told me that she had run away), and I haven't heard from her since.

In the current discourse of trafficking, as Bridget Anderson and Rutvica Andrijasevic argue in their article 'Sex, Slaves and Citizens: The politics of anti-trafficking', not only is 'trafficking' reduced to 'sex trafficking of women' while neglecting other types of labour trafficking, but also an automatic link between the phenomenon of trafficking and immigration has been intentionally forged by the authorities. This is particularly so since immigration policies and border controls were tightened all over Europe at the beginning of this century. Governments of the EU have blamed 'the growth of illegal immigration' for 'the growth of human trafficking'. Within this discourse, solutions to the ills of trafficking have concentrated exclusively on immigration controls. 'Combating trafficking' has become entwined with cracking down on 'illegal immigration'.

The UN's Palermo Protocol, signed by the UK in 2000 and ratified in 2006, is not, as many have recognised, a piece of human rights legislation for the protection of trafficking victims but an international mechanism for combating international organised crime and strengthening national borders. The Palermo Protocol includes a provision against trafficking as well as one against the smuggling of migrants. The direction of the anti-trafficking policies in Britain first became evident in 2000, in the Labour government's consultation paper 'Setting the Boundaries', published during the negotiations around the Palermo Protocol. 'Setting the Boundaries' called for a trafficking offence which did not see coercion or deception as necessary elements of trafficking. Following that, the Home

Office paper 'Stopping Traffic: Exploring the extent of, and responses to, trafficking in women for sexual exploitation in the UK', published the same year, also made no distinction between trafficking and prostitution in general. Then in 2002, the first piece of trafficking legislation entered the UK via Section 145 of the Nationality, Immigration and Asylum Act.

Within this framework, protection and support for trafficking victims always comes after immigration status and controls. The National Referral Mechanism (NRM), set up in 2009, treats a presumed victim who is a non-EEA (European Economic Area national simply as an immigrant by having his or her case examined by the UK Border Agency. The forging of the false link between trafficking and immigration clearly benefits the state, as Anderson and Andrijasevic argue. In this process, the role of the state in creating the conditions for trafficking – poverty, for example – has become largely forgotten.

The incidents of trafficking I've encountered in Manchester serve as an argument against this immigration-led anti-trafficking agenda. In my experience, the majority of women who have been deceived or coerced into the sex trade are, by and large, from within the EU. These women have come from the 'periphery' of the Union, compelled by poverty to leave their homes. Poverty and social exclusion are the most significant factors in both their migration and their potential deception into the west-European sex trade.

In the context of the current anti-trafficking discourse, statistics on trafficked victims should also be treated with care. My findings in the Chinese sex industry in Britain put a question mark alongside the statistics of trafficked migrant women found in the ACPO (Association of Chief Police Officers) report 'Setting the Record: The trafficking of migrant women in the England and Wales off-street prostitution sector', published in

August 2010. This piece of research was conducted under Project Acumen, commissioned by the ACPO migration business area, 'to gain a better understanding of the nature and extent of the trafficking of foreign nationals for sexual exploitation'.

The ACPO report categorised migrant women sex workers into three groups: those who were trafficked, those who were vulnerable and those who met neither threshold. Of the 17,000 migrant women identified, 2,600 were deemed to have been trafficked and a further 9,200 were deemed vulnerable to trafficking. The report said that most of those trafficked, 2,200, were from Asia, primarily from China.

There was no examination of how the data and information were gathered and collated. The clear and simple conclusion drawn from the ACPO report was that trafficking should be dealt with more intensely as an immigration crime. While the ACPO spokesman talked of 'shutting down trafficking routes into the UK', immigration minister Damian Green pledged to combat the international crime.

In reality, the high number of Chinese nationals found 'trafficked' is a statistic manufactured by current anti-trafficking practices. It is a result of the disproportionately higher number of police raids in the Chinese-run sex businesses. I talked to workers and owners of several Chinese brothels in London and the south-east, and found that police raids affected sex workers and maids much more than the owners of the businesses. Owners were rarely on the premises, leaving them to be run by maids. Workers were often arrested and deported while the owners simply changed their mobile phone numbers and opened a new business at another address.

In one north London brothel, the owner attended only in the evenings to collect the day's earnings. When the place was raided, the maid ran away, but the owner kept the brothel open and simply employed a new housekeeper, who knew nothing about the previous raid and the risk of an arrest until the next one, when they were caught. The owner, meanwhile, just looked for a new location.

The maid at the new premises, who has taken up sex work on the side, said, 'The boss doesn't care about our risks, so when the worst comes to the worst, we'll just have to say that we've been forced into work.' Fearing arrest and deportation, Chinese workers in most raids tell the police they have been trafficked, so to avoid the worst scenario – being sent back home.

I spoke to Mr Zhu, a massage parlour owner in Southampton, about how common this situation is. He said, 'Look, 99 per cent of Chinese sex workers are doing the work at their own will. When raided and arrested, many women will tell the police that they've been forced into the trade. This is based on their perception that Britain is a country that respects human rights and a trafficked victim will automatically receive care and protection rather than being deported. Reporting themselves as "trafficked victims" is therefore very common.'

He continued, 'However, many Chinese women workers began to realise that, actually, it does not help you gain any support by claiming to be a trafficked victim. They found that, in some cases, they were released sooner if they told the police they were doing sex work voluntarily. So you see, the police figures on "trafficked victims" might soon be going down again.'

Living in the Light

The sun just came out, shining through the clouds, following a brief but heavy shower in the early afternoon. Would there be a rainbow? Beata looked up at the blueness of the sky, embracing the short-lived glittering freshness of the air as she stood at the centre of a wide grassy expanse in Finsbury Park. Savouring this rare moment of calm, she took a deep breath and sat down on a bench.

But she never let her attention wander from her son. 'Tomasz! Careful!' She called out to him. But he was exploring, climbing a jagged metal fence with the reckless curiosity shown by ten-year-old boys the world over. He wouldn't listen. Beata ran over and grabbed him with both hands, lowering him to safety. He stared at his anxious mother with sensitive, heart-melting eyes, smiling innocently at her. She couldn't bear to scold him, instead holding him tightly in her arms.

'My Tomasz!' she said, kissing his forehead again and again.

This was the first time they'd been reunited in six months. He was the most understanding child in the world, so she told everyone. He knew she was working hard to make life better for him and never complained about his lonely existence being cared for by his grandparents. He never put pressure on her; he simply looked forward to the next time he would see her. And when the next school break came, she would again fetch him from Katowice to spend time with her in London.

During such precious reunions, they often took a stroll in her local park, sometimes staying there for hours. She enjoyed its tranquillity – for her, it was somewhere both physically and emotionally detached from the routine harshness of her daily working life. Somewhere she was unlikely to run into a punter and be reminded of her other self. She enjoyed simply watching Tomasz and seeing how he had grown in her absence. At this moment, he was watching a group of girls splashing around near the fountain. He looked at her and laughed. He was so carefree, and she wanted more than anything for him to stay that way. She wanted to give him a life filled with innocence and kindness. He was the purity within her. In him lay her future and her hopes.

In stark contrast to such moments of joy, Beata's working regime in the Soho flats remained a grim drag. While she was earning more than ever, she was still struggling to pay the extortionate rental charges. She dreaded the thought of a mounting debt that could well build up further if the number of punters didn't increase, which seemed unlikely in the continuing recession. She had long nurtured a dream of eventually setting up her own little business in London: a Polish deli. Self-employment seemed to her the only way to escape the routine exploitation that she'd experienced since setting foot in this country. To achieve that aim, however, she would need to save some of her earnings, something she hadn't been able to do for at least six months. It seemed that the longer she remained in the sex trade, the more tightly she became bound to it.

One night, after work, Beata wearily caught the tube back to Finsbury Park as usual. She had run out of energy, her mind blank, and she drifted off to sleep with the slow movement of the train. She didn't realise she was dozing on a stranger's shoulder. The man, realising she was exhausted rather than drunk, didn't move the slightest, allowing her to rest. When she awoke, she discovered she'd been leaning on him.

'Working late?' he asked, smiling amicably.

'Yes, too late,' Beata responded with an embarrassed smile. 'Was I using you as a pillow for long?'

'There's no problem,' he said with genuine kindness in his eyes, shrugging his shoulders. 'Happens all the time on the tube!'

She laughed. Yes, there must be many like her, working late every night and nodding off on the train back home. But she thought strangers on the London Underground would rarely strike up a conversation – most of them wouldn't even exchange eye contact without feeling uncomfortable.

'Where are you from, if you don't mind me asking?' she said.

'Kenya. I'm from Kenya,' he replied.

'Kenya! Ah, Africa!' Beata exclaimed. 'I can't even imagine being there … I am from Poland myself.'

'Really?' His eyes widened with curiosity.

'Have you met anyone from Poland before?' she asked.

'Oh yes, of course I have. And they're not all plumbers!' he joked. 'And have you met anyone from Kenya?'

'No, you're definitely the first!'

'So, what do you do for a living?' he asked.

She paused awkwardly. 'I, er, I work as a waitress.'

'Ah! Then we're both in catering – I'm a chef.'

There was a reassuring firmness in his voice. Beata looked at his face, intrigued by his large dark eyes that seemed to shine with genuine confidence.

'I have to buy you a coffee to thank you for letting me sleep on your shoulder,' said Beata, teasing. He laughed and said he would like that very much.

'My name is Richard,' he told her as they exchanged phone numbers.

Three days later, he called her. They met in Russell Square and Beata felt as though she was going to see a long-lost friend – it was both exciting and familiar. They went into a nearby Turkish café, eager to learn more about each other. Richard was a year older than her. He'd been working as a sous-chef in a central London restaurant for three years. Still new to the city, he was optimistic about his prospects and keen to build a life here. He had managed to save a little of his earnings and, despite the expense of living in London, had no regrets about leaving Kenya.

'I like this city very much. It is right here that you feel the world is in your hands! Although I'm a foreigner, I feel quite at home!' he said excitedly. 'It is here that people like you and I can meet.'

Richard's optimism was more than a breath of fresh air to Beata. He seemed to look at everything philosophically and was always positive in the face of difficulty. His smile was like a ray of sunshine, lighting up the dark and shadowy corners inside her. His manner soothed her. When she confessed she had been suffering from depression and felt unable to cope with the pressures of work and life, he listened to her attentively, able both to relate to her sorrow and empathise with her pain. At the same time, he never reinforced her negative emotions or patronised her, as most of her Polish friends would have. Rather, he picked up the positives and highlighted them for her.

When he laughed with her, she felt a flow of joy breaking down the thick four walls of solitude she had been locked inside for so long. At last she had found someone who understood and accepted her for who she was, someone able to really connect with her and lead her out of this prison. And, incredibly, her saviour was from a background that had nothing whatsoever in common with her own.

That very difference seemed to be the precious key that had unlocked the doors between them. Any baggage from the not-so-perfect past was now shed; she was suddenly a woman with no history – how liberating it was to feel that way! The memories of her broken marriage no longer mattered. Nor those of the poverty that had compelled her to leave home. Only the present was important; the here and now they passionately shared as migrants to a new home.

For the first time, Beata had found the natural connection she'd been searching for, but which her working life had always denied her. A connection made impossible by the distorted human relationships that she'd built around work. Now, she felt she had uncovered her lost self. 'I have found my angel, my very own angel,' she told Anna on the phone.

When Anna learned that Richard was from Kenya she laughed and said, 'Not all angels are white, then, are they?'

Beata's other Polish acquaintances back home were less accepting, their reactions ranging from disapproval to disgust that she should take an African for a lover. This may seem surprising for a nation so historically suppressed, but they lacked Beata's experience of living and working in a city as cosmopolitan as London, and to them the idea of a cross-cultural relationship was entirely alien. They questioned her choice openly, and some of them were downright rude. Yet in their own minds their behaviour wasn't racist.

Beata was deeply hurt and frustrated by such opprobrium. How could these people say they were her friends if they couldn't understand her relationships? She despised their parochialism and their ignorance of the wider world. 'London is made up of people from everywhere,' she said to Anna. 'Almost everyone I meet here is from outside the country.' Her Polish friends were clearly in need of a multicultural re-education, and the closer she grew to Richard, the more detached she found herself becoming from her old social circle back home.

Beata is the kind of woman who, when she loves, loves totally, and she was falling in love with Richard. But her work stood like an unscalable wall between her and happiness. She hated keeping secrets from him, and on numerous occasions resolved to tell him what she did for a living, but she had never been able to pluck up the courage to do so, fearing the pain she might see in his trusting eyes. Yes, she hated keeping secrets, but the thought of hurting him, of disillusioning him or, especially, of losing him was even worse.

Mia, the Taiwanese *xiaojie* I'd met in Stratford, felt sorry for me when Ah Qin gave me the sack. She offered to introduce me to Grace, another brothel owner for whom she worked regularly. Grace ran parlours in Finchley and Bounds Green, which she advertised in the local newspapers and on her web site. I was to discover later that Grace was well known for employing newcomers, both Chinese and Romanian. When I rang her, Grace's first question was whether I'd be both a maid and a part-time *xiaojie*: 'Have you done *zhuangzhong* before?' I detected her tone of disappointment when I said I was just a maid who offered no other services.

When Mia found out I had no experience in *zhuangzhong*, she urged me to 'try it out'. Many housekeepers end up doing *zhuangzhong*, she said. 'All you need is a makeover.' She studied me with a professional air. 'You've still got the face for the job. You need to do it when you don't look like an old lady yet.'

Mia was going to work in Grace's Bounds Green parlour that week, and Grace had agreed to take me on at Finchley. In the morning, Mia and I left the Stratford flat together. Mia insisted on taking me to McDonald's for breakfast before we got on the train. She seemed to feel genuinely sorry for me, having been sacked and not receiving a full wage, and wanted to feed me up before my job started with Grace. Then she said she was going to buy some face cream for me as a present. 'You need to look after yourself, Xiao Yun,' she said, examining my face with concern. I knew I looked exhausted after the work in Stratford.

I rang Grace for directions when I arrived in Finchley Central. Rather than giving me the address, she kept me on the phone and directed me through every turn and corner as I walked. When I eventually reached the building she told me to knock on the back door and her boyfriend Jamal would let me in. The door was opened by a well-built Middle-Eastern young man who led me up to a first-floor flat with two bedrooms and a large lounge that doubled as Grace's bedroom and the *xiaojies'* sitting room. A slim woman was having lunch at the table as I walked in. I guessed she was in her early forties. Her hair was brushed to one side and her face was pale and exhausted. She didn't look at all well. To her left, a long-haired middle-aged woman with high cheek bones was holding up her bowl of noodles with both hands, chewing noisily. She gave a slurpy greeting, introducing herself as Grace.

My cover story was that I'd come from Zhejiang province, a single mother with a seven-year-old daughter. I'd outstayed my business-visitor visa and had been working in Britain without papers for almost three years.

The sick-looking woman, who introduced herself as Ah Fen,

soon retreated into her room after lunch in a fit of coughing.
Grace followed her, shouting through Ah Fen's door, 'You've
been sick long enough! What luck I have!' Ah Fen just carried
on coughing. 'She's been ill for two days,' Grace informed me,
clearly infuriated.

Ah Fen was just as angry with the way Grace had treated her
during her illness. 'She's been cursing me all day long,' she told
me later. 'She told me to go to hell and asked me why couldn't
I die of my sickness.'

Grace proved to be an even worse version of Linda in Bedford,
constantly vulgar and managing to include a swearword in every
sentence she spoke, the English version of *niu-bi* being one of her
favourites. Her communication with Jamal was simply a stream of
filth to which her non-English-speaking *xiaojies* and maids would
listen open-mouthed, amazed at her fluency in the language. In
fact, she seemed barely able to put together a grammatical English
sentence, her default communicative mode being to scream at
him a lot. He appeared almost embarrassed, mumbling to her like
a scolded child, 'Why baby, why are you always like this?' They
fought even during meals. Ah Fen and I often sat eating with our
heads down, not knowing where to look.

Ah Fen came from Fuzhou, in Fujian, and had been in
Britain for four years. During the first two years, she worked
in catering, like many newly arrived Chinese. In the third year
she was laid off amid increasing raids on Chinese restaurants by
the immigration authorities. A friend of hers introduced her to
the sex trade. With no skills to find other work, she accepted
immediately. She told me it was the best decision she'd made
during her time in Britain, because since then her income had
gone through the roof and the money she'd been able to send
home was making a real difference to her family. 'In a good
week, I can earn £1,500 to £2,000,' she told me.

In the evening, two men turned up while Ah Fen was with a customer.

'Do you work as well?' they asked me.

'I'm a receptionist,' I replied.

They then asked Grace the same thing. She told them I didn't do sex work, and turned them away. But the pair returned within an hour, complaining that there was only one girl when Grace had told them that there would be two.

One of them asked me if I'd be willing to do a session with him and Ah Fen. 'Can you join in?'

I shook my head. Again, he repeated the request to Grace.

'No,' she said, sneering at me. 'Apparently she doesn't work.'

'So why the hell did you tell us there are two girls, then?' He was furious.

'I'm so sorry, darling.' She tried to placate him. 'Next time you come here, I give you a discount. Next week we have two girls. I promise!'

On the first night, Grace told me I could sleep on the sofa in the same room as her and Jamal. I didn't feel comfortable doing that, so I went to sleep on a mattress on Ah Fen's floor.

The next morning, Grace was arguing with her boyfriend again when I went into the main room to clean the floor. She shouted at him as he asked her for hundreds of pounds in cash. I overheard him tell her that he was going to see an estate agent to rent a flat for her new premises. Grace saw me looking and explained that her plan was to set up the new business herself and let me look after this one.

Grace thought Jamal was asking for too much money. It didn't appear that she trusted him – and, to be fair, he didn't look trustworthy either. There seemed to be no bond of affection between them; it was as though he was just hanging around her flat because he had nowhere else to go. There was something odd about their relationship, even beyond the fact that she was in her forties while he was in his early twenties. They could hardly understand each other, let alone communicate. When she shouted at him in her usual mixture of broken English and Chinese curses, he would try to hug and kiss her. It seemed clear that he was a kept man, but what was Grace getting in return? Presumably it was his legal status that made him useful. Or his body. It certainly wasn't his intellect.

The following day Ah Fen seemed even worse, but just after 9 a.m. an elderly customer came in and spent three hours with her. (He paid £80 per hour and gave her a £20 an hour tip.) Apparently, the man was a regular and always prepared to spend. 'He doesn't have intercourse with me, just enjoys touching and watching me,' Ah Fen told me at the end of the session. 'But even that was exhausting!'

Grace interrupted us. 'Your room needs a spray of vinegar,' she said harshly to Ah Fen, meaning that her room was infected by her illness. This was an insult, but again Ah Fen said nothing back.

Grace tried to find someone to replace Ah Fen as she became more ill, but had no luck. Once, when Ah Fen was busy, she even put on her 'work clothes' and said she was one of the girls, but the customer said he wanted someone slimmer and left. Grace spat curses after him, though it must have been humiliating for her to be rejected in my presence. (That punter had a lucky escape. Later that day I heard Grace telling a friend on the phone that she had a sexually transmitted disease.)

Ah Fen gave me her mobile phone and asked me to read out the names in her address book. 'My friend put them in for me, but I can't understand them,' she said. As I scrolled through the Chinese characters, I realised she was illiterate. This was the first time in England I'd met a Chinese migrant who couldn't read or write. Although she didn't reveal much about her background,

I imagined that she must have come from a village and had led a tough life before she left. She called her teenage son almost every day. She said she needed to hear his voice.

Grace kept up her campaign to talk me into doing sex work in order to help out with the business. She repeated the lecture every time a punter complained about there being only one working girl. Grace said she would help me dress up and look the part. I had the feeling she'd done this kind of recruitment many times before.

'You will be grateful to me for leading you into sex work,' said Grace, sitting on the sofa with her hair in a towel after a shower. 'No one in this trade can avoid doing it.'

Ah Fen had taken £540 that day, out of which she kept half. 'You see, Xiao Yun, where else are you going to make such quick cash? In a restaurant kitchen? In a factory?' Grace sneered and shook her head.

Ah Fen continued to exhibit an uncomplaining attitude towards Grace, her situation, her life. She appreciated that some people, people like her, were much less fortunate than others and had to start out from the bottom of society. 'You have to make the best of what you have, even if you have little,' she said. I looked at her tiny figure when she greeted each customer who came to her door. That body of hers, I thought to myself, is the only thing she believes she has, to keep herself and her family's heads above water. Ah Fen spoke no English other than 'how long?' (do you want?) and '£90' (per hour), '£50' (per half hour) and '£40' (per twenty minutes).

One day, Grace asked me to show her my iPhone. I carried it in my shirt pocket and had been using it to make sound recordings as part of my undercover work. 'Jamal's friend has the same phone and he's just lost it. Take the phone out of your pocket and let me have a look if it's the same one.'

'Are you accusing me of stealing?' I was infuriated.

'I just want to have a look. I'm going to call him to see if it's the same make.'

'Why don't you call him now?' I said.

Grace looked embarrassed and went into the front room.

Following that incident, she became harsher with me. She'd lost face because she hadn't been able to justify her accusation and she resented the fact that I'd challenged her. Her approaches to me to do *zhuangzhong* became more insistent. In the end, she called me into the front room. As I stood before her she said coldly to me, 'I have two choices for you: do *zhuangzhong*, or leave.'

'Why can't I stay as a housekeeper here?' I asked.

'I don't really need one,' she replied. 'Anyway, all my previous housekeepers have done sex work to help out. And they were grateful to me for giving them the chance to make a lot more money than just maiding. You understand?'

I remained silent and waited for her to continue.

'Besides, your ability to speak English is an asset and it will bring in more customers,' she added.

Still I said nothing, and she demanded a decision: 'I give you half an hour to consider it. Now get out.'

Thirty minutes later she called me back and I told her politely that I didn't think I wanted to do *zhuangzhong*, but that I would ask a friend's advice.

'You naïve, stupid cunt!' she shouted. 'Your bloody friend will only look down on you! What do you need advice for? This is not something you tell the world about!'

Then she tried a different tactic, using traditional moralism in an attempt to weaken my resolve. 'Don't you ever think about your daughter? And your parents? What is a little sacrifice for your family? Isn't this the reason why you are here, to make money for them?'

I listened quietly as I felt the weight of her argument. I looked at her, her tightened eyebrows and her intense gaze – she meant each of those words. She had been there before. Then she raised her voice slightly. 'If you don't bring cash back home, you are nothing.'

She believed in what she said and those words began to burden me – even though I was just a journalist working undercover. She knew that the fulfilment of familial duty was often assessed by material gain. For migrants, this is something at the heart of their work journey abroad. To succeed, or not, in supporting your family and accomplishing your mission was crucial for each and every migrant I met who was working in the sex trade. As Grace looked into my eyes accusingly, I began to feel that heavy weight of moral duty and responsibility on my shoulders. As a migrant myself (I still feel an 'outsider' today), I could imagine how difficult it must be for someone in my undercover persona's position to resist Grace's arguments.

In her early days in England, she had no doubt herself been judged and assessed – and much critiqued – against these values she was now evangelising. 'These days, even children judge their parents by money,' Grace said, smiling cynically. 'My son wasn't happy with me when I didn't send money home.'

I listened, wondering about her past, trying to imagine her as an exploited newcomer. Had she made the same sacrifices as other migrant mothers here, trapped in the role of absentee breadwinner for their families? That role seems the sole justification for the lives migrants lead here.

Grace continued with her assessment of 'success'. If you can feed your family with your earnings, you are average, she said. If you can build houses and really improve their lives, you're counted as successful. 'And if you can make so much money that you can afford an affluent lifestyle, then you are everyone's envy and your family's pride,' Grace said with conviction. She clearly wanted to achieve that affluence herself. She prayed to a smiling wealth Buddha every day, burning incense and placing fresh fruit and flowers in front of his pot belly. The pursuit of money by any means available is, in her eyes, a positive contribution to her future life and to her family. As long as she brings a lot of money home, she enriches the family name. Of course, they will never find out how she has accumulated her wealth.

In the end, she agreed that I could work for the rest of the week. I think she was still hoping she could change my mind.

Grace told me that I wasn't allowed to go to sleep until the flat closed at 2 a.m., even if there were no customers. I was utterly exhausted at the end of each day, having started work at 7.30 a.m. Grace became harsher as the week went by. Ah Fen said to me that Grace would treat me better if I'd agree to take up sex work. 'All you have to do is take one or two customers a day. No more than that. And see how you fit,' she said encouragingly. 'I can give you some work clothes. Why don't you try them on tomorrow? Grace will be so happy with you.'

Grace's verbal abuse lasted the entire week. If you believed her, I couldn't even do housekeeping, never mind *zhuangzhong*. From sweeping the stairs to cooking, she gave me her detailed criticism on a daily basis. Meanwhile, her campaign of persuasion carried on. One afternoon, she asked Ah Fen to train me to massage customers. 'You give them forty minutes of massage, heat them up and then give them sex,' said Grace, face down on her bed while Ah Fen sat on her back massaging her.

Then came the most unpleasant part of the training. 'Come over here,' Grace ordered me. 'Massage my forehead.' Her greasy forehead.

Later, three punters turned up while Ah Fen was working. Again, Grace tried to persuade me to take one. I refused, of course, which really angered her. She stormed into her room and quickly put on her work clothes, but was refused by all three punters, one after the other. I'd never seen her looking so humiliated. That was the last straw. 'Fuck off,' she said to me. 'You're just not for this job.'

I'd been sacked again.

Not long after my dismissal, I received a call from Grace. To my surprise, she wanted me to go back to work – not in Finchley but in Bounds Green, where she had just sacked another housekeeper, a Chinese man in his forties. She'd taken on a male housekeeper to improve safety and security, but now preferred a female, presumably because women could be trained to do profitable *zhuangzhong*. Perhaps she hadn't given up on me after all. Or maybe she just wouldn't admit defeat.

As I arrived at Bounds Green, a Romanian woman named Cathy was surprised and delighted to see me, a new female maid who could speak English with her. She hadn't previously been able to hold a conversation with anyone there. She soon made up for lost time, revealing to me how exploitative and abusive Grace was as an employer. Many Romanian women had been taken on by Grace as soon as they'd arrived in Britain. Some had had their work arranged even before they left home. Grace employed European women in order to 'provide variety' to customers, but she had never treated them with any respect. I could vouch for that myself, having heard her shouting constant abuse down the phone. Grace's pet name for Cathy was 'you ugly cunt'. Apart from verbal abuse, she treated the Romanian women like cargo, swapping them around in her premises as she pleased. Sometimes she had them working in both Bounds Green and Finchley on the same day, 'to cover busy times'. Refusal to go where they were told meant the sack.

My new position wasn't permanent. I was needed in Bounds Green just for one day. Two weeks later, I called Grace and asked for more housekeeping work. I wasn't really expecting her to say yes, but she did. She even seemed glad to hear from me. 'Come to Bounds Green tomorrow,' she said.

Grace opened the door herself when I arrived at 9 a.m. the next day. She didn't say much, but showed me to a broom-cupboard-sized room. 'This is yours,' she said, pointing to the coffin-sized space, which had room only for a single bed and a chest of drawers in which I was to put all the cash. Then she gave me a gift, to show good will. 'This is for you,' she said magnanimously, handing me a snack pack of watermelon seeds and nuts.

Grace didn't explain my readmission to the fold, but Mia, who was working there that week, told me the place had been raided by the police the previous day and the maid had run away. Grace was planning to hire a new housekeeper from Malaysia to work in Bounds Green and had got me back to cover the gap until he arrived.

Leaving me to hold the fort, Grace returned to Finchley. Soon Andrea, a twenty-five-year-old Romanian, arrived and I met her at the bus stop outside.

Grace's lack of respect for her Romanian workers became obvious when Mia told me I had to inform Andrea of the rules here: Chinese *xiaojies* are the 'priority' and customers are sent to them first. Non-Chinese women are treated as secondary, only 'helping out' and acting as *zhuangzhong* when either the *xiaojies* are busy or when the customers don't want a Chinese girl or they ask to 'double fly'. This was Andrea's first day, and she was furious when I told her the rules. She said she'd rather leave than work under such unfair restrictions. Grace tried to calm her down on the phone (Andrea was apparently quite popular among the punters in other brothels) and, in the end, a compromise was reached by which Andrea was allowed to keep her door open when punters arrived, so they could opt for her if they happened to notice her.

Beata carried on working in Soho while maintaining a relationship with Richard. She couldn't afford to quit the job, at least for the time being. As the relationship with him became more intense, she found herself becoming the liar that she detested. She would go to work at noon as 'a restaurant waitress in the West End', saying she couldn't see him in the evenings because she was too tired.

She had maintained the fiction for three months, and knew Richard had never doubted her: catering jobs in London are infamous for their long, anti-social hours. As a chef himself, he knew that only too well.

However, the more he trusted her, the more unbearably guilty she felt about not telling him the truth. More than once she imagined how she'd tell him. She rehearsed the story in her mind, over and over again. But when she saw him, the words failed her.

Then he asked her to move in with him. She was thrilled. This was the type of relationship she had always wanted: a meaningful, potentially long-term one with a decent man who relied on his own skill to earn a living. How could she let him down? How could she let herself down by allowing this chance of happiness to pass her by? Beata saw no option but to leave the sex trade. If she was going to live with him, she had to end all her ties with it straight away. Her mind was made up.

Predictably, Pam wasn't happy. 'We're short of people at the moment,' she said grudgingly. But Beata believed Pam and Trish were simply jealous. It was as if her departure finally meant that she had found an alternative to the grim and hopeless working life they offered her. She was no longer desperate and dependent on them. She was right; they weren't really short of workers. Within a few days, Beata's job was filled by a new woman who'd just arrived from Romania.

Beata's regular punters continued to ask for her. Losing Beata meant losing business. Pam became anxious and called Beata a fortnight after she'd left, pleading with her to return. But by now, Beata had found herself a new job in a new trade, tending bar at an Italian fast-food restaurant in central London. She'd had some previous experience of bar work back in Katowice, and fitted in well with the other mostly young migrant women who were accustomed to casual work and low wages.

So there she was, working five- and six-hour shifts for £5.80 an hour. Her colleagues were mainly temporary, some of them students, and most working no more than twenty hours per week. Beata found the short work hours far from sufficient to make ends meet – she had £86 to take home after fares – but the manager wouldn't increase her hours. The more 'temporary' you are, the fewer rights you have. She now understood the basic rule of casual employment in the catering capital of Europe.

Not only were the wages difficult to live on, the work regime was harsh and the manager had a foul temper and often bossed her about. All in all, this job wasn't much easier than sex work, and the hardship wasn't even compensated by good money! She dragged herself into work every day, wondering whether she'd made the right choice.

Beata's only consolation was that she could live with Richard and share her life with him openly. No more secrets or guilt.

She no longer had to live a double life. She moved out of her Finsbury bedsit and into Richard's one-bedroom flat in Lewisham. She had fought so long to reach this stage and was eager to rebuild her life. For the first time, Beata felt that she was truly living in Britain. She now had a place to call her own, a man she loved and a social life. She and Richard took trips together on their days off. She'd never been so happy.

Soon enough, they became inseparable and, almost inevitably, Richard proposed. Beata was naturally overjoyed, though she realised that, in some ways, her acceptance would herald a new set of difficulties. She now had to face the criticism of her friends and family.

'Richard is a skilled chef, a talented and hard-working young man,' Beata repeatedly told her parents and friends in Poland. But none of them could accept him. It was as if his personal qualities and capabilities were irrelevant. All that mattered to them were their 'cultural difference' and the colour of his skin. She tried to explain to them that London was a multicultural world city, but they didn't care. They argued with her bitterly and tried to convince her to change her mind. How could her own parents not be happy that their daughter had found a kind and caring man to look after her? Every time she called them, it ended in tears. It was so very unfair that they, her birth parents, were unable to see the man she loved as a human being.

Beata's parents refused to attend their wedding or even give it their blessing. They made it sound unlawful. Beata was heartbroken. She expected some prejudice, but she never imagined them taking it so far as to effectively disown her. She was utterly shocked and appalled by the racism of her family and friends. How could she carry on loving them? She had never felt so far from home.

When she and Richard finally married, only Richard's friends were there. Beata's parents did call to give their grudging acceptance of Richard as her husband, but they couldn't make it to the wedding and none of her friends wanted to be there either. She felt so alone, and also ashamed – ashamed to be Polish, ashamed to bring such humiliation to Richard and to their relationship.

Despite the contempt Beata's family and friends showed for him, Richard never held a grudge or blamed Beata for it. On the contrary, he respected her for her courage to abandon her familial and social circles to be with him. What she had done made him love her even more. He committed himself to looking after her as best he could, working all hours to pay the rent and save for their future. Beata, though, felt guilty that her wage at the restaurant was so meagre. She felt guilty for depending on him.

Beata wanted it to be fair. She thought about her failed marriage back home and was frightened of repeating her ex-husband's mistake: of becoming as dependent on Richard for money as Mariusz had been on her. But each day of cheap labour at the Italian restaurant reminded her of those early days of toiling in the salad factory and the sandwich bar. Deep down, she knew that the only job that would make her economically equal to Richard was selling sex in Soho.

The temptation for her to return to sex work was immense. It would be so easy – she was experienced now, and Pam would have her back like a shot. No, that was unthinkable. But she needed some way to increase her income. What if she were to work just two or three nights per week at the flat? As long as she didn't get drawn back to relying on it as her only job option, then that would be fine, wouldn't it? As she thought hard about these possibilities and tried to justify her return to the sex trade, a madam at a Soho flat rang offering work. Beata had worked there once to cover someone's leave. It wasn't a bad place and was always filled with punters.

She returned from work that evening, exhausted, to find yet another bill on the doormat. Richard wasn't home yet, still working overtime. She sat at their kitchen table alone, thinking of a hundred ways to help Richard by bringing in an extra income. She tried to pray – she hadn't done that for a very long time, ever since she felt God had stopped listening to her. She had found happiness at last, but she didn't seem able to hang on to it. She despised herself for her inability to earn a good living in the world 'above-ground'. Help me! she prayed. But where was she going to get help from? She had to depend on herself – just as when she'd decided to remain in the sex trade two years earlier. She must now go back to it. There was no alternative.

Beata made her plan: she would not resign from the bartending job, but would supplement her wages by part-time sex work. She would call the madam in Soho, and if that proved fruitless, she would call Pam. All she'd need would be two or three nights' work a week. No one would know about it.

The next morning, Beata awoke to the sound of her neighbour's music. It was one of her favourite songs by Marvin Gaye. The loud tunes from upstairs could keep her in bed listening for ages, although, despite their common taste in music, she'd never met the neighbours. 'I Heard it Through the Grapevine' filled the room. She turned her head and looked at Richard, still deeply asleep. He'd had a long day yesterday, working in the kitchen. He looked so innocent and kind, even in slumber. That innocence and kindness made her heart ache.

How could she even think of deceiving him and returning to sex work? What would that make her? She was aware of a suffocating pain in her chest as an immense feeling of guilt overwhelmed her. She couldn't possibly return to the working flats. She looked at her husband's face again. She caressed his curly black hair, kissing it, over and over again.

Going Home

Ming had been out of contact for months. The next time I managed to talk to her she had left Manchester and was working in a brothel in Portsmouth. She would travel to wherever the job was, north or south.

Ming had stumbled across her new position when she was introduced to a Chinese man whose friend was setting up in business on the south coast and was looking for staff. Her new boss was known as Da Ding, literally the Big Nail. When he picked Ming up from Southsea railway station, Ming was surprised to find that he was quite different from other parlour owners she'd met.

In his strong Hebei accent, Da Ding seemed to like to make fun of his own misfortunes. The first thing he said to Ming was that he had ended up running a brothel because he had run out of options. 'Coming to England was a real liberation for me and my family at the time. I thought to myself, I'm going to find every possible way to make money, even if it is a job involving carrying coffins,' he said with a wry laugh. 'And through these years, I've done all jobs under the sun, believe me. From dirty kitchen work to building site, and then to selling DVDs on the streets. Now I've got nowhere else to go. It's either running a brothel or returning home with half-empty hands.'

'You went to sell DVDs on the street?' Ming asked, surprised. Could Da Ding have once been as desperate as so many other Chinese migrants she'd met? As desperate as she had been?

'Sure I did!' Da Ding laughed again. 'But I couldn't really survive by selling DVDs. The last straw was when I was robbed by a gang of kids who lured me to an empty building site and forced me to give them everything I had in my rucksack ... £100 worth of DVDs. That was it, I thought to myself. And then two weeks later, someone told me there was a vacancy for a housekeeper in a brothel near Heathrow Airport. Without a doubt, I knew I had to take up that job.'

'So what happened then? Didn't the housekeeping job last?' Ming asked, looking at Da Ding and remembering her own days working as a brothel maid.

'I was getting £200 a week keeping the place, but it was very stressful, given the type of punters we used to have over there. One of them asked for a refund after he'd finished, and when I refused to open the door to him later on, he got violent and smashed the windows. *Xiaojie* got frightened and ran away. That place was doomed ... Then someone told me he knew a madam from Xian who was searching for a business partner. I thought to myself, why not? If you have to take risks working in this trade, you might as well go all the way and make more money.'

'So you opened a parlour, just like that?' Ming asked.

'Why the hell not? In England, you just don't know where life will take you. You've got to make cash while you can.'

Da Ding didn't have a posh car like Lao Chen, or the haughtiness of Linda and Sarah. He was much more down to earth. He and Ming caught the bus from the station to

Portsmouth's North End. Ming stared apprehensively from the window as they passed through the run-down streets. 'It's rough around here, a high crime rate, a lot of drunken locals,' Da Ding told her. 'We don't go out of the house unless it's necessary. Come on, this is our stop.' They walked silently into Havant Road, a quiet residential street. The parlour was an old two-storey, three-bedroomed terraced house.

'We only moved in a few weeks ago,' Da Ding explained as they entered the half-empty building. There was nothing in the lounge but two plastic chairs and a dining table. 'Business has just started up. Ay, not easy! The three of us, me and my partners, have invested £3,000 in total, so far … including the costs of rent and advertising. I've spent all my earnings from the DVD job. You will be our second *xiaojie*.'

A woman in her forties walked slowly down the stairs. Da Ding's business partner. She yawned and nodded at Da Ding. Then she turned to Ming. 'So you're here,' she greeted her. 'Come and sit down,' she pulled the chair towards Ming. 'Da Ding told me you're from the north-east, yes?'

Ming nodded.

'This is a new business, as you can see,' the woman said. 'Let me explain a few things.'

Ming listened attentively.

'You'll work here for two weeks, and then we'll have someone else for the two weeks after that. If you do well, we'll be able to book you back here next month.'

'OK,' said Ming.

'The rate here is £50 per half hour, £90 per hour. There's also escort service. We share the money half way, like everywhere else.'

Ming nodded. The rates were standard; other *xiaojies* had told her they had remained more or less unchanged over the last decade.

'The good thing about working here is that we pay a £100 daily base fee for the *xiaojie*,' the woman said, raising her eyebrow. 'So even when the worst time comes and there's few customers, you can still be sure to earn something every day.'

Another middle-aged woman came downstairs at this point – Da Ding's other business partner. Her hair was cropped to her white collar and she was wearing blue denim pedal pushers. She surprised Ming by speaking English to Da Ding. 'So tired! I'm so tired!' She shook her head hopelessly.

'Yes, yes,' Da Ding giggled, nodding to her. Like Ming, he couldn't speak more than a few words in English.

'You speak Mandarin?' Ming asked the woman. 'Where you from?'

The woman gave Ming a curious stare and smiled. 'I'm from Vietnam, darling,' she said, evading the question.

On most days, the two women were absent, and they left the daily chores to Da Ding. 'They think I'm new to the trade and I still need to learn the rules. They leave me in charge of all the housekeeping duties, and pay me £200 per week for that. So I'm working more like a maid here rather than their business partner,' Da Ding said cheerfully. 'Anyway, we're sharing the profits three ways, that's the important thing.'

The first few days were really quiet: no more than three punters a day. The men here appeared different from those in Nottingham or Manchester – they were even more aggressive. On the first day a white man arrived asking for a 'student'.

'Your boss told me you were a student,' he grumbled, 'but you look too old for one!' The Vietnamese woman had obviously lied to him on the phone.

Da Ding tried to calm the man down. 'She's good! Excellent service!' He put his thumb up and eagerly tried to sell Ming to the disappointed customer.

'No, no, I want a younger girl! A student!' The man became infuriated.

Ming stood listening silently as her merits were discussed. She'd never been so rudely rejected.

'For someone her age, I want half price,' the man argued, raising his voice impatiently.

The two women wouldn't have liked that. Da Ding had to let the man go. 'No, we don't do discount like that. I'm sorry. In two weeks' time we will have someone younger.'

Complaints from punters about age or appearance are obviously not a good sign for *xiaojies*. Ming thought she probably wouldn't be asked back after her initial fortnight. But Da Ding, having been a worker himself, was sympathetic. 'Sit down. Take a rest. No need to worry about punters like that. Either they like you or they don't. You'll just have to book yourself into the places where you're popular.'

Ming sighed. She knew that there was a limit to how long she'd be able to carry on. She needed to find as much work as she could before she was too old.

Da Ding tried to cheer her up. He told her about his past and the unusual jobs he'd done. He was from a village in Gaocheng, in Hebei province. 'I'm a peasant, you see,' he said merrily. 'My village had 4,000 residents who made a living growing sweetcorn and soybean, and half of them had left to make a better living abroad, in South Korea, Australia, Canada, the US and Europe. They were all aged between twenty-five and forty-five. There are few opportunities for the village youth – apart from agriculture, there is nothing. So people were leaving, wave after wave. At its height, around 500 villagers left in one go. Most went to South Korea.'

'How much does it cost to go there?' Ming asked, curious.

'South Korea is a much cheaper option, you see, costing

up to 40,000 yuan (£4,000). But our villagers have no proper papers when working abroad, so they tend to work in difficult circumstances, you know, without protection … and sometimes put their lives at risk. There was a big fire not long ago in a factory in South Korea, and most of the dead were from Gaocheng.'

Da Ding said his family land was only 4.5 *mu* (about three-quarters of an acre), which brought an annual income of 3,000–4,000 yuan. 'We used to be taxed heavily – 70 yuan for each *mu*. That was why people were leaving farming. I stopped working on the land in the 1990s and became a railway salesman, trying to bring in more income. My job was selling plastic toys to passengers on the Shijiazhuang–Beijing line. And I was bloody good at it!'

Ming had to smile at his comical facial expressions and that pair of large round childlike eyes that were now shining with nostalgia.

'And you know,' Da Ding recalled, revealing white teeth, 'I had charisma! Yes, I attracted many passengers, especially women! I was very good at holding my audience's attention. When I was younger I used to be a good Party member and made endless speeches in my village.'

'I can see what you mean,' Ming teased, smiling.

'I had talents beyond those of a toy salesman, though,' he said. 'I loved oil painting, and spent years developing a style of my own. I used to paint folk art.'

'Really? That is amazing!' Ming was genuinely impressed. She hadn't expected to find a folk artist in a place like this.

'But you know, in the villages people don't value art. They think about more practical matters – the weather, the crops, the harvests and their earnings,' Da Ding said with a shrug. 'In my village, painting was considered intellectual. I was seen as an idealist who thought he was too good for manual labour, "real" work. I didn't mind. To be honest, the villagers were right. I'd hated physical labour since I'd been made to join the village production team at eighteen. I frequently sneaked away when everyone was toiling in the fields, and sat in the shade under a tree, drawing the landscape around me. I truly enjoyed those rare stolen moments of solitude when I could simply concentrate on painting …'

Ming listened with growing incredulity. How had such a free spirit ended up here, in this dark hole of underground work in a foreign country?

'You know, I became a kind of a local celebrity later, through the sale of my art outside the village,' he continued, immersed in the memory. 'Eventually, I was given an award by the local council for my contribution to the cultivation of art in the region. I still have that certificate at home. Just as well I didn't bring it with me to England – that piece of paper would have revealed my true identity. Anyway, none of the villagers thought much about that achievement because, for them, an award for art wasn't real. Art wasn't real. They were only concerned about putting food on the table, and who can blame them? But you know, I suddenly became the talk of the village when I was invited to go on a two-week cultural visit, along with other much better-known Chinese artists, to Britain. I couldn't believe it myself – how could a peasant like me be given such an opportunity? For us, just going abroad was just unthinkable, let alone a cultural tour.'

'That is truly unbelievable,' Ming said, her eyes wide. 'You must have been gossiped about in every household in your village.'

'I'm sure I was,' Da Ding said, looking proud. 'I funded my trip to England with the money I'd earned from selling my paintings.'

'And as a painter, I guess you fell in love with the country the moment you saw it,' said Ming.

'During those two weeks, my eyes were opened. It felt like I was seeing clearly for the first time in my life. I thought to myself how different my paintings would have been if I had seen this place long ago ...'

'You must have seen much more of England than I ever have,' Ming said wistfully. 'I've spent most of my days inside these parlours.'

'You'd think so, but I'm not much better. In fact, I saw more in those first two weeks than I have in the years since. I was so impressed by how much space there was here ... and the rule of law and the institutions that work, you know what I mean. It is anarchy back home – only the fittest survive.'

Ming nodded. 'I felt exactly the same, until I started to work in this trade ... Anyway, what happened after your two-week cultural tour?'

'Remember, I had been a poor peasant all my life. I had a wife and child. I knew that this was the only opportunity I would ever have to improve life for them. I was a good Party member, but my loyalty to its ideals had not brought me and my family a secure livelihood. I was forced to make a choice. The night before the delegation was to return to China, I ran away.'

'You have courage, Da Ding,' Ming said sincerely. 'That was a brave decision to make. But a sensible one, too. I hope I'd have done the same.'

'Everyone I tell this story to says that. Of course, I'd soon outstayed my visa and become paperless.'

'Do you still paint?' Ming asked. 'Chinese paintings would sell for a good price here. Have you thought about that? Then you wouldn't have to be in this business.'

as utilising mystical 'ancient wisdom'. However, interwo
with these supposed medical benefits is a perception tha
'Oriental' females (in reality, migrant mothers trying to provide
for their families) are seen and treated as exotic (and erotic)
providers of sex to a largely white male clientele. This mystical
facade conceals a low-wage economy in which the imagery
and idea of 'Oriental' femininity are used to boost profits for
the 'respectable' medical side of the business while keeping
undocumented migrants at the bottom of the heap.

Deng's two friends are working as masseuses. They told me
that sex is one of the services they offered. They said this was
common practice in many Chinese medicine clinics in London.
'It is an open secret,' one of them said. I decided to talk to some
of the company's other employees and customers to find out
whether this was true.

One worker told me the masseuses, all in their thirties, are
mostly from the north-east of China and Fujian. The majority
are undocumented migrants who use their earnings to send
remittances home. Although the company officially offers only
massage and acupuncture, the masseuses have been offering sex
as an extra in order to boost their income and retain customers.
The sex services have become an 'unofficial' part of the
treatments provided and, according to the worker, are endowed
by the branch managers.

Another woman, who has been a masseur for two years,
said, 'If you are new, you'll feel the pressure to do the same, to
offer these extra services, because if you don't, you lose out, and
you can't keep customers like your colleagues. So many of us
have ended up doing it.'

Many men drop in during their lunch hour, for 'escapism'.
A former customer described his experience: 'The women
there would give you a massage and then launch into a "special

ogue" with you, where they indicate their willingness to
offer sex by making physical gestures, such as leaning on you
or crossing their legs on your arm.' Many customers would take
advantage of the 'extra service', even if it wasn't what they had
gone there for originally. After all, who would suspect anything
untoward behind the closed doors of a medical clinic?

'They are paid £35 per half hour for massage,' the man told
me. 'Customers are encouraged to buy six half-hour sessions.
If you buy six, then you get one session free. The masseuses
persuade you to buy these packages so that they look popular in
the clinic. It helps them to maintain a pool of regular customers.

'I got to know one of the women quite well. She was thirty-
four and had a daughter in Fujian. She worked seven days
a week without a break. She always talked about her family
during our sessions. She was very depressed about leaving her
child behind. Her aim was to support her family and eventually
buy a flat in China. She said I was her special customer. For
the extra service, her customers paid £20, which was called a
tip at the clinic. Even though we had those special sessions for
months, she'd never kiss me. I think it was because she saw
it as just her job. Something that she must do to earn more.
The closest we got emotionally was when she gave me a hug
and put her head on my shoulder. She told me that she was
exhausted.'

Grace rang, telling me to go to Finchley that Saturday for
housekeeping work. Had she sacked her new maid already? No
one could tell me.

When I arrived at lunchtime, the maid was still working
there. Her name was Jie, in her early fifties, from Shenyang.
She told me that she'd been doing *zhuangzhong* there and was

happy with the higher income: £200 as a housekeeper plus an extra £300–£400 per week from sex work.

The *xiaojie* this week was Ah Ling, a very approachable and chatty woman in her late thirties from rural Fuzhou in Fujian. She kept saying, 'We're from the countryside.' She had a seventeen-year-old son, who was being looked after by her husband. She told me she'd once tried to run her own business but had made losses. She'd then borrowed 200,000 yuan (£20,000) to pay for her to be smuggled into the UK in 2008.

'I wasted my first three years in England working in restaurants and takeaways doing tough work with little reward,' Ah Ling told me. 'A year ago, a friend of mine in the sex trade suggested I try doing this. She said, "Try it once and see if you are OK with it." It took me a couple of weeks to make my mind up, but eventually I took the plunge. Frankly, I had no real alternatives.'

'How do you feel about it now?' I asked.

'Now I regret not having started it as soon as I got here.'

Sex work had transformed Ah Ling's life. She had paid off all her debts within a year and was earning £600 a week. Her current aim was to pay for a new house back home for her family, and return after two more years of sex work.

It's not difficult to see why Ah Ling would recommend me to do the same. 'You don't want to waste your time here, Xiao Yun,' she urged. The time factor, the urgency to earn as much as possible as fast as possible, explains why many Chinese women make the same choice as Ah Ling.

At the same time, she admitted there was a high price to pay. 'I have to watch out for my health,' she said. 'Some of the punters play tricks with you and take off the condoms. Four times, punters have ejaculated when their condom was taken off.'

'Have you done anything about it?' I asked.

'I will. I am going to go for a health check … but I think it's OK,' Ah Ling said, shrugging her shoulders and trying to be optimistic. 'This kind of thing happens to every *xiaojie*.' She told me that she frequently gives oral sex without a condom, charging a £10 tip. She didn't seem to think it was unsafe. (Grace told customers on the phone that it was available, and certainly never warned the women about the health risks.)

The only service Ah Ling had turned down that day was when a punter asked for a 'golden shower' (for the woman to urinate in his mouth). 'I can't go to the loo yet,' she said, not wanting to offend the man. But Jie overheard and said she could do it — she was desperate for the money. But when she asked for £70, the man got upset and left, complaining: 'I did it in Edgware and it was £50!'

Ah Ling, Jie and I chatted about the work all night. Ah Ling said most of the women didn't like working for Grace because of her temper and her foul mouth, which was why Grace was always short of workers. Ah Ling seemed relaxed when Grace wasn't around. Grace came back from playing mah-jong just after half past ten, looking temperamental again. We all retreated to our rooms. There had been only six punters in total all day.

Jie was leaving to start work elsewhere as a *xiaojie*. She no longer wanted to be a maid or do *zhuangzhong*. She said she needed to earn fast. Time was not on her side. Although she knew full well that Jie wanted to get an early night to prepare for her new job the next day, Grace sadistically demanded that she stayed past midnight.

'It will take me two hours to get home by bus, on a Sunday,' Jie said to me, not knowing what to do.

I tried to plead her case with Grace. 'So you want Jie to go home, who's gonna be *zhuangzhong* then? You?' Grace said.

'Don't make me push you to do it.'

As Jie desperately wanted to leave, I decided to see what Grace would do if someone stood up to her. It is a maid's job to give wages to a *xiaojie* at the end of the day, so I went to the wardrobe in the front room where the money was kept and, in front of Grace, counted out Jie's money and handed it to her. 'Go home,' I said. Jie took the wages and left immediately. Grace simply sulked without a word.

Half an hour later, though, two customers arrived at once. Grace said to me, 'Take one,' and led one of the men into the room where I kept my luggage. I told her I wouldn't and started chatting with him instead. Grace got really upset, pouring out a torrent of abuse.

When Grace's boyfriend arrived back from his job in Scotland, we all retreated to our rooms to give them some privacy. Later, Ah Ling came to my room and tried to persuade me again. She said I could share a room with her in Elephant & Castle that cost just £70 per week. She said she'd prefer to live with someone in the trade. 'It is a small community and you don't want word to go round about what you do for a living.'

Ah Ling said that while she was waiting for transit in France (en route to the UK), she'd heard about Chinese prostitution in Paris but she hadn't given it another thought. It was the desperate economic situation here that led her to consider her friend's advice.

A 1 a.m., a customer rang the bell. When I led him to Ah Ling's room, she was half asleep. When she opened the door, I saw how exhausted she looked. She could hardly open her eyes.

'One hour,' the man said, his face expressionless.

I could see it was the last thing Ah Ling needed, but she had to say yes. Like Jie, she'd wanted an early night because she had to be up first thing in the morning to start a new job. I wasn't

…ing on top of the world myself, either. I showed him out at
…a.m. and went to bed with a cold and a temperature, feeling
like death warmed up.

A week later, Grace gave me an 'ultimatum'. 'Jie would very
much like to come back here to work,' she said, 'but if you
decide to do *zhuangzhong*, I will turn her down.'

Could she be serious?

'But you'll need to give me a definite answer by this evening,'
Grace went on. She said this in front of Popo, this week's working
girl, who wasn't impressed with the way Grace pressured me.

'I don't think you should push her,' said Popo, knitting her
thin eyebrows. 'Maybe Xiao Yun just can't take it mentally. If
you force her into sex work and something happens to her,
don't you think it would be your responsibility then? Do you
really want a bad name?'

Grace seemed affected by Popo's warning. Popo was a
business-minded woman from Hunan who had recently set
up her own small massage parlour employing one *xiaojie* each
week. To Grace, her words sounded like criticism from a rival.

Grace turned to me and quietly asked again, '*Zhuangzhong*
or not?'

'I need more time to consider it,' I said, trying to maintain
my cover for a while longer.

Grace wouldn't press the matter in front of Popo. She picked
up the phone and called Jie. I'd got the sack again. But although
Jie would resume her old job on Monday, Grace wanted me to
cover the maid's day off in Bounds Green.

Popo advised me not to go to Bounds Green to work for just
one day. 'Why are you putting up with all this? She's treating you
like a dog. You have to have some pride, even if you are poor.'

Grace's self-control didn't last long. That evening, she
physically pushed me through the door when I opened it to go

downstairs to receive a customer. Then she swore at me, 'Get out of the way, you cunt!'

Business was bad the following morning. No customers. Popo was frustrated and upset, saying she couldn't earn any money there. She told Grace she was leaving. Grace was furious, shouting and screaming abuse again. Popo left anyway. At least Grace now had someone else to be annoyed with.

She spent the next two hours calling all the *xiaojies* she knew, but as she was such an unpopular boss, few of them even answered the phone. Eventually, she called Ah Ling and pleaded with her to come to work that week. Ah Ling agreed. Mia too was asked to help out as a *zhuangzhong* – uncharacteristically, she agreed to work part-time for a week because she desperately needed a break after four months of non-stop working. Mia told me that she'd developed health problems since I'd last seen her. She often woke up with her arms numb, as though they were paralysed; she knew there was something wrong with her, but didn't have a GP to go to. 'I just need a break now,' she said.

It was the eve of Mia's birthday and she tried to celebrate it between sessions (she was booked to go out with a punter the following day). It was probably the first time in England that she'd actually relaxed for a moment and made time for some laughter. One of her regulars, an Irishman in his late forties, bought her a beautiful chocolate cake. He seemed to take great interest in East Asian women and visited every week, sometimes three times a day. He said he had money to spare, being a manager at a utility company. He'd also brought a bottle of red wine. Mia gathered us all – Ah Ling, Grace and me – in the front room for the cake and wine.

The Irishman sang 'Happy Birthday' and asked Mia to make a wish and blow out the candles. She closed her eyes, almost like a little girl, and did so. I could make a good guess what he'd wished for. But no matter how Ah Ling and I clapped and congratulated Mia and tried to foster a happy atmosphere, there was only sadness in the air.

Then the cake was cut and we all had a slice. Grace sat on the sofa behind us, trying to look happy and cheering Mia with a fake smile. She looked as though she'd rather be anywhere but here. I looked at Mia and felt really sorry for her: how sad it must be to celebrate your birthday with your pimp and a punter. Mia is truly alone in this country.

The Irishman left, but before Mia had time to finish her cake, the doorbell rang again and one of Mia's regulars, a younger man, arrived for a one-hour session. It tired her out. 'That one was really tough to do,' she told me afterwards. 'He took for ever to come!'

By midnight, Mia was still waiting for a text from her favourite punter 'Three' (his name is Sam, which in Chinese means three), with whom she had somehow become infatuated over the past month. But tonight he didn't text or call. She polished off the bottle of wine, looking sad. Her imagined relationships with some of her punters seemed the only contact she had with the outside world. It was her way of staying sane and human. She was under no illusions, though. She told me some 'romance' makes her work a little more bearable – and the time pass quicker. But when the romantic facade began to crack, she became anxious and depressed. Then she tried to tell herself that it was all pointless.

'It doesn't matter really. We have no future anyway,' Mia said, downing the dregs from her glass.

Ah Ling told me she was working extra hard now to save up to build a house in Fujian, which was going to cost her a million yuan. She would need to work another two to three years to accomplish that aim. 'But it's not just the house I'm worried about,' she said. 'I have to save up for my son and his future.' I could see that Ah Ling's working time in the sex trade was going to extend beyond her current plan.

She said she couldn't afford to go out with punters like Mia did, partly because she was worried she might be seen by other Fujianese migrants and partly because she wanted to spend every penny and every minute of her working time earning for her son. She said she didn't want to be distracted.

Grace had told me not to cook for Ah Ling. She was trying to give me less to do to make me look redundant. She used the excuse that my cooking was bad and too oily and that I used too much rice, so no one should eat my food. She was determined to isolate me. To both deflect her abuse and carry on with my undercover job, I bought my own food from the corner shop. But it didn't stop her. When she saw my open tin of tuna in the fridge, she deliberately knocked it over.

'Sweep it up! Hurry! Sweep it up! Now!' she shouted and screamed. She was in a state of mad fury and nothing could stop her.

When I tried to do some washing-up, she came up and pushed me aside, shouting, 'I don't want you to touch this! Go away!'

I began to fear her presence, her voice and her words. I was counting the hours until I could leave.

My wages were due, but in the early evening Grace left to play mah-jong without a word. It was obvious she didn't intend to pay my wages. The sympathetic Ah Ling cooked Fujianese seafood congie for us in the evening and we ate together in the front room, chatting about work and home.

Grace came back at 1 a.m. She seemed disappointed that

was still there – she'd expected me to have left without my money. (Jie was due to replace me the following day.) She called me into the front room and asked how much I'd paid Ah Ling that day (£95). Then she gave me £130 to give to Mia and sent me out. Five minutes later she came to Mia's room with £100.

'Can't be more than this – for you,' she said, speaking to me but looking at Mia, who was drinking a glass of wine on the bed. 'You didn't do your work and this is all I can give you.'

That worked out at about £8 per day.

I wanted to prolong my undercover work, so I called Grace a week later and said I didn't have anywhere to live and wondered if she could put me up for a few days. In return, I said I'd do maiding work free of charge, opening the door to customers and so on. She said, 'OK, come here.'

When I arrived at Finchley, Jie was leaving for the day. She said she wouldn't have been able to have a day off if I hadn't been coming back. (Grace didn't believe in giving maids time off.) Jie was getting frustrated with the job only after one week since returning to Grace – all because of Grace's temper. She was talking about finding massage work somewhere else rather than work as a *zhuangzhong* here.

There was a Romanian girl called Laura and a middle-aged Chinese woman called Jessica working that week. They had both just come from the Bounds Green flat. Jessica was trying to persuade Laura to leave, saying there weren't enough customers for both of them. Following a quiet morning, Grace summoned Laura back to Bounds Green to work.

Jessica and I chatted, and she said she knew of a place in Bath where I could get work as a maid. She said I wouldn't get abused over there, because the boss was never around. 'Grace is too harsh for anyone,' she said. Of course, she also tried to persuade me into sex work with the usual offer: if I didn't want to go straight into it, I could start with massage …

Grace had been out dining and gambling with her boyfriend. On their return, she was in a bad mood. Her boyfriend told me they had lost a few hundred pounds in the casino. Jessica and I decided it would be wise to steer clear of her.

Shortly after midnight, just as I was dozing off, Grace sent a customer into Jie's bedroom, where I was sleeping, without even knocking. The punter stood right beside my bed, staring at me, while Grace banged on Jessica's door to wake her up.

Jie came back the next morning. Again she complained that she wouldn't have been able to have a day off if I hadn't come back. 'For Grace, the only time when you can have a day off is when you leave the job.'

That afternoon, Grace started shouting that £700 had disappeared from under her pillow. I thought it strange that someone who loved money so much would hide such a sum so carelessly. There seemed to be no doubt in her mind that one of us was responsible.

'The money was here and it's gone! She took it, no doubt!' Grace didn't say who she meant by 'she'. It made everyone nervous. When we all denied knowledge, she began to suspect her boyfriend, who apparently had a habit of taking money from her. She called him, shouting at him on the phone, and then suddenly passed the phone to me.

'Jamal wants to speak to you,' she said.

I picked up the phone, and heard his aggressive voice in my ear: '*You took the money! If you don't spit it out now, I will report it to the police!*'

He saw me as an easy target because he thought I had no papers and had to depend on Grace for my accommodation. So far as he knew, I was homeless and desperate. It was an obvious trick: his aggression and accusation without a shred of evidence vere an attempt to shift the blame from him to me, in the belief I'd pay up to avoid a police visit.

I called his bluff. 'You can't accuse me of anything without evidence. Go and call the police! Go ahead!'

He hadn't expected that and was almost lost for words. I put the phone down on him while he was still stammering out a response.

When he returned he ignored me, going straight into the front room and starting to argue with Grace. 'Are you calling me a thief? Don't you trust me?' we heard him screaming from behind the closed door.

We were all worried what might happen next. Even Jessica's customer got scared. Jessica had to interrupt the session to ask Grace and Jamal to keep the noise down as they were frightening the punters.

Jie, who had no papers, was fretting that Jamal might make good on his threat to call the police. She kept asking me to translate what they were saying. I tried to reassure her that no one in their right mind would bring the police to a brothel owned by his girlfriend. Sure enough, Jamal soon stormed out again.

Later, a customer arrived and asked for me. 'I'm just the housekeeper,' I told him. 'I'll do the housekeeping for you,' he said with a smile. He didn't seem to want Jessica or Jie. He asked Grace whether I could do a session with him.

Jessica, clearly not wanting to lose the punter, then suggested she did the session while I observed. 'You'll get a £10 tip for just watching us,' she added.

I said no. I recalled Ming's experience; I knew what that could lead to. Predictably, Grace became angry with me again for losing a customer. At this point, Jamal returned and joined in the verbal abuse. Grace moaned about me to Jie and Jessica for a while longer before returning to the main room to carry on the earlier argument with Jamal.

It had been a stressful day, to say the least. Now that Jie had returned, I was demoted to sleeping on her floor. I didn't sleep well.

The next day, Grace again attempted to cajole me into sex work. She never seemed to tire of trying. She kept it up all day. It was well known that she was continually short of staff because few people would work for her more than once. Her *xiaojies* didn't usually return and her maids rarely stayed long.

Yet another customer came and asked if I would work. This time, Grace asked the punter to talk me into it. He was Chinese, a regular, and had seen both Jessica and Jie already. He just wanted someone different and I happened to be the only new person around. Grace sent him to see me in Jie's small room.

'Come on, give it a try,' he said with an encouraging wink.

Eventually he left without a session with anyone, which again put Grace in a bad mood.

Jessica was distraught at being turned down. It wasn't the first time that day, and she hadn't earned much. She'd seen just two punters. 'It's pitiful,' she said, worried that she needed to earn more and that Grace would be upset. That evening I heard her whispering to Grace that it might have something to do with the way I stood at her door when the customers came in. She was implying that I didn't try hard enough to 'sell' her to the men. I understood Jessica's anxiety both to earn and to please the boss, and so I didn't make a fuss about it. I was there under false pretences, after all.

I was woken up by Jie screaming in her dreams. She sounded as if she was struggling for help ... 'It must have been a nightmare,' she told me in the morning. Jie wouldn't talk in depth about her problems – she wasn't the kind of person to open up easily – but I could see she was always anxious: about her income, her job insecurity and her future in this country. Her mood would swing from day to day, depending on how much she'd earned.

To make matters worse, Jie was scolded by Grace for being overweight (which she wasn't in the least). It was because two punters had turned down both Jie and Jessica the previous night. Understandably, Jie felt wounded by Grace's remarks, though she didn't dare argue with her. But she wasn't prepared to put up with it, either. While Grace was off collecting cash in Bounds Green, Jie was calling round to find new work.

Over the dumpling breakfast Jie had prepared, Jie and Jessica talked about the £700 that Grace claimed had been stolen. They didn't believe she'd really lost it.

'She must have miscounted the cash or forgotten where she'd put it,' said Jessica.

They both agreed it was uncharacteristically careless of her.

'It's that poor sod Jamal I feel sorry for,' said Jessica. 'Now he's trying his best to get back in her good books. He said he's bringing over a BMW to show her later. What a pair!'

I suspected that Grace had invented the entire episode in order to exercise her authority. One thing I'd learned during the past month was that she was a manipulative liar, capable of manufacturing an environment in which every worker was under immense pressure and frightened of being noticed. The fear she generated enabled her to control her workers better.

Despite her constant stream of invective, Grace knew that I was useful to her. She asked for my help negotiating the rental of another flat in Bounds Green. Perhaps 'asked' is the wrong word. 'Xiao Yun! Get over here!' she screamed. She ordered me around like this all the time, as if I were her servant.

Then she started singing karaoke from her laptop. She announced to Jie and Jessica that she'd entered a singing

'Oh yes, I never gave up painting – it was all that kept me sane during my time working in restaurants and takeaways and on building sites. But I don't think the British appreciate my artwork. It's too raw, too rural for them. They prefer more refined, traditional Chinese watercolours.'

'I still find it strange that you've ended up in this line of work, Da Ding,' said Ming. 'You don't fit here.'

'You have to fit where there is work, you should know that by now,' Da Ding smiled.

Ming nodded with a sigh. 'It's true. Hardship makes us stronger.'

'Not always. In China, I always saw myself as a strong-willed man who had not yet succeeded. In England, I see myself as a vulnerable, weak person, barely surviving on the edge of society, grabbing any crumbs there are to keep myself afloat and my family fed and clothed. Hardship has robbed me of my pride. Look where I am now.'

His words brought tears to Ming's eyes. His story said a lot about her own. And until now, no one had summarised it so clearly.

Da Ding fetched some photographs he'd been sent by his wife. 'Look at her,' he pointed to a short-haired, plainly dressed woman in her late forties who stood in front of a huge metal door. 'She's an easygoing character, my wife, a very warm-hearted person.'

Ming pointed to the door behind her. 'Is this your house?'

'Yes, yes,' Da Ding nodded enthusiastically. 'This two-storey house is built by my hard work in England. They completed construction just last year.'

'You've done so well.'

'Not only me. All over the village, you can tell when someone in the household has gone abroad to work by the look of the house. There's a three-storey house built by a man who went to South Korea, it's much more luxurious than mine.'

He sighed. 'I'm not the type to remain content with a life of hardship and scarcity. I'm not the type to live with unsatisfactory conditions. I had to be here to make a difference to my family's life. My son wouldn't have been able to get married without my working here. The wedding ceremony cost 10,000 yuan [£1,000]. He was finally able to marry last year, to a young woman from a sweetcorn farming family in the neighbouring village. They are now living in a large room designed especially for them, in this new house built with my earnings.'

'I'm also saving up for my daughter,' Ming said. 'Does your son farm?'

'He'd like to, but it's not possible. Although the heavy tax system has been replaced by a tiny annual subsidy of 50 yuan per *mu*, they still depend mainly on what I send home. My son has found himself a job as a builder in Shijiazhuang, earning 1,000 yuan per month. It's barely enough to support him and his wife.'

Da Ding sighed again. 'We all pay a huge price for this. Look at where we've ended up now. But you know, we can all say that we're lucky enough to have survived here.'

Ming nodded, reflecting on her own experience.

Da Ding continued. 'Some aren't so lucky. A man from my village committed suicide in prison in England after being arrested at a cannabis farm. He didn't want to work there but what choice did he have? Immigration raids have kept many restaurants and takeaways from employing people without papers. He couldn't bring himself to tell his wife that he was in jail and there was no way he could pay back the money he'd borrowed to come here.'

He saw the sad look on Ming's face, and asked, 'I assume you won't stay in this trade for long, will you?'

competition and was preparing two songs for it. Awful Chin.
pop songs. Jie and Jessica quickly retreated to their rooms whr.
Grace carried on singing hard and loud, as if she wanted to tell
everyone that she had other things going on in her life; that she
didn't exist only to make money but had 'outside interests' too.
All night we heard her wailing voice echoing pathetically in the
hallway.

Late that night, after the lonely singing session, Grace said
to me that she would have to get me ready for sex work in the
morning. 'Time's running out,' she said. 'You're not finding any
work for yourself. You are wasting your own time. I will sort
you out tomorrow. You'll make money.'

I was exhausted, having spent all day answering calls from
annoying and repulsive punters on three phone lines.

'How old are the girls?' asked the latest.

'The girls are in their mid twenties,' I lied for the umpteenth
time.

'Have you got anything younger?'

'Is mid twenties not young enough for you?' I ran out of
patience and put the phone down.

I'd been ordered to monitor three phone lines. Grace was
trying to make me do as much free work as possible. Jie was
feeling better because she'd earned £190 from seven punters the
previous day. She had a smile on her face today.

Grace lectured me about sex work again – the need to earn
for the family. She said I was useless if I couldn't support my
family, my parents. She asked Jie to 'train' me, to get ready for
customers. Jie didn't, of course. It wouldn't have been in her
interests to do so, for, as Jessica reminded her, if I were to take
up the role of *zhuangzhong* here, there would be no job for Jie.

tried to fob Grace off by saying, quite truthfully, that I
ouldn't be as well suited to the job as the two women she
already employed.

'You shouldn't feel inferior to those two,' Grace scoffed.
'You'll earn more than them because you're younger and you
speak English.' She told me she'd done sex work for three months
before setting up as a madam. She'd bought three houses back
home so far, costing 5 million yuan, with the profits she'd made.

'Aren't you envious?' She stared at me with her sharp eyes. 'I
bet you are!'

The following day Jie was depressed again, having earned
only £70. She was spending her free time looking at herself in
the mirror, worrying about being fat.

Grace spent the morning practising her karaoke. 'Look at me!
and look at yourself!' she said, holding a dildo as a microphone.
'I have earned a lot of money and now I have leisure time, to
sing and do what I want. What about you? *You have nothing*
and you can only rely on the mercy of others and you can only
beg for help. And I am the only person who can help you.'

I remained quiet.

Finally, she cracked. 'Why did your mother give birth to
you? You useless cunt.'

I told her I had a job interview, but she wouldn't allow me
to go out. 'Why do you need a job interview? It's useless! You
won't get the job anyway!' she sneered, ordering me back to the
phones.

When Grace left for the karaoke competition, she told Jie
and Jessica I wasn't to leave the building. All I was to Grace
was a source of free labour and, with a bit of luck, a future
zhuangzhong.

'No, just for a while longer,' said Ming solemnly. 'An.
things improve at home, I will stop.'

'Me too. I feel my days are numbered here. Entering t.
trade is just the last resort. But deep down I know it isn't fo.
me.'

One day, another punter arrived expecting to find a student
working there after speaking to Da Ding's Vietnamese partner.
He agreed to a half-hour session with Ming instead, but asked
for a refund afterwards.

'You've had your session. We can't refund you,' Da Ding
argued.

'Your boss lied to me about the girls here,' the punter became
angry. 'She's not a student. I want my money back!'

Da Ding shook his head.

'Do you want me to call the police? You cunt!' the man
started waving his fist.

Da Ding still said no. Surely the customer was just bluffing?
Shortly after the man left he phoned Da Ding and said, 'I've
called the police and told them where you are and what you're
doing. Now you'd better run!' He laughed and hung up.

Da Ding had £1,000 in cash that his partners had given him
to cover running costs. That would be evidence enough for the
police to charge him with living on immoral earnings. There
was no way to tell whether the punter had been serious, but Da
Ding couldn't take the chance. He certainly didn't want to risk
being arrested. He told Ming they should leave the house for a
few hours, just in case.

At first they wandered North End's back streets aimlessly,
but still they didn't feel safe. 'We need to be further away,' said
Da Ding, leading her to a park near the centre of town. 'They
definitely won't find us here,' he said. They found a bench and
sat watching the passers-by. Da Ding was anxiously looking

watch every five minutes, worrying about whether the
were searching the house and what they might find. He
n't had time to remove the evidence that the place was run
s a brothel: the bins filled with damp tissue, the soiled bed
sheets, the packets of condoms and KY jelly.

Two women strolled past with prams, each holding a cornet.
'Do you want an ice cream?' Da Ding offered. 'I saw a sign
for them at the café just now.'

'No, thanks,' Ming said without a smile. 'Da Ding, will
everything be all right?'

There had been no calls from the two business partners. No
calls from the estate agent from whom they'd rented the house.
That must mean that the police hadn't been. Mustn't it? Five
hours later, Da Ding decided that it would be safe for them to
return. No one had been there. Everything was as they'd left it.
'Let's hide the cash somewhere, just in case they do turn up,' Da
Ding said to Ming, reaching into his pocket.

He decided that the safest hiding place was the back garden.
He dug a hole and carefully buried the notes in a sealed plastic
bag. But although the money was now secure, Ming no longer
felt safe. Just the thought of a police raid had spooked her. She
went to her room and started packing.

'I'd stay till the end of the booking if I were you,' Da Ding
advised. 'The punters always try to scare us. That's a common
trick they play. We take precautions, but we don't need to take
them too seriously.'

Ming dubiously agreed to stay on, and it seemed that Da
Ding was right. The police never came. All that happened was
that the same punter started to send text messages to Da Ding,
asking if the students were working.

When the two weeks were up, Ming left as originally agreed.
Da Ding accompanied her on the bus back to Southsea station.

'Where are you working tomorrow?' he asked, it was usual for *xiaojies* to go from one booking to without a day's break.

'London,' Ming answered. 'A parlour in London.'

A minute later, Da Ding turned to her and said, 'You know, there is one thing I'd really like to do before I leave England.'

Ming stared at his bright round eyes, wondering where his next adventure would be.

'I want to go to London, to Highgate Cemetery.'

'What for?'

'To pay my respects at Marx's grave.'

Ming hasn't been in England long enough to know about Marx's grave. But she imagined, with a smile, the sight of Da Ding bringing flowers to the cemetery. Did this old-time-party-member-turned-brothel-owner still have some idealism in his cells?

I met Da Ding for myself a while later. As it turned out, he left the trade two weeks after Ming's departure. Neighbours had informed the police about the parlour and his two partners decided to close it down and relocate. Da Ding decided that the stress of dealing with difficult punters and the ever-present threat of a police raid weren't for him. He decided to come back to London and start a new career as a professional gambler.

For two months, Da Ding had been playing the tables in the Empire casino in Leicester Square. In the first twenty days, he made £1,000. He sent the money home immediately, though he told his wife that he'd got a new job as a kitchen porter. When I met him, he was convinced that he would continue to make at least £1,000 a month. As he was in the casino all the time, day and night, he thought he might as well sleep there, to cut sts. A number of other Chinese migrants were doing ; they simply found a spare sofa to sleep on. So far as I , he's still there.

Since Ming left Portsmouth, I have not been able to reach her by phone. It appears that she has changed her mobile number. I tried to find her via Da Ding, but all he'd heard was that she was working in a Chinese medicine clinic in the West End. Did that mean she'd left the sex trade? Although I haven't managed to find her, my subsequent meanderings in Chinese medicinal circles lead me to believe this might not be the case.

An acquaintance of mine called Deng introduced me to Mr Li, one of the managers of a chain of Chinese medicine clinics. Li was well respected by migrants from his home town, having found jobs for many of them. Connections and patronage are important for new arrivals, and for well-established migrants like Li, such networks are the basis of his clientele. As Deng put it, it's a mutually beneficial thing. Deng was grateful and always talked proudly of his friend Li, whom he felt had brought honour to their home town. Two of Deng's friends were among those helped by Mr Li. There was a lot of competition for their jobs, and Deng was very thankful to his manager friend.

The company has twelve branches in London, most of them in the West End. These clinics now form part of the tourist landscape in and around Chinatown. On Little Newport Street, those well-dressed women Ming had noticed during her earlier job-seeking trip in Chinatown, or others like them, can still be found standing outside, soliciting customers. Many of their clients are tourists.

'It is believed that Chinese herbs, acupuncture and Chinese massage are making great contributions towards Man's health and longevity,' says the company's advertising literature. Private 'alternative' health care has been promoted in beautiful language

My undercover work was finished, but Grace continued to c
me with offers of work. 'My maid in Bounds Green has left,' she
said one day. 'I can give you a job there.'

I found out later from Mia, who was working there at the
time, that the flat had been raided by the police on several
occasions, and the maid, who had no papers, wouldn't continue.

'So Grace offered me the job knowing that I might get
arrested?' I said to Mia.

'Why would she care?' replied Mia.

Mia was leaving England and had wanted to meet up to
say goodbye. Remarkably, she had achieved her aim of earning
£20,000 in four months. She had worked herself to the bone
almost literally to earn an average of £1,600 per week. When
we had our last dinner in a Notting Hill pub, Mia showed me
the neat list of her weekly earnings she'd made at the back of
her diary – the figure ranged from £1,200 to £2,800. She had
worked herself almost to death each day, often existing on only
four hours' sleep.

As usual, Mia drank a whole bottle of red wine as we talked.
'As a friend, Xiao Yun, I really advise you to do something to
increase your earnings here,' she said. 'The fastest way to do it is
to do the same work as me. This will help you …' She gave me
the list of all the contacts she'd made in the sex trade and urged
me to book myself into as many brothels as possible.

'Xiao Yun, I'd like to see you make lots of money and achieve
your aim in being here. When I come back to England in future,
I'd like to see you having become a boss of some sort, having
your own place and able to spend in high-class restaurants …'

'I just want to be able to send money home,' I said, for as far
as Mia was concerned I was still a housekeeper who was afraid
to dip her feet in the water.

'Well, *xia hai* is the only way to enable you to do that fast.'

used the same Chinese expression I'd heard from Ming to
escribe entering the sex trade: 'going into the sea'. 'Your family
cannot wait for ever.'

Before we parted, Mia embraced me and said this had been
her happiest day in England.

On the way home, Grace called me again. She had finally
opened the new premises in Bounds Green (one of those flats
whose rental I'd negotiated) and would like me to go and work
there for her. She didn't tell me that the old premises had been
closed down following yet another police raid.

Acknowledgements

I would like to thank all the women who shared their life stories with me. Their courage and perseverance are so inspiring. Their strong will is humbling. Their names have been changed to protect their identities.

I would like to thank my editor, Rukhsana Yasmin, so much, for her lasting enthusiasm for this project and her warm encouragement and advice throughout. I am so fortunate to have met such a committed editor – and such a kind and lovely person.

Big thanks to my wonderful publisher, Lynn Gaspard, who offered her excellent advice and kind support from start to finish. Many thanks to Trevor Horwood, my copy-editor, for his thorough and excellent work and his good ideas for improvement.

Many thanks to Nigel Mathers, a sexual health specialist who now lectures at the University of Sheffield and who generously offered to review the early chapters of my first draft, and novelist Betsy Tobin, who kindly acted as my 'test reader' and offered her brilliant and invaluable advice.

I would also like to thank Anna Miralis, my commissioning editor at Channel 4, for her support and encouragement in my undercover work. Many thanks to Nick Broomfield, who directed the Channel 4 documentary, for appreciating the issues and committing so much time and effort to making the film.

For useful advice and assistance, my thanks to the organisations who have been working tirelessly to improve the health and well-being of workers in the sex trade: Doctors of the World UK, Lotus Bus, Project: London, Open Doors, CLASH and X: talk.

Finally, many thanks to John Davies for his support, as always.